DATE DUE			

THE REBIRTH OF LEARNING

GENERAL EDITOR

Charles M. Sherover

I. THE SPIRIT OF THE CLASSICAL WORLD
WADE C. STEPHENS

II. THE REBIRTH OF LEARNING
The First Twelve Centuries
WILLIAM BRYAR
and
GEORGE L. STENGREN

III. SACRED AND SECULAR
1200–1500
GEORGE L. STENGREN

IV. SEPARATION AND RECONSTRUCTION
1500–1700
GEORGE L. STENGREN

V. THE ENLIGHTENMENT
The Proper Study of Mankind
NICHOLAS CAPALDI

VI. ROMANTICISM AND EVOLUTION
The Nineteenth Century
BRUCE WILSHIRE

VII. CRISIS IN MEANING
Dilemmas of 20th-Century Civilization
EDWARD C. CELL
and
JACK F. PADGETT

VIII. THE SPIRIT OF AMERICAN CULTURE
GERALD E. MEYERS

The Spirit of Western Civilization

THE REBIRTH
OF LEARNING

The First Twelve Centuries

AN ANTHOLOGY

SELECTED, EDITED, AND WITH INTRODUCTIONS BY

William Bryar
and
George L. Stengren

G. P. PUTNAM'S SONS : NEW YORK

Copyright © 1968 by

Educational Resources Corporation

Library of Congress Catalog
Card Number: 67-23119

PRINTED IN THE UNITED STATES OF AMERICA

Contents

V. THE DEVELOPMENT OF JUDAIC TRADITION

VI. MEETING OF EAST AND WEST

THE REBIRTH OF LEARNING

Foreword

THIS volume and the two that follow it together portray the continuity of the first seventeen centuries of the Christian era—what has been viewed as the central period of Western civilization. The three volumes are divided as follows: the first through the twelfth centuries, the thirteenth throught the fifteenth centuries, the sixteenth and seventeenth centuries.

This study of the central period begins in the first century with Philo of Alexandria, interpreter of the Old Testament in the languages of Greek philosophy, and concludes with the German Leibniz, inventor of the calculus. We move from imperial Byzantium to the colonies of the New World. In the course of things, we witness the division of Christianity into Orthodox, Catholic, Protestant. We see together the divisions of monotheism: Judaism, Christianity, and Islam. The same central period will manifest pantheism, humanism, and rationalism. It will contain extraordinary works in natural science, in law, in literature, in philosophy, in theology.

In seeking freedom and scope in the treatment of this central period of seventeen centuries, we shall not always follow usual and useful categories, such as patristic, scholastic, and baroque; or Hellenistic Age, Middle Ages, Renaissance, Reformation, Enlightenment. We shall instead attempt to define the dominant preoccupations of the period at significant points and to group its ideas in line with these. We shall, thus, be bound neither by strict chronological divisions nor by divisions between various fields of study.

Certain general emphases, however, have been most helpful. The polarity of sacred and secular has allowed us to see varied dimensions within the same thought or event or institution or work of literature. By describing together the intellectual and social and religious aspects of the areas studied, especially the three dimensions in relation to one another, additional depth has been attained.

As we consider the first twelve centuries, seen in terms of rebirth of learning, a succession of striking figures comes to mind: Origen, Augustine, John Scotus Erigena, Avicenna, Maimonides, Abelard. The twelve centuries witness a remarkable succession of meetings of East and West, or the cultural, political and religious movements centered in one or the other.

These twelve centuries can be seen as the time of transformation of the heritage of the ancient world. They comprise as well the age preparatory to the full institution of universities. They provide the songs of valor and the songs of love which stand at the beginning of vernacular literatures, literatures of power in the formation of ideals and peoples.

These languages and peoples, religions and institutions, ideas and customs, are present in various ways in the modern world, the world of the eighteenth, nineteenth, and twentieth centuries. The confluence of historic Rome and Athens and Jerusalem, which is a special concern of our study of these twelve centuries, has shaped the world and the culture in which we live. The interest of the first twelve centuries, however, does not lie uniquely in their antecedents or in their influence on later times. They have more than sufficient resources and vitality in themselves to command our attention.

The general structure of the volume, the Foreword, and the introductory essays for each of the six chapters are primarily the responsibility of William Bryar, of Hunter College of the City University of New York. The editing of the selections, some original translations done specifically for this volume, and the prefatory notes to the selections are primarily the responsibility of George L. Stengren, of Iona College.

I.

*Byzantium and the
Tradition of the East*

CONTEMPORARY differences between Russia and the greater part of Eastern Europe on one hand and Western Europe and the Americas on the other have signal historical antecedents. The major precedent lies in the division between the Eastern Roman Empire, which continued until A.D. 1453, and the Western Roman Empire, which gave way to barbarian invasions one thousand years earlier. Gradual separation took place within the Christian Church between the Eastern Orthodox and the Western Catholic peoples. In the East contact with Islam was more direct. In the West, with the lack of political unity, there was need of special search for moral unity.

The early centuries of the Christian era, in Egypt, in Cappadocia, in Byzantium, witnessed a fusion of biblical and Hellenistic thought in both East and West. Some scholars maintain that the religion of today, or its "religion-less" equivalent, must move beyond both Greek and Semitic categories, especially beyond the influence of the foundational period with its fusion of Hellenistic philosophy and biblical writing. Whatever the case, we do well to know the terms of the choice to be made, terms perhaps best seen in their origin in these early centuries.

The city of Byzantium embodied the traditions of the East, from the time of its establishment as a capital in A.D. 330 by Emperor Constantine. It is said by some that our present age is in a special way the end of the "Constantinian era," that is, the integration of religious and intellectual and political life in a single social scheme. These thinkers hold that today these three dimensions of life have gained sufficient strength and autonomy so that we have entered a new era, an era in which each kind of life will reach its maturity in development relatively independent of the others.

We can better judge, perhaps, the values of the hope of the "Constantinian era" by way of some reflection on the specific hope of

Byzantium. Here was to be the integration of the values of the three great centers of antiquity: Athens, Rome, and Jerusalem. Intellectual, political and religious life were to flourish through mutual support and enrichment.

We have, then, mentioned three contemporary issues which suggest a study of the sources in the tradition of the East. These issues, subjects deserving of study in their contemporary context as well, are: differences between Russia and America, questions of dehellenizing religious teaching, efforts to separate school, church and state from each other.

In Philo of Alexandria, Origen, Gregory of Nyssa, and Justinian, four representatives of the tradition of the East, we may see the initial blending of the classical and the biblical heritages which has so greatly influenced the development of Western civilization. Philo, Origen, and Gregory were similar in manifesting a deep relationship between a life of religious devotion and concern for what are at times the highest reaches of intellectual life. The use of sophisticated and subtle concepts in the discussion of religious matters was not a matter of mere academic exercise. It was important for these men, and for their traditions, that religious practice be informed by a religious mind, and that no parts of difficult religious teaching be put aside or fail to be used for the deepening or enrichment of life.

They insisted on attending with great care to seemingly conflicting facets of religious teaching. This care was not a love of paradox. Only through penetration of the two sides of apparently contradictory teaching did they think it possible to avoid distortion by oversimplification, to safeguard both the life of the mind and the life of action. For example, God is immutable, and yet God is responsive to the changing needs and prayers of men. God is the universal cause of the world of creatures, and yet men are free.

The theological pursuits of the East gave rise to the decrees and definitions of the ecumenical councils of the Christian Church, and thereby determined much of subsequent religious and secular thought. Sophistication, subtlety and imaginativeness in the interpretation of religious writings provided a kind of basis for development of humanistic disciplines.

The tradition of the East has given history a special ideal of the fusion of the social, intellectual and religious dimensions of human life.

The four authors—Philo of Alexandria (25 B.C.–A.D. 50), Origen (A.D. 186–255), Gregory of Nyssa (A.D. 330–394), Justinian (A.D. 483–565)—are representative of this historic period and source of our civilization. They were not isolated individuals but part of a general movement of innovation.

Philo of Alexandria, in view of his birth in 25 B.C. and by virtue of his influence, stands rightly at the beginning. He belonged to the Jewish religious community in the great center of Hellenistic learning, the city of Alexandria. His work broke the ground for the interrelation of the secular learning of classical antiquity and biblical teaching. His writings provided an important example for subsequent intellectual life in the worlds of Judaism, Christianity, and Islam, and in the areas of secular concern which paralleled their developments. His example directly influenced Origen and Gregory. He represented the Jewish community at the court of the Roman Emperor Caligula in A.D. 39.

Origen's position in the development of Western civilization is also associated with the intellectual center of Alexandria, in his case in the third century A.D. He is generally regarded as the most learned of Christian writers prior to the time of the Council of Nicaea, which began in A.D. 325. The comprehensive character of his thought provided a definite advance in the Christian community, although he maintained a number of religious and philosophical views that were not generally acceptable. He died in A.D. 255 as a result of sufferings in the persecution of the Roman Emperor Decius.

Origen's *Dialogue with Heraclides* reports a discussion of the orthodoxy of Bishop Heraclides before a synod of bishops. This dialogue examines the Christian doctrine of God as one and three, the implication of trinitarian teaching in the life of public prayer, the doctrine of the coexistence of humanity and divinity in Christ, and the doctrine of the immortality of the human soul. The hammering out of what is today often considered standard teaching is very much a part of the life and the interest for us of Origen and his period.

Gregory of Nyssa in the fourth century was one of the Greek or Eastern Fathers of the Christian Church, as Augustine was recognized as one of the Latin or Western Fathers. He explicitly continued and developed the work of Philo and Origen. While Bishop of Nyssa in Cappadocia, a region of Asia Minor, Gregory played an important part in the Council of Constantinople in A.D. 381 and for some time exerted considerable influence in the capital of the Eastern Empire.

Gregory's work is the first real example of systematic mystical theology, theology concerned with the dynamics of the religious man in his most nearly perfect movement toward present union with God. He offers a dynamic and affective, rather than a relatively static and scientific, theology of man. It is in this emphasis that we meet the beginning of the continuing strain in theological tradition which will, perhaps, be of most interest to contemporary man in his preoccupation with self-identity and personal fulfillment. Gregory's writings are best read as the beginning of a comprehensive effort to unfold the vital growth of volitional and emotional life.

Justinian, whose reign as emperor in the sixth century A.D. saw the last period in which the unity of the eastern and western regions of the Mediterranean was restored, stands as a special symbol of Byzantium. In his political and military policies, as well as in the celebrated legal code which bears his name, there was a univeralism that is suggestive of both Roman civilization and biblical teaching. In the code there was embodied an intellectualism which was characteristic of the Greek intellectual inheritance and of religious teachers such as Philo, Origen, and Gregory of Nyssa. The code, as revised by Napoleon, remains to this day as the basis of the legal system of most of Europe, apart from the United Kingdom.

Even a brief consideration of the Justinian Code illustrates something of the amplitude of the civilizing force of the tradition of the East. From the same Justinian came the orders for the building of the Church of St. Sophia (Holy Wisdom), which stands today after transformation by Islamic conquerors. This remarkable work of art and architecture, symbol of empire, brings to mind the developing liturgical poetry and music which were to be a prime unifying and civilizing influence for countless barbarian peoples who were, over the centuries, to enter Western civilization.

1. PHILO: How the Passions Help the Soul

Philo of Alexandria (25 B.C.-A.D. 50) was an important Jewish thinker of the Hellenistic period. At the same time that he was a devout Jew, his interpretation of the Bible and Judaism seems to depend more on philosophic sources derived from Greek philosophy than on the Jewish tradition. In his *Allegorical Interpretations** he makes extensive use of Greek learning in interpreting the Old Testament and Jewish practice. Although he emphasized allegorical interpretation, he pointed out that allegorical meanings may be coupled with literal meanings of texts or customs. His philosophical orientation derived in good part from the platonic tradition.

His rambling style, which allows him to cover a whole multitude of topics under a seemingly simple heading, provides the receptive reader with considerable information and interest. The openness of his way of inquiry accounts in part for his broad influence in subsequent intellectual and religious life.

BOOK II

I. "And the Lord God said, It is not good that the man should be alone, let us make for him a helper corresponding to him" (Gen. ii. 18). Why, O prophet, is it not good that the man should be alone? Because, he says, it is good that the Alone should be alone: but God, being One, is alone and unique, and like God there is nothing. Hence, since it is good that He who IS should be alone—for indeed with regard to Him alone can the statement "it is good" be made— it follows that it would not be good that the man should be alone. There is another way in which we may understand the statement that God is alone. It may mean that neither before creation was there anything with God, nor, when the universe had come into being, does anything take its place with Him; for there is absolutely nothing

* The selection is taken from Books II and III, trans. Colson and Whitaker (Cambridge, Mass.: Loeb Classical Library and Harvard University Press). Used by permission.

which He needs. A yet better interpretation is the following. God is alone, a Unity, in the sense that His nature is simple not composite, whereas each one of us and of all other created beings is made up of many things. I, for example, am many things in one. I am soul and body. To soul belong rational and irrational parts, and to body, again different properties, warm and cold, heavy and light, dry and moist. But God is not a composite Being, consisting of many parts, nor is He mixed with aught else. For whatever is added to God, is either superior or inferior or equal to Him. But there is nothing equal or superior to God. And no lesser thing is resolved into Him. If He do so assimilate any lesser thing, He also will be lessened. And if He can be made less, He will also be capable of corruption; and even to imagine this were blasphemous. . . .

II. It is not good that *any* man should be alone. For there are *two* races of men, the one made after the (Divine) Image, and the one moulded out of the earth. For the man made after the Image it is not good to be alone, because he yearns after the Image. For the image of God is a pattern of which copies are made, and every copy longs for that of which it is a copy, and its station is at its side. Far less is it good for the man moulded of the earth to be alone. Nay, it is impossible. For with the mind so formed, linked to it in closest fellowship, are senses, passions, vices, ten thousand other presences. With the second man a helper is associated. To begin with, the helper is a created one, for it says, "Let us *make* a helper for him"; and, in the next place, is subsequent to him who is to be helped, for He had formed the mind before and is about to form its helper. In these particulars again, while using terms of outward nature he is conveying a deeper meaning. For sense and the passions are helpers of the soul and come after the soul. In what way they help we shall see: let us fix our attention on their coming later than the soul.

III. In the view of the best physicians and natural philosophers the heart is thought to be formed before the whole body, by way of a foundation, or as the keel in a ship, the rest of the body being built upon it; and they assert that accordingly even after death it still beats, and decays after the body, as it came into existence before it. In just the same way, it is thought, the princely part of the soul is older than the soul as a whole, and the irrational portion younger. The creation of this the prophet has not as yet related, but he is going to describe it. The irrational portion is sense and the passions which are the offspring of sense, unquestionably so if they are not the result of any choice of our own. This helper then is later born and of course created.

Now let us consider the point which we deferred, *how* the help is given. How does our mind apprehend the fact that an object is white or black, except by using sight as a helper? How does it become aware that the musician's voice is sweet or on the other hand out of tune, save by using the sense of hearing as a helper? How does it recognize that perfumes are pleasant or disagreeable, except by using as an ally the sense of smell? How does it distinguish savours, except by means of the taste acting as its helper? Things smooth and rough, again, how but by touch? Moreover, there are, as I have said, helpers of another kind, namely the passions. For pleasure and desire contribute to the permanence of our kind: pain and fear are like bites or stings warning the soul to treat nothing carelessly: anger is a weapon of defence, which has conferred great boons on many: and so with the other passions. This shows also that the prophet was perfectly right in saying that the helper must be one "corresponding to him." For in very deed this helper is intimately allied to the mind, as though a brother of one blood with it: for sense-perception and passions are parts and offspring of one soul with it.

IV. There are two species of this helper: the one has its sphere in the passions, the other in sense-perception. At present He will produce the former only, for he says, "And God moulded moreover out of the earth all the wild beasts of the field, and all the birds of the heaven, and led them to Adam to see what he would call them: and whatever Adam called a living soul, this was its name" (Gen. ii. 19). You see who are our helpers, the wild beasts, the soul's passions: for after saying, "Let us make a helper corresponding to him," he adds the words, "He moulded the wild beasts," implying that the wild beasts are our helpers. These are not properly called our helpers, but by a straining of language; in reality they are found to be our actual foes, just as the allies of states sometimes turn out to be traitors and deserters, and in private friendships flatterers prove enemies instead of comrades. He uses the terms "heaven" and "field" as synonyms, meaning the mind. For the mind is like the field in having countless sproutings and upgrowths, and like heaven again in having natures brilliant and godlike and blessed. The passions he likens to wild beasts and birds, because, savage and untamed as they are, they tear the soul to pieces, and because like winged things they light upon the understanding; for the assault of the passions is violent and irresistible. The addition of "further" to "formed" is by no means otiose. How do we see this? Because above also he mentions the forming of the wild beasts before the creation of man, as we see from these words referring to the sixth day: and He said, "Let the earth bring forth the living soul after its kind, four-footed animals and creeping things and wild beasts" (Gen. i. 24). . . .

BOOK III

I. "And Adam and his wife hid themselves from the presence of the Lord God in the midst of the forest of the garden" (Gen. iii. 8). He introduces a doctrine showing that the bad man is an exile. For if virtue is a city peculiar to the wise, the man who has no capacity to partake of virtue has been driven away from the city, in which the bad man is incapable of taking part. It is accordingly the bad man only who has been driven away and sent into exile. But the exile from virtue has by incurring such exile hidden himself from God. For if the wise, as being His friends, are in God's sight, it is evident that all bad men slink away and hide from Him, as is to be expected in men who cherish hatred and ill-will to right reason. The prophet, moreover, finds proof that the bad man is without city or dwelling-house, in the account of Esau, the hairy man, crafty in wickedness, when he says, "Esau was skilled in hunting, a countryman" (Gen. xxv. 27); for vice, that hunts after the passions, is by nature unfit to dwell in the city of virtue. Rather, in utter senselessness, it follows after rustic grossness, the life of the untrained. Jacob, the man full of wisdom, belongs to a city, and as a dwelling-house he occupies virtue. The prophet says of him: "But Jacob was a simple man dwelling in a house" (*ibid.*). It accords with this too that the mid-wives, since they feared God, made houses for themselves (Exod. i. 21); for such (souls) as make a quest of God's hidden mysteries— and this is what is meant by "saving the males' lives" or "bringing the males to the birth"—build up the cause of virtue, and in this they have elected to have their abode. By these instances it has been made clear how the bad man is without a city or home, being an exile from virtue, while the good man has received it as his lot to have wisdom for both city and dwelling.

II. Let us see next how a man is said actually to hide himself from God. Were one not to take the language as figurative, it would be impossible to accept the statement, for God fills and penetrates all things, and has left no spot void or empty of His presence. What manner of place then shall a man occupy, in which God is not? The prophet elsewhere bears witness of this saying, "God in heaven above and upon the earth beneath and there is none else but He" (Deut. iv. 39). And again, "Here stand I before thou (wert made)" (Exod. xvii. 6); for before every created thing God is, and is found everywhere, so that no one could possibly hide himself from God. And why should we marvel at this? Whatever should happen, we could never escape or hide ourselves from those, even among things created, that are essential elements of creation. For instance, let a man fly, if he can, from earth or water or air or sky or the world at large. A man must needs have all these round him, for no one shall ever be able to escape out of the world. Then, seeing a man is power-less to hide himself from the parts of the world or from the world itself, would he be able to escape the eye of God? By no means. Why then does it say "they hid themselves"? The bad man thinks that God is in a place, not containing but contained; and for this reason he imagines that he can hide from Him, fancying that God, the Author of all things, is not in that part, which he has chosen for his lurking-place.

III. It is possible to take it in this way. In the bad man the true opinion concerning God is hidden in obscurity, for he is full of darkness with no divine radiance in him, whereby to investigate realities. Such an one is in banishment from the divine company, like the leper and the man with an issue. The former combines as joint causes God and creation, which are natures mutually hostile, for he shows two different colours, whereas there is one single Cause, even He who doeth all. The man with an issue, on the other hand, deriving everything from the world, and making it return into the world, imagines that nothing has been created by God, associating himself with the opinion of Heracleitus, in his advocacy of such tenets as "fullness and want," "the universe one," and "all things interchange." So the divine word saith, "Let them send forth out of the holy soul every leper, and everyone that hath an issue, and everyone that is unclean in soul, both male and female" (Numb. v. 2), and eunuchs with the generative organs of the soul cut away, and fornicators, deserters from the rule of One, to whom entrance into the assembly of God is absolutely forbidden (Deut. xxiii. 2). But wise reasoning, so far from hiding themselves, are keenly desirous to be manifest. Do you not see that Abraham "was still standing before the Lord and drew nigh and said, 'Destroy Thou not the just man together with the impious one'" (Gen. xviii. 22f.), the one that is manifest and known to Thee together with him who shuns and avoids Thee? For this one is impious, but he that stands before Thee and avoids Thee not is just. For the only justice is that Thou, O Master, shouldst be honoured. A pious man is not found with the same ease as an impious one. We have to be content with a just man. This is why He says, "Destroy not a just together with an impious man." For no one honours God as He deserves but only as is just. It is impossible to requite even our parents with boons equal to those which we have received from them—for it is out of the question to requite by becoming their parents. How must it not be impossible to recompense or to praise as He deserves Him who brought the universe out of non-existence? For it was an exercise towards us of every virtue.

IV. Through three seasons, then, O soul, that is throughout the whole of time with its threefold divisions, make thyself ever manifest to God, not dragging after thee the weak feminine passion of sense-perception, but giving forth as incense the manly reasoning schooled in fortitude. For the sacred word (Deut. xvi. 16) enjoins that at three seasons of the year every male is to show himself before the Lord the God of Israel. For this reason Moses also, when he is being established as one standing open before God, avoids Pharaoh, the symbol of dispersion, for he boasts saying that he knows not the Lord (Exod. v. 2). "Moses," we read, "withdrew from Pharaoh's presence and settled in the land of Midian" (Exod. ii. 15), or in the examination of the things of nature, "and sat on the well," waiting to see what draught God would send to quench the thirst of his soul in its longing for that which is good. So he withdraws from the godless opinion of Pharaoh, which the passions follow as their leader, and withdraws into Midian, the sifting-place, to inquire whether he is to be still or to dispute again with the evil man for his destruction; he considers whether, if he attack him, he shall prevail to win the victory, and so he is kept there waiting upon God, as I have said, to see whether He will bestow upon a deep reasoning faculty free from shallowness a stream sufficient to drown the onrush of the king of the Egyptians, the onrush, that is, of his passions. And he is deemed worthy of the boon: for, having taken the field in the cause of virtue, he does not abandon the warfare till he beholds the pleasures prostrate and out of action. This is why Moses does not fly from Pharaoh, for that would have been to run away and not return, but, like an athlete taking an interval to regain his breath, "withdraws," that is, brings about a cessation of arms, until he shall by divine words have raised forces of wisdom and every other virtue to aid him in renewing the attack with irresistible power.

But Jacob, "Supplanter" that he is, acquiring virtue with great toil by wiles and artifices, his name having not yet been changed into "Israel," runs away from Laban and all his belongings, tints and shapes and material bodies generally, whose nature it is to inflict wounds on the mind through the objects of sense. For since when facing them he was not able completely to vanquish them, he flies, fearing defeat at their hands. And in doing so he is thoroughly deserving of praise; for Moses says, "Ye shall make the sons of the seeing one cautious" (Lev. xv. 31), not bold and aiming at what is beyond their capacity.

V. "And Jacob stole away unawares to Laban the Syrian, in that he told him not that he fled. So he fled with all that he had; and passed over the river, and set his face toward the mountain of Gilead" (Gen. xxxi. 20f.). It is thoroughly in accordance with true principles that he is said to have concealed the fact that he is running away and not made it known to Laban, who represents the way of thinking governed by objects of sense. For instance, if thou hast caught sight of beauty and been captivated by it, and if it is like to be a cause of stumbling to thee, fly secretly from the vision of it, and give no further report of it to thy mind, that is to say, do not give it another thought or ponder it: for to keep on recalling anything is the way to engrave on the mind distinct outlines of it, which injure the mind and often bring it to ruin against its will. The same principle holds in the case of every kind of attraction by the avenue of whatever sense it may reach us; for here safety lies in secret flight; but recalling the attractive object in memory, telling of it, turning it over, spells conquest and harsh slavery for our reasoning faculty. If, therefore, O my mind, thou art in imminent danger of falling a prey to some object of sense that has shown itself, never report

it to thyself, never dwell on it, lest thou be overcome and plunged
into misery. Nay, rush forth at large, make thy escape, choose the
freedom of the wild rather than the slavery of the tame.

VI. Now (let us ask) why, as though Jacob were not aware that
Laban was a Syrian, does he say, "Jacob kept Laban the Syrian in
the dark"? In this likewise there is a point not without pertinence.
For "Syria" means "Highlands." Jacob, therefore, the mind in training, when he sees passion grovelling low before him, awaits its onset
calculating that he will master it by force, but when it is seen to be
lofty, stately, weighty, the first to run away is the mind in training,
followed by all his belongings, being portions of his discipline,
readings, ponderings, acts of worship, and of remembrance of noble
souls, self-control, discharge of daily duties; he crosses the river of
objects of sense, that swamps and drowns the soul under the flood
of the passions, and, when he has crossed it, sets his face for the
lofty high-land, the principle of perfect virtue: "for he set his face
towards the mountain of Gilead." The meaning of this name is
"migration of witness"; for God caused the soul to migrate from the
passions that are represented by Laban, and bore witness to it how
greatly to its advantage and benefit its removal was, and led it on
away from the evil things that render the soul low and grovelling up
to the height and greatness of virtue.

For this reason Laban, the friend of the senses and the man whose
actions are regulated by them and not by the mind, is vexed, and
pursues him, and says, "Why didst thou run away secretly" (Gen.
xxxi. 26), but didst not remain in the company of bodily enjoyment
and of the teaching that gives the preference to bodily and external
good things? But in addition to fleeing from this view of life, thou
didst carry off my soundness of sense as well, Leah and Rachel to wit.
For these, while they remained with the soul, produced in it sound
sense, but when they removed elsewhither they left behind to it
ignorance and indiscipline. This is why he adds the words "thou didst
rob me" (ibid.), that is, didst steal my good sense.

VII. What, then, his good sense was, he is going to explain; for
he adds "and didst carry away my daughters as prisoners of war:
and if thou hadst told me, I would have sent thee forth" (ibid.).
Thou wouldst not have sent forth those at variance one with another;*

* The things mutually at variance are true "well-being" and the lower
delights, represented by the "music and tabrets and harp," which, as Philo
takes it, are to go with those released.

for hadst thou really sent forth and liberated the soul, thou wouldst have stripped from it all voices belonging to the body and senses: for it is in this way that the understanding is delivered from vices and passions. But as it is, thou *sayest* that thou art ready to send her forth free, but by thy actions thou ownest that thou wouldst have detained her in prison; for if thou hadst sent her on her way with "music and tabrets and harp" and the pleasures that suit each several sense, thou wouldst not really have sent her forth at all. For it is not from thee only, O Laban, friend of bodies and of tints, that we are running away, but from all too that is thine: and this includes the voices of the senses sounding in harmony with the operations of the passions. For we have made our own, if so be that we are under virtue's training, a study absolutely vital which was Jacob's study also, to consign to death and destruction the gods that are alien to the soul, the gods moulded in metal, the making of which Moses has forbidden (Lev. xix. 4); and these are a means of dissolving virtue and well-being, and a means of forming and giving fixity to wickedness and passions, for that which undergoes moulding, if dissolved, grows fixed and firm again.

VIII. We read as follows: "And they gave Jacob the strange gods, which were in their hands, and the ear-rings which were in their ears, and Jacob hid them under the terebinth that was in Shechem" (Gen. xxxv. 4). These are bad men's gods. And Jacob is not said to receive them, but to hide and destroy them. This is in every point perfectly accurate. For the man of sterling worth will take nothing to make him rich in the products of evil, but will hide them secretly and do away with them. In like manner when the king of Sodom is artfully attempting to effect an exchange of creatures without reason for reasonable beings, of horses for men, Abraham says that he will take none of the things that are his but will "stretch out" his soul's operation, which he figuratively called his "hand," "to the Most High God" (Gen. xiv. 22), for that he would not take of all that was the king's "from a cord even to a shoelace," in order that he may not say that he has conferred wealth on the man whose eyes were open, by giving him poverty in return for his wealth of virtue. The passions are always hidden away and placed under guard in Shechem—"shoulder"* is the meaning of the name—for he that devotes toil to pleasures is prone to keep pleasures well guarded. But in the case of the wise man

* Or "shouldering," *i.e.* "toil."

the passions perish and are destroyed, not for some short period but "even to this day," that is, always. For the whole age of the world is made commensurate with to-day, for the daily cycle is the measure of all time. For this reason too Jacob gives as a special portion to Joseph Shechem (Gen. xlviii. 22), the things of the body and of the senses, as he is occupied in toiling at these things, but to Judah who openly acknowledges God he gives not presents, but praise and hymns and hallowed songs from his brethren (Gen. xlix. 8). Jacob receives Shechem not from God, but by dint of "sword and bow," words that pierce and parry. For the wise man subjects to himself the secondary as well as the primary objects, but, having subjected them, does not keep them, but bestows them on him to whose nature they are akin. Mark you not that, in the case of the gods also, though apparently receiving them, he has not really done so, but hid them and did away with them and "destroyed" them for ever from himself? What soul, then, was it that succeeded in hiding away wickedness and removing it from sight, but the soul to which God manifested Himself, and which He deemed worthy of His secret mysteries? For He says: "Shall I hide from Abraham My servant that which I am doing?" (Gen. xviii. 17). It is meet, O Saviour, that Thou displayest Thine own works to the soul that longs for all beauteous things, and that Thou hast concealed from it none of Thy works. That is why it is strong to shun evil and always to hide and becloud and destroy passion that works cruel havoc.

IX. In what manner, then, the bad man is in banishment and hiding himself from God we have shown; let us consider now where he hides himself. "In the midst," it says, "of the wood of the garden" (Gen. iii. 8), that is in the centre of the mind, which in its turn is the centre of what we may call the garden of the whole soul: for he that runs away from God takes refuge in himself. There are two minds, that of the universe, which is God, and the individual mind. He that flees from his own mind flees for refuge to the Mind of all things. For he that abandons his own mind acknowledges all that makes the human mind its standard to be naught, and he refers all things to God. On the other hand he that runs away from God declares Him to be the cause of nothing, and himself to be the cause of all things that come into being. The view, for instance, is widely current that all things in the world tear along automatically independently of anyone to guide them, and that the human mind by itself established arts, professions, laws, customs, and rules of right treatment both of men and animals on the part of the state and in our conduct whether as individual persons or as members of communities. But thou perceivest, O my soul, the difference of the two opinions; for the one turns its back on the particular being, created and mortal mind, and whole-heartedly puts itself under the patronage of the universal Mind, uncreated and immortal; the other opinion on the contrary, rejects God, and by a grievous error calls in to share its warfare the mind that is insufficient even to help itself.

X. This is the ground for Moses' words, "If the thief be found where he has just broken through and be smitten and die, there is no blood-guiltiness for him: but if the sun have risen upon him, (then he) is liable, he shall die in requital" (Exod. xxii. 1 f.). For if a man cleave and break through the tenet that stands firm in its soundness and uprightness, testifying of unlimited power as belonging to God alone, and he be found where he has broken through, that is, in the pierced and cloven doctrine that is conscious of a man's own mind at work but not of God, he is a thief abstracting what belongs to another; for all things are God's possessions, so that he who assigns anything to himself is appropriating what is another's, and he receives a blow grievous and hard to be healed, even self-conceit, a thing akin to boorish ignorance. Moses does not make distinct mention of the man who strikes, for he is no other than the man who is struck; just as the man who rubs himself is also rubbed, and the man who stretches himself is also stretched; for in his own person he is at the same time active and passive, employs the force and submits to its effect. Even so he that steals what is God's and assigns it to himself, is the victim of the outrage inflicted by his own impiety and self-conceit. A good thing it would be should he die when struck, that is to say permanently fail of the accomplishment of his purpose; for he must then be held to be less a sinner. For wickedness presents itself now as stationary, now as moving. It is wickedness in motion that is ripe for filling up its full measure by carrying its designs to completion, and so it is worse than stationary wickedness. If, therefore, the understanding which fancies itself and not God to be the cause of all that comes into existence die, that is, shrink into inactivity, blood-guiltiness does not pertain to it; it has not gone the full length of abolishing the living doctrine which ascribes to God the totality of powers. But if the sun shall have risen, that is the mind that shines so brilliantly in us, and shall have conceived the notion that it discerns all things, and decides all things, and that nothing ever escapes it, he is guilty, he shall die in requital for the living doctrine which he destroyed, which acknowledges God as the sole Cause. For he is found futile and dead indeed in himself; he has come forward as the author of a lifeless, mortal, and erroneous doctrine.

XI. In keeping with this the sacred word pronounces a curse on one setting up in secret a graven or molten image, the work of the hands of the craftsman (Deut. xxvii. 15). For why, O mind, dost thou hoard and treasure in thyself those wrong opinions, that God is as the graven images are, of this or that kind, God the Being that is without kind, and that He the incorruptible is, as the molten images are, corruptible? Why dost thou not rather bring them forth into the open, to the end that thou mayest be taught the things which it behoves thee to learn from those who study the truth? For thou fanciest thyself one versed in science because thou hast conned over methods of persuasion unworthy of an educated man, wherewith to combat the truth. But thy science proves itself no science, in that thou refusest to submit to healing treatment of thy soul's sore malady of ignorance.

XII. That the bad man sinks down into his own incoherent mind as he strives to avoid Him that IS, we shall learn from Moses who "smote the Egyptian and hid him in the sand" (Exod. ii. 12). This means that he took full account of the man who maintains that the things of the body have the pre-eminence and holds the things of the soul to be naught, and regards pleasures as the end aim of life. For having noted the toil imposed by the king of Egypt on him who sees God—and the king is wickedness whose lead the passions follow—he sees the Egyptian man, that is, human and perishable passion, beating and outrageously treating the seeing one; and having looked round upon the whole soul in this direction and in that, and seen no one standing, save God who IS, but all other things tossing in wild confusion, after smiting and thoroughly reckoning up the lover of pleasure, he hides him in his mind, which is a congeries of disconnected grains, devoid of cohesion and union with the beautiful and noble. So this man has been hidden away in himself. But the man of a character the reverse of his flies indeed from himself but takes refuge in the God of those that are.

XIII. And for this reason he says, "He led him forth abroad and said, Look up to heaven and count the stars" (Gen. xv. 5). These we would fain take in in one all-encompassing view, being insatiable in our love of virtue, but we are powerless to take the measure of the riches of God. Yet thanks be to the Lover of Giving, for telling us in this way that He has set for Himself in the soul seeds far-shining, radiant, full charged with meaning, as he has set the stars in heaven. But is not "abroad" a superfluous addition to "led him forth"? For who is ever led forth within? But it may be that this is what he means; He led him forth to outermost space, not just to one of the outside spaces, one that can be encompassed by others. For just as in our houses the women's apartments have the men's quarters outside them and the passage inside them, and the courtyard door is outside the court but inside the gateway, even so, in the case of the soul too, that which is outside one part can be inside another part. We must take what he says in this way; He led forth the mind to the outermost bound. For what advantage would it have been for it to leave the body behind and take refuge in sense-perception? What gain in renouncing sense-perception and taking shelter under the uttered word? For it behoves the mind that would be led forth and let go free to withdraw itself from the influence of everything, the needs of the body, the organs of sense, specious arguments, the plausibilities of rhetoric, last of all itself.

XIV. For this reason he glories elsewhere saying "The Lord, the God of heaven, and the God of the earth, who took me out of my father's house" (Gen. xxiv. 7); for it is not possible that he whose abode is in the body and the mortal race should attain to being with God; this is possible only for him whom God rescues out of prison. For this reason Isaac also, the soul's gladness, when he meditates and is alone with God, goes forth, quitting himself and his own mind; for it says, "Isaac went forth into the plain to meditate as evening was drawing near" (Gen. xxiv. 63). Yes, and Moses, the word of prophecy, says, "When I go forth out of the city," the soul to wit (for this too is the city of the living being giving him laws and customs), "I will spread out my hands" (Exod. ix. 29), and I will spread open and unfold all my doings to God, calling Him to be witness and overseer of each one of them, from whom evil cannot hide itself, but is forced to remove all disguises and be plainly seen.

When the soul in all utterances and all actions has attained to perfect sincerity and godlikeness, the voices of the senses cease and all those abominable sounds that used to vex it. For the visible calls and summons the sense of sight to itself, and the voice calls the sense of hearing, and the perfume that of smell, and all round the object of sense invites the sense to itself. But all these cease when the mind goes forth from the city of the soul and finds in God the spring and aim of its own doings and intents.*

XV. For truly are "the hands of Moses heavy" (Exod. xvii. 12); for inasmuch as the bad man's doings are light and windy, those of the wise man will be weighty and immovable and not easily shaken. Accordingly they are steadied by Aaron, the Word, and Hor, which is "Light"; and life has no clearer light than truth. The prophet's aim therefore is to show thee by means of symbols that the doings of the wise man are upheld by the most essential of all things, the Word and Truth. And so, when Aaron dies, that is, when he is made perfect, he goes up into Hor, which is "Light" (Numb. xx. 25); for the end of the Word is Truth, which casts a beam more far-reaching than light. To this it is the earnest endeavour of the Word to attain.

Mark you not, that when he had received from God (Exod. xxxiii. 7) the Tent, namely, wisdom, in which the wise man tabernacles and dwells, he fixed and made it fast and strongly established it, not in the body, but outside it? For to represent the body he uses the figure of a camp, the quarters of an army full of wars and all the evils that war produces, a place that has no part in peace. "And it was called 'the tent of testimony,' " wisdom testified to by God. Yes, for "everyone that sought the Lord went out to it." Right finely is this said. For if thou are seeking God, O mind, go out from thyself and seek diligently; but if thou remainest amid the heavy encumbrances of the body or the self-conceits with which the understanding is familiar, thou mayest have the semblance of a seeker, not thine is the quest for the things of God. But whether thou wilt find God when thou seekest is uncertain, for to many He has not manifested Himself, but their zeal has been without success all along. And yet the mere seeking by itself is sufficient to make us partakers of good things, for it always is the case that endeavours after noble things, even if they fail to attain their object, gladden in their very course those who make them. Thus it is that while the bad man, who shuns virtue and hides

* Exod. ix. 29 is still being handled.

himself from God, takes refuge in his own mind, a sorry resource, the good man, on the other hand, who runs away from himself, returns to the apprehension of the One, thus winning a noble race and proving victor in this grandest of all contests. . . .

2. ORIGEN: The Incarnate God

Origen (A.D. 186-255) was an Alexandrian Christian. His *Dialogues with Heraclides** is taken from a recently discovered papyrus. The work gives an account of the examination by this learned teacher of a certain Bishop Heraclides. In the course of the examination there is discussion of a number of key religious teachings: unity and trinity in God, the nature of Christ, the immortality of the soul. His works are both of pastoral and theoretical significance. As with Philo, Origen represented an extraordinary advance in the effort to employ intellectual means for deeper appreciation of the meaning of religious teaching.

Dialogue of Origen with Heraclides and the
Bishops with him concerning the Father
and the Son and the Soul¹

THE TEXT

After the bishops present had raised questions concerning the faith of the bishop Heraclides, that he might confess before all the faith which he held, and after each one had said what he thought and asked questions, Heraclides said:

I also believe what the sacred Scriptures say: "In the beginning was the Word, and the Word was with God, and the Word was God. He was in the beginning with God. All things were made by him, and without him nothing was made."² Accordingly, we hold

* The selection is taken from *Alexandrian Christianity*, Vol. II, ed. Oulton and Henry Chadwick (Philadelphia: Westminster Press, 1954). Used by permission.

¹ The original scribe only wrote the title in the final colophon at the end of the work: "Dialogues of Origen: with Heraclides and the bishops with him." A later reviser added to this final colophon "Concerning the Father and the Son and the Soul" and also inserted this full title at the head of the work.

² John 1:1-3.

the same faith that is taught in these words, and we believe that
Christ took flesh, that he was born, that he went up to heaven in the
flesh in which he rose again, that he is sitting at the right hand of
the Father, and that thence he shall come and judge the living and
the dead, being God and man.

Origen said: Since once an inquiry has begun it is proper to say
something upon the subject of the inquiry, I will speak. The whole
church is present and listening. It is not right that there should be
any difference in knowledge between one church and another, for
you are not the false church.

I charge you, father Heraclides: God is the almighty, the uncreated,
the supreme God who made all things. Do you hold this doctrine?

Heracl.: I do. That is what I also believe.

Orig.: Christ Jesus who was in the form of God,[3] being other than
the God in whose form he existed, was he God before he came into
the body or not?

Heracl.: He was God before.

Orig.: Was he God before he came into the body or not?

Heracl.: Yes, he was.

Orig.: Was he God distinct from this God in whose form he existed?

Heracl.: Obviously he was distinct from another being and, since
he was in the form of him who created all things, he was distinct
from him.

Orig.: Is it true then that there was a God, the Son of God, the
only begotten of God, the first born of all creation,[4] and that we
need have no fear of saying that in one sense there are two Gods,
while in another there is one God?

Heracl.: What you say is evident. But we affirm that God is the
almighty, God without beginning, without end, containing all things
and not contained by anything; and that his Word is the Son of the
living God, God and man, through whom all things were made,[5]
God according to the spirit, man inasmuch as he was born of Mary.[6]

Orig.: You do not appear to have answered my question. Explain
what you mean. For perhaps I failed to follow you. Is the Father God?

Heracl.: Assuredly.

[3] Phil. 2:6.
[4] Col. 1:15.
[5] John 1:3.
[6] Cf. Rom. 1:3.

Orig.: Is the Son distinct from the Father?

Heracl.: Of course. How can he be Son if he is also Father?

Orig.: While being distinct from the Father is the Son himself also God?

Heracl.: He himself is also God.

Orig.: And do two Gods become a unity?

Heracl.: Yes.

Orig.: Do we confess two Gods?

Heracl.: Yes. The power is one.

Orig.: But as our brethren take offence at the statement that there are two Gods, we must formulate the doctrine carefully, and show in what sense they are two and in what sense the two are one God. Also the holy Scriptures have taught that several things which are two are one. And not only things which are two, for they have also taught that in some instances more than two, or even a very much larger number of things, are one. Our present task is not to broach a problematic subject only to pass it by and deal cursorily with the matter, but for the sake of the simple folk to chew up, so to speak, the meat, and little by little to instil the doctrine in the ears of our hearers. . . . Accordingly, there are many things which are two that are said in the Scriptures to be one. What passages of Scripture? Adam is one person, his wife another. Adam is distinct from his wife, and his wife is distinct from her husband. Yet it is said in the story of the creation of the world that they two are one: "For the two shall be one flesh."[7] Therefore, sometimes two beings can become one flesh. Notice, however, that in the case of Adam and Eve it is not said that the two shall become one spirit, nor that the two shall become one soul, but that they shall become one flesh. Again, the righteous man is distinct from Christ; but he is said by the apostle to be one with Christ: "For he that is joined to the Lord is one spirit."[8] Is it not true that the one is of a subordinate nature or of a low and inferior nature, while Christ's nature is divine and glorious and blessed? Are they therefore no longer two? Yes, for the man and the woman are "no longer two but one flesh," and the righteous man and Christ are "one spirit." So in relation to the Father and God of the universe, our Saviour and Lord is not one flesh, nor one spirit, but something higher than flesh and spirit,

[7] Gen. 2:24; Matt. 19:5.
[8] I Cor. 6:17.

namely, one God. The appropriate word when human beings are joined to one another is flesh. The appropriate word when a righteous man is joined to Christ is spirit. But the word when Christ is united to the Father is not flesh, nor spirit, but more honourable than these —God. That is why we understand in this sense "I and the Father are one."[9] When we pray, because of the one party let us preserve the duality, because of the other party let us hold to the unity. In this way we avoid falling into the opinion of those who have been separated from the Church and turned to the illusory notion of monarchy, who abolish the Son as distinct from the Father and virtually abolish the Father also. Nor do we fall into the other blasphemous doctrine which denies the deity of Christ. What then do the divine Scriptures mean when they say: "Beside me there is no other God, and there shall be none after me," and "I am and there is no God but me"?[10] In these utterances we are not to think that the unity applies to the God of the universe . . . in separation from Christ, and certainly not to Christ in separation from God. Let us rather say that the sense is the same as that of Jesus' saying, "I and my Father are one."

It is necessary to study these doctrines because there has been much disturbance in this church. Often people write and demand a signature of the bishop and of those they suspect, asking that they should give their signatures in the presence of all the people, that there may be no further disturbance or dispute about this question. Accordingly, with the permission of God and secondly of the bishops, thirdly of the presbyters, and also of the people, I will again say what I think on this subject. Offering is universally made to Almighty God through Jesus Christ inasmuch as, in respect of his deity, he is akin to the Father. Let there be no double offering, but an offering to God through God. I shall seem to be speaking in a daring manner. When we pray let us abide by the agreements.[11] If the word: "Thou shalt not respect the person of man, nor allow thyself to be impressed by the person of the mighty"[12] is not realized . . . If this is

[9] John 10:30.

[10] Isa. 43:10; Deut. 32:39.

[11] . . . the general idea of this corrupt passage is an appeal to the universal sense of the church. It is likely that Origen means the agreed formulas of liturgical prayer: *lex orandi lex credendi.* . . .

[12] Lev. 19:15. The quotation is odd . . . and the passage, the text of which is more corrupt than any other in the Dialogue, was not understood by the original scribe. The general sense is that if unauthorized people interfere, there will be chaos and the authorized ministry deprived of all meaning.

not realized . . . these agreements, it will give rise to fresh disputes. . . . If a man is a bishop or a presbyter, he is not a bishop, he is not a presbyter. If he is a deacon, he is not a deacon, nor even a layman. If he is a layman, he is not a layman, nor is there a meeting of the congregation. If you assent, let these agreed usages prevail.

Some people raise the objection that, with reference to the problem of deity, while I have thus attributed deity to Jesus Christ substantially, I have professed before the church my faith that at the resurrection the body which rose had been a corpse. But since our Saviour and Lord took a body, let us examine what the body was. The church alone in distinction from all the heresies that deny the resurrection confesses the resurrection of the dead body. For from the fact that the firstfruits were raised from the dead, it follows that the dead are raised. "Christ the firstfruits"[13]; on that account his body became a corpse. For if his body had not become a corpse, capable of being wrapped in a grave-cloth, of receiving the ointment and all the other things applied to dead bodies, and of being laid in a tomb[14]—these are things that cannot be done to a spiritual body. For it is entirely impossible for that which is spiritual to become a corpse, neither can that which is spiritual become insensible. For if it were possible for that which is spiritual to become a corpse, we would have reason to fear lest after the resurrection of the dead, when our body is raised, according to the apostle's saying, "It is sown animate, it is raised spiritual,"[15] we shall all die. . . . In fact "Christ being raised from the dead dies no more."[16] And not only Christ, but those who are Christ's,[17] when they are raised from the dead, die no more. If you agree to these statements, they also with the solemn testimony of the people shall be made legally binding and established.[18]

What else is there to be said concerning the faith? Do you agree to this, Maximus? Say.

Maximus: May everyone hold the same doctrines as I do. Before God and the Church I both give my signature and make my oath.

[13] I Cor. 15:12 ff.
[14] I Cor. 15:44.
[15] Matt. 27:59; Mark 15:46; Luke 23:53.
[16] Rom. 6:9.
[17] I Cor. 15:23.
[18] The procedure appears to have been that at the end of the synod the doctrinal decisions would have been formally set forth, and the congregation would have declared their adherence thereto.

But the reason why I raised a certain question was in order that I might be in no doubt or uncertainty at all. For the brethren know that this is what I said: "I need the help of my brother and instruction on this point." If the spirit was truly given back to the Father, in accordance with the saying, "Father, into thy hands I commend my spirit,"[19] and if without the spirit the flesh died and lay in the tomb, how was the tomb opened and how are the dead to rise again?

Orig.: That man is a composite being we have learnt from the sacred Scriptures. For the apostle says, "May God sanctify your spirit and your soul and your body," and "May he sanctify you wholly, and may your entire spirit and soul and body be preserved unblameable at the coming of our Lord Jesus Christ."[20] This spirit is not the Holy Spirit, but part of the constitution of man, as the same apostle teaches when he says: "The spirit bears witness with our spirit."[21] For if it were the Holy Spirit he would not have said: "The spirit bears witness with our spirit." So then our Saviour and Lord, wishing to save man in the way in which he wished to save him, for this reason desired in this way to save the body, just as it was likewise his will to save also the soul; he also wished to save the remaining part of man, the spirit. The whole man would not have been saved unless he had taken upon him the whole man. They do away with the salvation of the human body when they say that the body of the Saviour is spiritual. They do away with the salvation of the human spirit, concerning which the apostle says: "No man knows the things of man except the spirit of man that is in him."[22] ... Because it was his will to save the spirit of man, about which the apostle said this, he also assumed the spirit of man. At the time of the passion these three were separated. At the time of the resurrection these three were united. At the time of the passion they were separated —how? The body in the tomb, the soul in Hades, the spirit was put in the hands of the Father. The soul in Hades: "Thou shalt not leave my soul in Hades."[23] If the spirit was put into the hands of the Father, he gave the spirit as a deposit. It is one thing to make a gift, another thing to hand over, and another to leave in deposit. He who

[19] Luke 23:46.
[20] I Thess. 5:23. ...
[21] Rom. 8.16.
[22] I Cor. 2:11.
[23] Ps. 16 (15):10; Acts 2:27.

makes a deposit does so with the intention of receiving back that which he has deposited. Why then had he to give the spirit to the Father as a deposit? The question is beyond me and my powers and my understanding. For I am not endowed with knowledge to enable me to say that, just as the body was not able to go down to Hades, even if this is alleged by those who affirm that the body of Jesus was spiritual, so also neither could the spirit go down to Hades, and therefore he gave the spirit to the Father as a deposit until he should have risen from the dead. . . . After he had entrusted this deposit to the Father, he took it back again. When? Not at the actual moment of the resurrection, but immediately after the resurrection. My witness is the text of the gospel. The Lord Jesus Christ rose again from the dead. Mary met him and he said to her: "Touch me not."[24] For he wished anyone that touched him to touch him in his entirety, that having touched him in his entirety he might be benefited in body from his body, in soul from his soul, in spirit from his spirit. "For I am not yet ascended to the Father." He ascends to the Father and comes to the disciples. Accordingly he ascends to the Father. Why? To receive back the deposit.

All the questions about the faith which disturbed us have been examined. But we must realize that at the divine tribunal we are not judged for faith alone,[25] as if our life were left unexamined, nor for our life alone, as if our faith were not subject to scrutiny. We are justified on the ground that both are correct. We are punished for both if both are incorrect. There are some, however, who will not be punished for both, but for one of the two: some for their faith because it is defective, but not because their life is lacking in right conduct; others, again, will not be punished for their faith, but will be for their life, on the ground that they have lived a life contrary to right reason. My opinion is that in the Proverbs of Solomon these two kinds (I mean that which concerns our belief and knowledge and that which concerns our manner of life) are mentioned by Solomon in the following words: "Who shall boast that he has a pure heart? Or who shall present himself saying that he is free from sins?"[26] The difference between these we take to be this: the "heart" means the thought, the "sins" refer to actions. "Who shall boast that he has a pure heart"

24 John 20:17.
25 Cf. James 2:24.
26 Prov. 20:9.

which is undefiled by the knowledge falsely so-called,[27] undefiled
by falsehood? Or "who shall present himself saying that he is free
from sins," having done nothing amiss in his practical conduct? If
then we wish to be saved, let us not be concerned about faith to the
neglect of practical conduct of life, nor again let us place our confidence in our life. Let us realize, let us comprehend, let us believe that
it is on the ground of both that we either receive our acquittal or
blessedness, or receive the opposite of these. The things that are
liable to punishment, therefore, are not merely the terrible and
fearful sins which should not even be named,[28] whether sins of life
or of thought, but also sins commonly thought to be of less importance. That is why, it seems, the apostle puts side by side with
acts which are abominable, infamous, and revolting (if I may so
say) things which are regarded by most people as of little significance.
What does he say? "Be not deceived; neither fornicators, nor adulterers, nor effeminate men, nor homosexuals, nor thieves, nor drunkards, nor revilers, shall inherit the kingdom of God."[29] You see that
together with such gross sinners as the homosexual person, the effeminate man, the adulterer, the fornicator, he enumerates the drunkard,
the reviler—sins thought by all of us to be of small account, so that
we may be taught that it is not for the great sins alone that we are
excluded from the kingdom of God, but also for these which are
commonly supposed to be of minor significance. Therefore, let us
not revile, nor be drunkards, nor extort, nor steal, nor do anything
wrong, even if we are "deceived."

If there is any further point to raise concerning the Rule of faith,
mention it. We will speak still further upon the Scripture.

Dionysius said: Is the soul the blood?

Orig.: It has come to my notice, and I say this with full knowledge
of the facts, that some of the folk here and in the neighbourhood
suppose that after the soul has departed this life it is incapable of
feeling, but is in the tomb, in the body. And I know that on this
question I was impelled to deal very severely with the other Heraclides and Celer his predecessor, so severely in fact that I would
have preferred to leave the subject and to go away. But for the sake
of honour and for the subject under debate he summoned us to deal

[27] I Tim. 6:20.
[28] Eph. 5:3.
[29] I Cor. 6:9-10. . . .

with it. We agreed to discuss the matter; he made a statement . . .[30] how the former cleared himself before us as though before God, by his orthodox statements.

Accordingly, the question posed by the beloved Dionysius forces our hand. I shall first set out the passages which trouble them, lest any one of them be omitted, and by God's permission we will answer each one of them in accordance with your request. The disturbing passage is as follows: "The soul of all flesh is blood." This text has terribly distressed those who have not understood it. Also, "Ye shall not eat the soul with the flesh; pay strict heed to see that you eat no blood; ye shall not eat the soul with the flesh."[31] The disturbing text is this one. For the other distressing texts are far less emphatic in expressing the idea suggested here. For my part, according to my measure of understanding, and praying for assistance in reading the divine words (for we are in need of help lest our minds should conceive ideas diverging from the truth),[32] I have found that incorporeal things are given the same names as all the corporeal things, so that just as corporeal things apply to the outer man, those which are given the same names as corporeal things apply to the inner man. The Bible says that man is two men: "For if our outward man perish, yet our inward man is renewed day by day," and "I rejoice in the law of God after the inward man."[33] These two men the apostle everywhere shows to be distinct. In my judgment he would not have ventured to invent this notion out of his own head, but rather said this because he had clearly understood statements in the Scriptures which are obscurely expressed. Some people imagine that there is a mere repetition when in the story of the creation of the world after the creation of man we read "God took dust of the earth and formed man."[34] The corollary of this interpretation is that it is the body which is the part "after the image,"[35] and that God is given a human form, or that the form of God[36] is shaped like the

[30] The sense is not clear and was not understood by the scribe. Whether Heraclides or Celer cleared himself before Origen is obscure.

[31] Lev. 17:11 f; Deut. 12:23.

[32] Origen often says that divine grace and prayer are necessary for interpreting the Scripture rightly. . . .

[33] II Cor. 4:16; Rom. 7:22.

[34] Gen. 2:7.

[35] Gen. 1:26.

[36] Cf. Phil. 2:6.

human body. But we are not so crazy as to say either that God is composed of a superior and an inferior element so that that which is in his image is like him in both elements, which constitute God in his completeness, or that that which is in his image consisted rather in the inferior part and not in the superior.[37]

The questions are highly delicate. We need hearers who have an acute understanding. I therefore charge those who listen to pay heed to themselves lest they should make me liable to the accusation of casting holy things to the dogs, to shameless souls. For the barkers, like dogs, those who think only of fornication and abuse, do nothing but yelp like dogs, and it is not right for me to cast holy things before such folk. So also I charge my hearers that they do not make me liable to the accusation of laying splendid pearls, which we try to collect like good merchants, before people steeped in the impurities of their bodies, and who are therefore called swine.[38] For I would say that a person who continually steeps himself and wallows in the filth of life and makes no attempt to live a pure life, a holy life, is simply a swine. If then, because the kingdom of heaven is like a merchant seeking goodly pearls, I find the goodly pearls, and having bought them at the price of weariness and sleeplessness I fling them before pleasure-loving souls, and those who are steeped in the filth of the body and in impurity, then I also will be a transgressor because I am casting pearls before swine. But when the swine have got the pearls, because they do not perceive their beauty nor see their excellence, they tread them under foot by speaking evil of what was rightly said, and not only do they trample the pearls under foot, but they also turn and rend those who supplied them with the pearls.

I beseech you, therefore, be transformed. Resolve to learn that in you there is the capacity to be transformed, and to put off the form of a swine, which is in an impure soul, and the shape of a dog, which is that of a man who barks and reviles and pours out abuse. It is also possible to be transformed from the shape of snakes; for a wicked man is described as a serpent and "the offspring of vipers."[39] If, then, we are willing to understand that in us there is the power to be transformed from being serpents, swine, and dogs, let us learn from the apostle that the transformation depends upon us. For he

[37] The text here is corrupt.
[38] Matt. 7:6.
[39] Cf. Matt. 23:33. . . .

says this: "We all, when with unveiled face we reflect the glory of the Lord, are transformed into the same image."[40] If you are like a barking dog, and if the Word has moulded and transformed you, you have been transformed from being a dog to being a man. If you were impure and the Word came to your soul and you submitted yourself to the moulding of the Word, you changed from being a swine to being a man. If you were a savage beast, and heard the Word that tames and softens, that changes you into a man, by the will of the Word you will no longer be called a serpent, the offspring of vipers. For if it were impossible for these serpents, serpents in their soul because of wickedness, to be changed, the Saviour (or John) would not have said: "Do therefore fruits worthy of repentance."[41] After repentance you are no longer a serpent, the offspring of vipers.

Since it is our task to speak about man, and to inquire whether the soul of man is not blood, and since this subject required us to discuss in detail the doctrine of the two men, and as we have come to a mysterious subject, I beseech you that you do not cause me to be accused of casting pearls before swine, of throwing holy things to the dogs, of flinging divine things to serpents, of giving the serpent a share in the tree of life. That I may avoid this accusation, be transformed, put off evil, quarrelling, wrath, strife, anger, division of opinion,[42] that there may not be any further schisms among you but that "you may be firmly established in the same mind and the same judgment."[43]

To speak makes me embarrassed, and not to speak makes me embarrassed. Because of those who are worthy I would speak, lest I be accused of depriving of the word those able to understand it. Because of the unworthy I shrink from speaking for the reasons I have given, lest I should be flinging holy things to dogs and casting pearls before swine. It was the work of Jesus only to know how to distinguish among his hearers between those without and those within, so that he spoke to those without in parables, but explained the parables to those who entered into his house.[44] To remain without

[40] II Cor. 3:18.
[41] Luke 3:8; cf. Matt. 3:8.
[42] Cf. Col. 3:8.
[43] I Cor. 1:10.
[44] Cf. Mark 4:11; Matt. 13:36. . . .

and to enter into the house have a mystical meaning. "Why should I judge those that are without?"[45] Every sinner is without. That is why those without are addressed in parables in case they should be able to leave the things without and enter within. To enter the house has a mystical meaning: he who enters Jesus' house is his true disciple. He enters by holding the doctrine of the church, by living a life according to the teaching of the church. "Within" and "without" are spiritual terms.

You see how long an introduction I have given in order to prepare my hearers: I shrink from speaking. When I am on the point of speaking I put it off. What is my purpose in doing this? To shape my discourse so as to heal the souls of my hearers.

At the creation of man, then, there was first created the man that is "after the image," in whom there was nothing material. He who is in the image is not made out of matter. "And God said, Let us make man in our image and likeness, and let them have dominion"[46] and so on. And when God made man he did not take dust of the earth, as he did the second time, but he made him in the image of God. That that which is in the image of God is understood as immaterial and superior to all corporeal existence not only by Moses but also by the apostle is shown by his words, as follows: "Putting off the old man with his deeds and putting on the new which is renewed in the knowledge of him who created him."[47]

Therefore in each one of us there are two men. Why does Scripture say that the soul of all flesh is blood? It is a great problem. Just as the outward man has the same name as the inward man, so also this is true of his members, so that one may say that every member of the outward man has a name corresponding to what is true of the inward man.

The outward man has eyes, and the inward man also is said to have eyes: "Lighten my eyes lest I sleep in death."[48] This does not refer to these eyes, nor to physical sleep, nor to ordinary death. "The commandment of the Lord, luminous, enlightens the eyes."[49]

[45] I Cor. 5:12.
[46] Gen. 1:26-27. Origen follows Philo . . . in interpreting Gen. ch. 1 of the creation of the archetypal Image; Gen. ch. 2 describes the making of material man of the dust of the earth.
[47] Col. 3:9.
[48] Ps. 13 (12):3.
[49] Ps. 19 (18):8.

By keeping the commandments of the Lord we do not become more sharp-sighted physically but by keeping the divine commands we become more sharp-sighted in mind. The eyes of our inward man see with greater perception: "Open my eyes and I shall comprehend the wonders of thy Law."[50] It is not that his eyes were veiled; but our eyes are our mind. It is for Jesus alone to unveil them, that we may be able to understand the Scriptures and comprehend what is obscurely expressed.

The outward man has ears, and the inward man also is said to have ears. "He that has ears to hear, let him hear."[51] They all had ears as organs of physical sense; but they had not all succeeded in having the inward ears which are purified. To possess the latter sort of ears is not part of our natural constitution; the former are part of our nature. And because the former sort of ears are part of our nature the prophet says, "Hear ye deaf, and ye blind, look and see. Who is deaf but my servants, and who is blind but those who are their lords? Even the servants of God are blinded."[52] That to become deaf is what we bring upon ourselves—let us pay attention: what I am saying will affect all of us; it is necessary to describe the inward man to discover what the blood is—that to become deaf in respect of the inward ears is something we bring upon ourselves, hear the declaration of the prophet: "Sinners are alienated from the womb; they have erred from the womb. They have spoken lies. Wrath is upon them after the likeness of the serpent, like a deaf adder which stops her ears, which does not hear the voice of those who enchant her and the incantation pronounced by a wise man."[53] And all of you also who are aware that you are responsible, if you hear the word and the incantation pronounced by a wise man and listen to the enchanting words, so that he may check your wrath and iniquity, and if, then, you shut your ears, and do not throw them wide open to accept what is said, then to you apply the words: "Wrath is on them after the likeness of the serpent like a deaf adder which stops her ears, which does not hear the voice of those who enchant her and the incantation pronounced by a wise man."

The outward man has nostrils with which to smell, and so per-

[50] Ps. 119 (118):18.
[51] Matt. 11:15, etc.
[52] Isa. 42:18.
[53] Ps. 58 (57):3-5. . . .

ceives good and bad smells; and the inner man with different nostrils perceives the good smell of righteousness and the bad smell of sins. Of the good smell the apostle teaches us when he says, "We are a sweet savour of Christ unto God in every place, among them that are saved and them that are perishing; to the one a savour of death unto death, to the others a savour of life unto life."[54] And Solomon also says in the Song of Songs, putting the words into the mouth of the daughters of Jerusalem: "After thee we will run to the odour of thy perfumes."[55] As, then, we perceive with our nostrils good and bad smells in the world of sense, so also for the inward man there is a perception of the good smell of righteousness such as the apostle had, and an evil smell of sins, which is possessed by the person whose divine senses are in good health. What is the evil smell of sins? That of which the prophet says this: "My sores have become foul and rotten in face of my foolishness."[56]

The outward man has the sense of taste; and the inner man also has a spiritual taste, of which it is said: "Taste and see that the Lord is kindly."[57]

The outward man has physical touch. The inner man also has touch, that touch by which the woman with the issue of blood touched the hem of Jesus' garment.[58] She touched it. For he witnessed to the fact saying, "Who touched me?" Yet just before Peter said to him, "The crowds throng you and you say, Who touched me?" He imagined that those who touched him, touched by physical, not spiritual, contact. Those, therefore, who thronged Jesus did not touch him. For they did not touch him by faith. Only the woman, who had a sort of divine touch, touched Jesus and by this was healed. And because she touched him with a divine touch, power went out from Jesus at her divine touch. He says therefore: "Who touched me? For I have felt power to go forth from me." Concerning this more divine touch John says: "And our hands have handled concerning the word of life."[59]

In this way we possess other hands, concerning which it is said: "Let the lifting up of my hands be an evening sacrifice."[60] For it is

54 II Cor. 2:15-16.
55 S. of Sol. 1:4.
56 Ps. 38 (37):5.
57 Ps. 34 (33):8; I Pet. 2:3.
58 Luke 8:45-46; Mark 5:29-32.
59 I John 1:1.
60 Ps. 141 (140):2.

not when I lift up these hands, while the hands of my soul hang down instead of being lifted up by holy and good works, that the lifting up my hands becomes an evening sacrifice. I also have feet of a different kind, concerning which Solomon commands me saying, "Let not thy foot stumble."[61]

There is a curious saying in Ecclesiastes. To anyone that does not understand it it will seem meaningless, but it is for the wise man that Ecclesiastes says: "The wise man has his eyes in his head."[62] In what head? Every man, even the blockhead and the fool, has his bodily eyes in his bodily head. But "the wise man has his eyes" (those of which I have already spoken, which are enlightened by the Lord's commandment[63]) "in his head," in Christ, since "Christ is the head of a man,"[64] the apostle says. The thinking faculty is in Christ.

"My belly, my belly is in pain,"[65] says Jeremiah. In what belly is he in pain? That in which we too feel pain, that by which, when it is in travail bringing the people to birth[66]; "I suffer pain in my belly and my sense"—not these senses, but those of my heart.

Even if I pass on to the fine parts of the body, I see them in the soul under an unfleshly form. "Lord, reprove me not in thine anger; chastise me not in thy anger. Have pity on me, Lord, for I am feeble. Heal me Lord, for my bones are troubled."[67] What bones of the prophet were troubled? The constitution of his soul and the firmness of his mind was troubled, and he implored the Lord for the restoration of those bones. "Our bones are scattered in Hades."[68] What bones of the speaker were scattered in Hades? Consider, I pray you, the sinner, consider his frame in the domain of sin, in the domain of the dead, in the domain of evil, and you will say of such a man that his bones are scattered. "All my bones will say, Lord who is like unto thee?"[69] They are the bones which speak, converse with, and perceive God, whereas these bones are incapable of perception, as is shown by the sons of physicians; when they saw off a man's

61 Prov. 3:23.
62 Eccles. 2:14.
63 Cf. Ps. 19 (18):8.
64 I Cor. 11:3.
65 Jer. 4:19.
66 Cf. Gal. 4:19.
67 Ps. 6:2-3.
68 Ps. 141 (140):7.
69 Ps. 35 (34):10.

bones, he does not feel the saw. "All my bones will say, Lord who is like unto thee?" All the bones are those which belong to the inner man.

The inner man has a heart. "Hear me, ye who have lost your heart."[70] They possessed a heart, that of the body; it was not that heart which they lost. But when a man neglects to cultivate his intellectual life, and in consequence of much idleness his thinking capacity has atrophied, he has lost his heart, and it is to such a person that the words are added: "Hear me, ye who have lost your heart."

"The hairs of your head are all numbered."[71] What hairs? Those by virtue of which they were Nazirites in a spiritual sense.

Thus you have all the parts of the visible body in the inner man. Do not doubt, then, concerning the blood also because it has the same name as physical blood, like the other members of the body. It is that which belongs to the inner man. It is that blood which is poured forth from a sinful soul. For "The blood of your souls shall be required."[72] It does not say "your blood" but "the blood of your souls." And "I will require the blood at the hand of the watchman."[73] What kind of blood does God require at the hand of the watchman, but that which is poured forth from the sinner? Thus the heart of the fool perishes, and it is said, "Hear me, ye who have lost your heart," because there is poured forth the blood and the vital power of the soul.

If one comprehends what the soul is, and that it belongs to the inner man, and that it is in that part there is the element which is "in the image," it is clear that Paul was right when he said: "For it were better to depart and to be with Christ."[74] Before the resurrection the righteous man is with Christ and in his soul he lives with Christ. That is why it is better to depart and to be with Christ. But according to you who say that the soul remains in the tomb with the body, it has not left the body, it does not rest, it does not dwell in the paradise of God, it does not repose in the bosom of Abraham.[75] According to you who maintain such absurd doctrines it would not be better to depart and to be with Christ. For one is not with Christ as soon

70 Isa. 46:12.
71 Matt. 10:30.
72 Gen. 9:5.
73 Ezek. 33:6.
74 Phil. 1:23.
75 Luke 16:23.

as one departs if the soul is the blood. If the soul remains in the tombs, how can it be with Christ? But according to my view and that of the word of God, the soul which has departed from the troubles, the sweat, and the body, that which can say, "Lord now lettest thou thy servant depart in peace,"[76] is that which departs in peace and rests with Christ. It is thus that the soul of Abraham understood the words: "As for thee, thou shalt go in peace to thy fathers, having lived to a good old age."[77] He departed to his fathers. What fathers? Those of whom Paul says: "For this cause I bow my knees to the Father of whom all fatherhood is derived."[78] In our view it was in this sense that Aaron was set free.[79] Also it is written in Ecclesiastes concerning the just man who has fought a good fight, who is departing from the fetter of the body, that "From the house of the prisoners he will go forth to be a king."[80] Thus I am persuaded to die for the truth, thus I readily despise what is called death. Bring wild beasts, bring crosses, bring fire, bring tortures. I know that as soon as I die, I come forth from the body, I rest with Christ. Therefore let us struggle, therefore let us wrestle, let us groan being in the body,[81] not as if we shall again be in the tombs in the body, because we shall be set free from it, and shall change our body to one which is more spiritual. Destined as we are to be with Christ, how we groan while we are in the body!

Bishop Philip came in, and Demetrius, another bishop, said: Brother Origen teaches that the soul is immortal.

Orig.: The remark of father Demetrius has given us the starting point for another problem. He asserted that we have said the soul is immortal. To this remark I will say that the soul is immortal and the soul is not immortal. Let us first define the meaning of the word "death," and determine all its possible senses. I will try to show all its meanings not by appealing to the Greeks, but all its meanings as found in the divine Scripture. Perhaps one more learned than I will point out other senses also. But for the present I am aware of three kinds of death. What are these three kinds of death? According to

[76] Luke 2:29.
[77] Gen. 15:15.
[78] Eph. 3:14.
[79] Num. 20:29.
[80] Eccles. 4:14.
[81] II Cor. 5:2, 4.

the apostle, a man may live unto God and die unto sin.[82] This death is a blessed thing. A man dies to sin. This death my Lord died. "For in that he died, he died unto sin."[83] I know also another sort of death, according to which a man dies to God; concerning this it was said: "The soul that sins, it shall die."[84] And I know of a third kind of death, according to which we commonly suppose that those who are separated from the body die. For "Adam lived nine hundred and thirty years and died."[85]

There being, then, three kinds of death, let us see whether the human soul is immortal in respect of the three kinds of death, or if not in respect of the three, yet in respect of some of them. The death that is a matter of moral indifference all men die. It is that which we consider dissolution. No soul of man dies this death. For if it did so, it would not be punished after death. It is said: "Men shall seek for death and shall not find it."[86] In this sense every human soul is immortal. But in the other meanings, the soul in one sense is mortal, and blessed if it dies to sin. It is of this death that Balaam spoke when he prophesied, praying by divine inspiration: "May my soul die among the souls of the just."[87] Concerning this death Balaam made his astonishing prophecy, and by the word of God he made for himself a splendid prayer. For he prayed that he might die to sin that he might live unto God. And this account he said: "May my soul die among the souls of the just and my posterity be like their posterity." There is another death in respect of which we are not immortal, although we have the power by exercising vigilance to avoid death. And perhaps that which is mortal in the soul is not for ever mortal. For in so far as it gives way to sin, so that the word is realized which says, "the soul that sins, it shall die,"[88] the soul is mortal and dies a real death. But if it is found firmly established in blessedness so that it is inaccessible to death, because it has eternal life, it is no longer mortal but in this sense has even become immortal. How is it that the apostle says of God: "He who alone has im-

[82] Rom. 6:2.
[83] Rom. 6:10.
[84] Ezek. 18:4.
[85] Gen. 5:5.
[86] Rev. 9:6.
[87] Num. 23:10.
[88] Ezek. 18:4.

mortality"?[89] On investigation I find that Christ Jesus "died for all apart from God."[90] There you have the explanation how God alone has immortality.

Let us therefore take up eternal life. Let us take up that which depends upon our decision. God does not give it to us. He sets it before us. "Behold, I have set life before thy face."[91] It is in our power to stretch out our hand, to do good works, and to lay hold on life and deposit it in our soul. This life is the Christ who said: "I am the life."[92] This life is that which now is present in shadow, but then will be face to face.[93] "For the spirit before our face is Christ of whom we may say, In his shadow we shall live among the nations."[94] If the mere shadow of life that is yours offers you so many good things, that shadow which Moses had when he prophesied, that shadow which Isaiah possessed when he saw the Lord Sabaoth sitting upon a throne high and lifted up, which Jeremiah had when he heard the words: "Before I formed thee in the womb, I knew thee, and before thou didst come forth from the womb I sanctified thee," which Ezekiel had when he saw the Cherubim, when he saw the wheels, the ineffable mysteries[95]: what sort of life shall we live when we are no longer living under the shadow of life but are in life itself. For now "our life is hid with Christ; but when Christ, who is our life, shall appear, then shall we also appear with him in glory."[96] Let us haste towards this life, groaning and grieving that we are in this tent, that we dwell in the body. So long as we are present in the body, we are absent from the Lord.[97] Let us long to be absent from the body and to be present with the Lord, that being present with him we may become one with the God of the universe and his only begotten Son, being saved in all things and becoming blessed, in Jesus Christ, to whom be the glory and the power for ever and ever. Amen.

[89] I Tim. 6:16.

[90] II Cor. 5:15; Heb. 2:9, which Origen knows in both readings (a) "apart from God," (b) "by the grace of God" (*Comm. in Joann.*, I, 35 (40); XXVIII, 18 (14)). He regarded the first as the correct text.

[91] Deut. 30:15.

[92] John 11:25; 14:6.

[93] I Cor. 13:12.

[94] Lam. 4:20.

[95] Isa. 6:1; Jer. 1:5; Ezek. 1:15; 10:1.

[96] Col. 3:3-4.

[97] II Cor. 5:6, 8.

3. GREGORY OF NYSSA: Entering The Dark Cloud*

Gregory of Nyssa (A.D. 330-394) was personally associated with two other Fathers of the Eastern Christian Church—his brother, Basil the Great, and his friend, Gregory Nazianzen. All three came from Cappadocia, in their time a part of the Eastern Roman Empire, today a part of Turkey. The extensive writings† of Gregory of Nyssa include much material which blends metaphorical and allegorical language with philosophical language. His immediate purposes in writing were often quite practical and related to the personal development of his readers. He provided much to influence the later intellectual life of Western civilization, as we can especially see in Augustine and Bernard of Clairvaux.

But what now is the meaning of Moses' entry into the darkness and of the vision of God that he enjoyed in it? The present text (Exod. 24.15) would seem to be somewhat contradictory to the divine apparition he has seen before. There he saw God in the light, whereas here he sees Him in the darkness. But we should not therefore think that this contradicts the entire sequence of spiritual lessons which we have been considering. For the sacred text is here teaching us that spiritual knowledge first occurs as an illumination in those who experience it. Indeed, all that is opposed to piety is conceived of as darkness; to shun the darkness is to share in the light. But as the soul makes progress, and by a greater and more perfect concentration comes to appreciate what the knowledge of truth is, the more it approaches this vision, and so much the more does it see that the divine nature is invisible. It thus leaves all surface appearances, not only those that can be grasped by the senses but also those which the mind itself seems to see, and it keeps on going deeper until by the operation of the spirit it penetrates the invisible and incomprehensible, and it is there that it sees God. The true vision and the

* Chapter 15, "The Life of Moses," 376C-377A; ed. Danielou, ii. 162-164.
† The selections are taken from chapters 15, 17, 75, 77 and 83 of *From Glory to Glory: Texts from Gregory of Nyssa's Mystical Writings*, selected and with an introduction by Jean Danielou, S.J., translated and edited by Herbert Musurillo, S.J. (New York: Charles Scribner's Sons, 1962). Used by permission.

true knowledge of what we seek consists precisely in not seeing, in an awareness that our goal transcends all knowledge and is everywhere cut off from us by the darkness of incomprehensibility. Thus that profound evangelist, John, who penetrated into this luminous darkness, tells us that *no man hath seen God at any time* (John 1.18), teaching us by this negation that no man—indeed, no created intellect —can attain a knowledge of God.

4. GREGORY OF NYSSA: The Abyss of Knowledge*

. . . So too no created being can go out of itself by rational contemplation. Whatever it sees, it must see itself; and even if it thinks it is seeing beyond itself, it does not in fact possess a nature which can achieve this. And thus in its contemplation of Being it tries to force itself to transcend a spatial representation, but it never achieves it. For in every possible thought, the mind is surely aware of the spatial element which it perceives in addition to the thought content; and the spatial element is, of course, created. Yet the Good that we have learned to seek and to cherish is beyond all creation, and hence beyond all comprehension. Thus how can our mind, which always operates on a dimensional image, comprehend a nature that has no dimension, especially as our minds are constantly penetrating, by analysis, into things which are more and more profound. And though the mind in its restlessness ranges through all that is knowable, it has never yet discovered a way of comprehending eternity in such wise that it might place itself outside of it, and go beyond the idea of eternity itself and that Being which is above all being. It is like someone who finds himself on a mountain ridge. Imagine a sheer, steep crag, of reddish appearance below, extending into eternity; on top there is this ridge which looks down over a projecting rim into a bottomless chasm. Now imagine what a person would probably experience if he put his foot on the edge of this ridge which overlooks the chasm and found no solid footing nor anything to hold on to.

* Chapter 17, Commentary on Ecclesiastes, sermon 7, 44. 724D-732D. See Introduction to Selection 3.

This is what I think the soul experiences when it goes beyond its footing in material things, in its quest for that which has no dimension and which exists from all eternity. For here there is nothing it can take hold of, neither place nor time, neither measure nor anything else; it does not allow our minds to approach. And thus the soul, slipping at every point from what cannot be grasped, becomes dizzy and perplexed and returns once again to what is connatural to it, content now to know merely this about the Transcendent, that it is completely different from the nature of the things that the soul knows.

Thus it is, then, that when reason touches on those things which are beyond it, that is the *time to keep silence* (Eccles. 3.7); rather it keeps the wonder of that ineffable power within the secret of our conscience, fully aware that great men have spoken not of God but rather of his works, saying: *Who shall declare the powers of the Lord?* (Ps. 105.2) and *I will relate all thy wonders* (Ps. 9.2), and *Generation and generation shall praise thy works* (Ps. 144.4). This is what they discuss and this is what they have to say in their attempt to translate reality into words. But when their discourse touches on that which transcends all knowledge, it is rather silence that they prescribe in what they tell us. For they tell us that *of the magnificence of the glory of His holiness there is no end.* Ah, the wonder of it! Why does the sacred text fear to approach the glory of the divine mystery, so that it has not even expressed any of those effects which are outside His nature? It does not say that God's essence is without limit, judging it rash even to express this in a concept; rather it merely marvels at the vision *of the magnificence of His glory.* But once again he is unable to see the substance of this glory; he is merely in amazement at the glory of His holiness. He is far from being concerned with the exact nature of God's essence; he has not the power to show admiration for the least of God's manifestations; for he does not admire God's *holiness,* nor even *the glory of His holiness,* but merely attempts to admire *the magnificence of the glory of His holiness,* and even here his powers fail. His mind, then, did not comprehend the ultimate limit of what he admired; and hence he says: *Of the magnificence of the glory of His holiness there is no end.*

Thus in speaking of God, when there is question of His essence, then is the *time to keep silence.* When, however, it is a question of His operation, a knowledge of which can come down even to us, that is the *time to speak* of His omnipotence by telling of his works and explaining His deeds, and to use words to this extent. In things, however, which go beyond this, the creature must not exceed the bounds of its nature, but must be content to know itself. For indeed, in my view, if the creature never comes to know itself, never understands the essence of the soul or the nature of the body, the cause of being, how beings arise from one another by generation, how being comes from non-being and is resolved into non-being, how the universe is harmoniously constructed out of contraries—if the creature does not know itself, how can it ever explain things that are beyond it? Of such things it is *time to keep silence;* here silence is surely better. There is, however, *a time to speak* of those things by which we can in our lives make progress in virtue.

5. GREGORY OF NYSSA: The Successive Purifications*

. . . The soul that looks up towards God, and conceives that good desire for His eternal beauty, constantly experiences an ever new yearning for that which lies ahead, and her desire is never given its full satisfaction. Hence she never ceases *to stretch herself forth to those things that are before,* ever passing from her present stage to enter more deeply into the interior, into the stage which lies ahead. And so at each point she judges each great marvelous grace to be inferior to what is yet to come, because each newly won grace always seems to be more beautiful than those she has previously enjoyed. It was in this way that Paul died daily (I Cor. 15.13). For each moment that he participated more deeply in life he died to all that was past, forgetting those graces which he had already attained. . . .

But there is still another interpretation that we can discover in the text, quite in harmony with what we have already considered. The soul, having gone out at the word of her Beloved, looks for Him but does not find Him. She calls on Him, though He cannot be reached by any verbal symbol, and she is told by the watchmen that she is in love with the unattainable, and that the object of her

* Chapter 75, *ibid.,* 1029A-1037C. See Introduction to Selection 3.

longing cannot be apprehended. In this way she is, in a certain sense, wounded and beaten because of the frustration of what she desires, now that she thinks that her yearning for the Other cannot be fulfilled or satisfied. But the veil of her grief is removed when she learns that the true satisfaction of her desire consists in constantly going on with her quest and never ceasing in her ascent, seeing that every fulfillment of her desire continually generates a further desire for the Transcendent.

Thus the veil of her despair is torn away and the bride realizes that she will always discover more and more of the incomprehensible and unhoped for beauty of her Spouse throughout all eternity. Then she is torn by an even more urgent longing, and through the daughters of Jerusalem she communicates to her Beloved the dispositions of her heart. For she has received within her God's special dart, she has been wounded in the heart by the point of faith, she has been mortally wounded by the arrow of love. And *God is love*.

6. GREGORY OF NYSSA: The New Creation*

The establishment of the Church is a re-creation of the world. In the Church there is a new heaven, as the Prophet said (Is. 65.17). Here too there is a new firmament, which is, as Paul tells us, faith in Christ (1 Tim. 3.15). A new earth is formed, and it drinks up the rains that pour down upon it. Man is created once again, for by his rebirth from on high he is renewed according to the image of his Creator. There is also a new light, of which He speaks: *You are the light of the world* (Matth. 5.14); and again: *Among whom you shine as lights in the world* (Phil. 2.15). And there are many stars rising on the firmament of faith. And there should be no wonder that there are so many stars numbered by God in this world and called by name, for their names, says their Creator, have been written in heaven. For it is in this sense that I understand the Creator of the new universe to say to His luminaries: *Your names are written in heaven* (Luke 10.20). This is not the only striking thing about the

* Chapter 77, *ibid.*, 1049B-1052A. See Introduction to Selection 3.

new creation, that the Word has created in it a multitude of stars. There are also many suns, that light up the world with the rays of good works. For thus does their Creator speak: *Let your light shine before men* (Matth. 5.16); and, again: *Then shall the just shine as the sun* (Matth. 14.43).

Anyone who gazes upon the visible universe and sees the wisdom that has been impressed upon the beauty of all creatures, can argue from the visible to the invisible beauty, the fountainhead of all Wisdom, Whose influence brought all creatures into being. So too, anyone who looks upon the universe of this new creation reflected in the Church, can see in it Him Who is all in all, and thus through things that are intelligible and understandable he may be led by our faith to an awareness of the Transcendent.

And so these maidens request the soul who is rising up towards perfection to reveal her Beloved to them; and she paints a picture of her love in terms of the mysteries of salvation. She shows how the whole Church is but the one Body of her Spouse; and in her description of His beauty she attributes a particular meaning to each one of His members, but it is only by the union of all of the particular members that the beauty of the Body is complete.

7. GREGORY OF NYSSA: The Unity of All Men*

One is my dove, my perfect one: She is the only one of her mother, the chosen one of her who bore her (Cant. 6.8). This verse is more clearly explained by the Lord's words in the Gospel. There in giving *all power* to His disciples by His blessing, in His prayer to the Father he grants many other favors to those who are holy; and He adds this, which is the crown of all blessings, that in all the diversity of life's decisions they should never be divided greatly in their choice of the good; but He prays that all *may be one* (John 17.22), united in a single good, so that linked *in the bond of peace* (Eph. 4.3), as

* Chapter 83, *ibid.*, 1116D-1120A. See Introduction to Selection 3.

the Apostle says, through *the unity of the* Holy *Spirit,* all might become *one body and one spirit,* through the *one hope* to which they have all been called.

But it would be better here if we would quote the actual words of the Gospel. *That they all may be one,* He says, *as Thou, Father, in me, and I in Thee; that they also may be one in us* (John 17.21). Now the bond of this unity is *glory* (John 17.22), and no one, who would seriously consider the Lord's words, would deny that this *glory* is the Holy Spirit. For He says: *The glory which thou hast given me, I have given to them* (John 17.22). Actually He gave His disciples this glory when He said to them: *Receive ye the Holy Ghost* (John 20.22). And He Himself received this glory when He put on human nature, though He had indeed always possessed it since before the beginning of the world. And now that His human nature has been glorified by the Spirit, this participation in the glory of the Spirit is communicated to all who are united with Him, beginning with His disciples.

Hence He says: *The glory which thou hast given me, I have given to them: that they may be one, as we also are one: I in them, and they in me: that they may be made perfect in one* (John 17.22-23). He who grew quickly from childhood *unto a perfect man, unto the measure of* that spiritual *age* (Eph. 4.13), though born of a slave and a bondwoman, was honored with the royal dignity and received the Spirit by his detachment and his purity—this is the perfect dove on whom the Bridegroom looks when He says: *One is my dove, my perfect one: she is the only one of her mother, the chosen one of her who bore her* (Cant. 6.8). Surely we know who the mother of the dove is, since we know the tree by its fruits. When we consider man, we cannot doubt that he is born of man. Similarly, if we look for the mother of the chosen dove, we will recognize her in none other than that Dove we spoke of. For the nature of the parent is always visible in the offspring. But the offspring of the Spirit is spirit. Hence, if the offspring is a dove, then surely its mother must be that Dove that came down from heaven to the Jordan, as John testifies. This is the Dove that the maidens call blessed, and the queens and concubines praise (Cant. 6.8). For the path to that blessed happiness is one that is open to all souls from every rank; and that is why the text says: *The daughters saw her, and will bless her: the queens and concubines will praise her* (Cant. 6.8).

All men are drawn to desire that which they praise and bless. So the daughters bless the Dove. And they too would desire above all to become doves. And the fact that the concubines praise the Dove testifies too to their earnest desire to attain what they praise, until that day when all men shall be made one, when all will look to the same end, when God will become all in all and all evil will be destroyed, and all men will be united together in harmony by their participation in the Good.

8. JUSTINIAN: On Justice and Law

Justinian (483–565) was Emperor in Byzantium from A.D. 527 to 565. He commissioned a codification of law for the entire Roman Empire; this work is known as *The Institutes.** The early sections indicate the rigorous effort to proceed in a rational order.

Justinian's military successes resulted for a time in a reunification of the eastern and western regions of the Mediterranean world. His closing of the philosophical schools in Athens in 529 led to further movement of Greek thought into Syria, Persia and other lands beyond the direct influence of the Greeks. His legal code was to provide the basis for church and civil law in subsequent centuries.

PROOEMIVM

In the name of Our Lord Jesus Christ.

The Emperor Caesar Flavius Justinian, conqueror of the Alamanni, the Goths, the Franks, the Germans, the Antes, the Alani, the Vandals, the Africans, pious, prosperous, renowned, victorious, and triumphant, ever august,

To the youth desirous of studying the law:

The imperial majesty should be armed with laws as well as glorified with arms, that there may be good government in times both of war and of peace, and the ruler of Rome may not only be victorious over

* The selection is taken from *The Institutes of Justinian*, trans. J. B. Moyle (Oxford: The Clarendon Press, 1913). Used by permission.

his enemies, but may show himself as scrupulously regardful of justice as triumphant over his conquered foes.

With deepest application and forethought, and by the blessing of God, we have attained both of these objects. The barbarian nations which we have subjugated know our valour, Africa and other provinces without number being once more, after so long an interval, reduced beneath the sway of Rome by victories granted by Heaven, and themselves bearing witness to our dominion. All peoples too are ruled by laws which we have either enacted or arranged. Having removed every inconsistency from the sacred constitutions, hitherto inharmonious and confused, we extended our care to the immense volumes of the older jurisprudence; and, like sailors crossing the mid-ocean, by the favour of Heaven have now completed a work of which we once despaired. When this, with God's blessing, had been done, we called together that distinguished man Tribonian, master and ex-quaestor of our sacred palace, and the illustrious Theophilus and Dorotheus, professors of law, of whose ability, legal knowledge, and trusty observance of our orders we have received many and genuine proofs, and specially commissioned them to compose by our authority and advice a book of Institutes, whereby you may be enabled to learn your first lessons in law no longer from ancient fables, but to grasp them by the brilliant light of imperial learning, and that your ears and minds may receive nothing useless or incorrect, but only what holds good in actual fact. And thus whereas, in past time even the foremost of you were unable to read the imperial constitutions until after four years, you, who have been so honoured and fortunate as to receive both the beginning and the end of your legal teaching from the mouth of the Emperor, can now enter on the study of them without delay. After the completion therefore of the fifty books of the Digest or Pandects, in which all the earlier law has been collected by the aid of the said distinguished Tribonian and other illustrious and most able men, we directed the division of these same Institutes into four books, comprising the first elements of the whole science of law. In these the law previously obtaining has been briefly stated, as well as that which after becoming disused has been again brought to light by our imperial aid. Compiled from all the Institutes of the ancient jurists, and in particular from the commentaries of our Gaius on both the Institutes and the common cases, and from many other legal works, these Institutes were submitted to us by the three learned men aforesaid, and after reading and examining them we have given them the fullest force of our constitutions.

Receive then these laws with your best powers and with the eagerness of study, and show yourselves so learned as to be encouraged to hope that when you have compassed the whole field of law you may have ability to govern such portion of the state as may be entrusted to you.

Given at Constantinople the 21st day of November, in the third consulate of the Emperor Justinian, Father of his Country, ever august.

BOOK I

TITLE I
OF JUSTICE AND LAW

Justice is the set and constant purpose which gives to every man his due. Jurisprudence is the knowledge of things divine and human, the science of the just and the unjust.

Having laid down these general definitions, and our object being the exposition of the law of the Roman people, we think that the most advantageous plan will be to commence with an easy and simple path, and then to proceed to details with a most careful and scrupulous exactness of interpretation. Otherwise, if we begin by burdening the student's memory, as yet weak and untrained, with a multitude and variety of matters, one of two things will happen: either we shall cause him wholly to desert the study of law, or else we shall bring him at last, after great labour, and often, too, distrustful of his own powers (the commonest cause, among the young, of ill-success), to a point which he might have reached earlier, without such labour and confident in himself, had he been led along a smoother path.

The precepts of the law are these: to live honestly, to injure no one and to give every man his due. The study of law consists of two branches, law public, and law private. The former relates to the welfare of the Roman State; the latter to the advantage of the individual citizen. Of private law then we may say that it is of threefold origin, being collected from the precepts of nature, from those of the law of nations, or from those of the civil law of Rome.

TITLE II
OF THE LAW OF NATURE, THE LAW OF NATIONS, AND THE CIVIL LAW

The law of nature is that which she has taught all animals; a law not peculiar to the human race, but shared by all living creatures, whether denizens of the air, the dry land, or the sea. Hence comes the union of male and female, which we call marriage; hence the procreation and rearing of children, for this is a law by the knowledge of which we see even the lower animals are distinguished. The civil law of Rome, and the law of all nations, differ from each other thus. The laws of every people governed by statutes and customs are partly peculiar to itself, partly common to all mankind. Those rules which a state enacts for its own members are peculiar to itself, and are called civil law: those rules prescribed by natural reason for all men are observed by all peoples alike, and are called the law of nations. Thus the laws of the Roman people are partly peculiar to itself, partly common to all nations; a distinction of which we shall take notice as occasion offers. Civil law takes its name from the state wherein it binds; for instance, the civil law of Athens, it being quite correct to speak thus of the enactments of Solon or Draco. So too we call the law observed by the Roman people the civil law of the Romans, or the law of Quirites; the law, that is to say, which they observe, the Romans being called Quirites after Quirinus. Whenever we speak, however, of civil law, without any qualification, we mean our own; exactly as, when "the poet" is spoken of, without addition or qualification, the Greeks understand the great Homer, and we understand Vergil. But the law of nations is common to the whole human race; for nations have settled certain things for themselves as occasion and the necessities of human life required. For instance, wars arose, and then followed captivity and slavery, which are contrary to the law of nature; for by the law of nature all men from the beginning were born free. The law of nations again is the source of almost all contracts; for instance, sale, hire, partnership, deposit, loan for consumption, and very many others.

Our law is partly written, partly unwritten, as among the Greeks. The written law consists of statutes, plebiscites, senatusconsults, enactments of the Emperors, edicts of the magistrates, and answers of those learned in the law. A statute is an enactment of the Roman people, which it used to make on the motion of a senatorial magistrate, as for instance a consul. A plebiscite is an enactment of the commonalty, such as was made on the motion of one of their own magistrates, as a tribune. The commonalty differs from the people as a species from its genus; for "the people" includes the whole aggregate of citizens, among them patricians and senators, while the term "commonalty" embraces only such citizens as are not patricians or senators. After the passing, however, of the statute called the lex Hortensia, plebiscites acquired for the first time the force of statutes. A senatusconsult is a command and ordinance of the senate, for when the Roman people had been so increased that it was difficult to assemble it together for the purpose of enacting statutes, it seemed right that the senate should be consulted instead of the people. Again, what the Emperor determines has the force of a statute, the people having conferred on him all their authority and power by the *lex regia,* which was passed concerning his office and authority. Consequently, whatever the Emperor settles by rescript, or decides in his judicial capacity, or ordains by edicts, is clearly a statute: and these are what are called constitutions. Some of these of course are personal, and not to be followed as precedents, since this is not the Emperor's will; for a favour bestowed on individual merit, or a penalty inflicted for individual wrongdoing, or relief given without a precedent, do not go beyond the particular person: though others are general, and bind all beyond a doubt. The edicts of the praetors too have no small legal authority, and these we are used to call the *ius honorarium,* because those who occupy posts of honour in the state, in other words the magistrates, have given authority to this branch of law. The curule aediles also used to issue an edict relating to certain matters, which forms part of the *ius honorarium.* The answers of those learned in the law are the opinions and views of persons authorized to determine and expound the law; for it was of old provided that certain persons should publicly interpret the laws, who were called jurisconsults, and whom the Emperor privileged to give formal answers. If they were unanimous the judge was forbidden by imperial constitution to depart from their opinion, so great was its authority. The unwritten law is that which usage has approved: for ancient customs, when approved by consent of those who follow them, are like statute. And this division of the civil law into two kinds seems not inappropriate, for it appears to have originated in the institutions of two states, namely Athens and Lacedaemon; it having been usual in the latter to commit to memory what was observed as law, while the Athenians observed only what they had made permanent in written statutes.

But the laws of nature, which are observed by all nations alike, are established, as it were, by divine providence, and remain ever fixed and immutable: but the municipal laws of each individual state are subject to frequent change, either by the tacit consent of the people, or by the subsequent enactment of another statute.

The whole of the law which we observe relates either to persons, or to things, or to actions. And first let us speak of persons: for it is useless to know the law without knowing the persons for whose sake it was established.

TITLE III
OF THE LAW OF PERSONS

In the law of persons, then, the first division is into free men and slaves. Freedom, from which men are called free, is a man's natural power of doing what he pleases, so far as he is not prevented by force or law: slavery is an institution of the law of nations, against nature subjecting one man to the dominion of another. The name "slave" is derived from the practice of generals to order the preservation and sale of captives, instead of killing them; hence they are also called *mancipia,* because they are taker from the enemy by the strong hand. Slaves are either born so, their mothers being slaves themselves; or they become so, and this either by the law of nations, that is to say by capture in war, or by the civil law, as when a free man, over twenty years of age, collusively allows himself to be sold in order that he may share the purchase money. The condition of all slaves is one and the same: in the conditions of free men there are many distinctions; to begin with, they are either free born, or made free.

II.

*The Foundation of
the West*

TODAY, with the questioning of so many traditions in social, religious, and intellectual life, the life span of Augustine, A.D. 354-430—years of decline of the Western Roman Empire—appears to be particularly relevant. For, though we are more and more impressed by the way in which the whole of Western civilization underlines the importance of its beginnings in the East, we are also increasingly drawn to the life and thought of Augustine. Institutions and practices which owe much to Augustine are at present subject to unremitting challenge from within and from without the circles which bespeak allegiance to his spirit. The challenge comes with respect to political, ecclesiastical and other institutions of common life, with respect to the union of intelligence and volition and emotion in the mind's work of looking inward, with respect to the securing of personal and communal objectives through the ascertainment of moral law.

Political unity in Western Europe and in the Atlantic region, theological traditions common to Catholic, Lutheran and Calvinist, monasticism and its offshoots in education are all in some way related to the tradition of Augustine. In the West the failure of Western Roman power in the fourth century A.D. to hold against barbarian invasions called forth, partly under the influence of Augustine's thought, a whole political history of rule and association that is significantly different from the imperial rule of Byzantium and its successors in the East.

What is involved in this development is the rule of a multiplicity of nations, or peoples, within a single framework of civilization. At the present time we realize that the coming age must determine whether this Augustinian tradition of long term moral unity in the West is to be replaced by a new, more detailed and comprehensive unity. In a world of atomic stalemate the older, looser unities seem to some quite anachronistic; to others, they seem more than ever in need of transformation and vivification.

Problems of institutional life, whether in political, religious or educational domains, call to mind great themes of Augustine's masterwork, the *City of God*. In the concurrent themes of the City of God (The Heavenly City) and the City of Man (the Earthly City) there is the decisive double sense of divine things in simultaneous relevance to, and transcendence of, the world about us. In face of the fall of the Western Roman Empire, Augustine's theology was neither one of obvious flight nor of obvious commitment. The relevance of theological teaching to all human things, yet its allowance of their own developments, remains one of the most profound aspects of Augustine's intellectuality.

The power of integration within Augustine's thought has in the course of history led lesser men to associate his name with efforts to reduce all knowledge to theology, to subordinate all social units to a single political power, to assimilate all religious life to some theocratic system. Augustine's efforts to find an integrative perspective illuminative of all areas of knowledge, reality and action does not warrant any such domination of life and spirit. In short, the basic character of his answers comes in response to his own most basic question, a question of integrity.

Contemporary emphasis on depth psychology, and on phenomenological method in philosophy, bear comparison with some aspects of the thought of Augustine and of authors associated with his tradition. Augustine's other masterwork, the *Confessions,* reveals a deep sense of inwardness and of the subjective, a probing of consciousness, of the affections, of the self. Yet, there is no corresponding denial of the objective or universal or intellectual. The data of consciousness are plumbed with a view to ascertaining the most fundamental realities of the universe, and also with a view to a most subtle use of the intellect in matters of the will. These facets of Augustine's thought ground in the history of philosophy the tradition which includes Boethius, Anselm, Bonaventure, Descartes, Pascal, Hegel, Kierkegaard.

Together with a sense of inwardness, Augustine demonstrated a profound sense of objective law. He found a proper work of man to lie in the discernment of law through reason and revelation. Augustine's emphasis on law may reflect in turn the ancient schools of rhetoric, the stoic philosophy, the Roman tradition. In him, especially, there was concern for a law of *conscience,* a law of fulfillment, a law related to a continuously developing use of intellectuality. As such, law is not simply a matter of divine commandments or of imperial or ecclesiastical decrees. It does not deny these but seeks a more subtle, more insightful, more helpful way of giving unity to movement within human experience.

After consideration of the specific character of the thought of Augustine, particularly as it has shown itself in political and psychological and moral questions, we may consider Augustine first in relation to the tradition of the East, and then in the context of the foundation of the West. With respect to the East, the influence of Plotinus on Augustine was very great, and the thought of Plotinus requires special consideration.

Plotinus, who was thought to have been born in Egypt in A.D. 203, and to have died in Italy in A.D. 270, and whose chief work is the *Enneads,* might be called the last great intellectual figure of classical antiquity. His work is well characterized as a fusion of Plato and Aristotle. Plotinus did not address himself to the problems of Judaism or Christianity. For Plotinus, the ultimate principle of explanation, whether in the order of being or in the order of knowledge, was the transcendent "One," and beyond the "One," only emanations from it. Thus, Plotinus presents a truly comprehensive, dialectical scheme, in the manner of Plato. In the manner of Aristotle, the scheme was fixed, i.e., not to be followed by other, equally comprehensive frameworks. Whereas Plato passes through a succession of dialectical efforts which seek to unify all being and thought, Plotinus stops with the single scheme in which all things emanate from "the One." Whereas for Aristotle the order of knowledge differs from the order of being, and different intellectual problems require the discovery of different basic principles of solution, Plotinus' principle of explanation is comprehensive and unified. We have, thus, a prototype of neoplatonism, a combination of platonic and aristotelian factors, sacrificing through the combination important differentiating marks of each.

In Plotinus, Jewish and Christian and Islamic thinkers were to find a version of philosophy, a comprehensive scheme, which was far more congenial than most alternative, comprehensive schemes. There were always some religious thinkers to note the difficulties for religious teaching inherent in comprehensive formulations, especially difficulties for biblical teaching on divine and human freedom, and to emphasize the specifically religious character of religious teaching. With respect to Augustine, the long term encounter with the thought of Plotinus was to yield positions acceptable to the Christian religious community. Unlike such thinkers as John Scotus Erigena, Augustine was to incorporate elements of Plotinus without creating the impression of losing Christianity in the process. Indeed, in time some were to give positive religious sanction to this way of thinking in Augustine.

Augustine stands as a Father with respect to the Christianity of the Latin world and of the world of Northern Europe. He stands behind the Latin or Catholic, and the Protestant or Evangelical, behind Bonaventure and Aquinas, Calvin and Luther. He has not been so related to the Eastern or Orthodox Christianity of Asia Minor, of Greece, of Russia. We look to Augustine for a key to differences between East and West. At the same time we do well to remember that all three branches of Christianity seek at once to be orthodox and catholic and evangelical.

It has been commonplace to note the influence of the Hellenistic philosophy of Plotinus on Augustine, and of neoplatonism in general on the Augustinian tradition, but we should not overlook the role played in Augustine's thought by the writings of Cicero and Seneca. Their special influence may have given Augustine's intellectuality a rhetorical emphasis which helps explain the specific quality of his thought. Difference may be founded also in the need of the Western Church *to rule* in the place of an effective empire, a need leading Augustine to evolve a special legalism within the religious ethos in view of the lawlessness in secular life.

For all the academic interest there has been in the speculative thought of Augustine, it is desirable to consider that the ultimate concern of his thought, taken as a whole, may be primarily not with understanding and knowledge, however important he may have thought these to be. Consider the *use* of the mind, the kind of turning inward, the mind and its concepts being the right track and means for reaching divine things. The practical or pragmatic in the Western temperament may, in Augustine's work, use the mind in fortifying and ennobling man's attitudes, in turning him toward a life in accord with, joined to, divine things. As Dante will later use poetry as *means* in the teaching of a theology, so Augustine's teaching of theology may be *means* with a direct view to conversion of life.

The legacy of Augustine to the West prompts reference to the history of Western monasticism, of the Western Empire and the Papacy, of the schools and universities. Augustine's rule for common religious life was to provide a basis for the whole history of Western monasticism, including the celebrated rule of Benedict. The original Benedictine, the Cluniac and the Cistercian monastic movements are particular and timely developments through the centuries of this inspiration. The Benedictine Anselm, author of the *Monologium* and the *Proslogium,* was to cultivate an area of Augustinian thought and make a well-remembered step in the history of philosophy. What interests us here is that his writing has the character of monastic meditation.

Both developments of continuation in the West, the Holy Roman Empire begun with Charlemagne, and the special form of the Papacy after the fall of the imperial power in the Western Empire, recall the thought of Augustine's *City of God.* The tensions obtaining in the West between Church and State, and the special points of fusion, reflect in a measure some special characteristics of Augustine's vision, as well, perhaps, as they reflect the special divisions and issues characteristic of the West.

In the thirteenth century the standard textbook for the study of theology was to be the *Sentences* of Peter Lombard, in large part a compilation of teachings of Augustine. We may consider the place of the monastery libraries and schools and writings in the development of education in the West, with a view to the importance of the Augustinian writings in these centers. In Church and State, in monastery and school, separated and related as these were, we find the evidence of the presence of Augustine in the foundation of the West.

The influence of Augustine may be viewed profitably in relation to two other thinkers: Boethius (A.D. 480-524) and Anselm of Canterbury (1033-1109). Boethius is most widely known as the author of the *Consolation of Philosophy.* Educated at Athens, he had a facility in Greek that was a rarity in the West at that time. His translation of classical writings in logic provided the basic textbooks during the first millennium of Christianity in Europe and were its main link with the writings of classical antiquity before the twelfth century. Boethius did much to set the tone of medieval education and his own philosophic statements reflected the influence of Plotinus, and more particularly, the writings of Augustine.

Anselm is probably best known for his arguments for the existence of God. On philosophic foundations drawn from Augustine's adaptation of Platonism, he formulated what has come to be known as the "ontological" argument for the existence of God. The response to this argument, and reformulation of it, have made of the argument a touchstone for identifying basic divisions within philosophy at the various stages of its history. Anselm took as a central theme the Augustinian conviction of the necessity of faith for understanding. Anselm's most purely philosophic works manifest this Augustinian characteristic. Yet, following Augustine, Anselm had a high regard for the autonomy of each type of knowledge: reason is not subservient to faith and faith is not reduced to what may be known through reason. Each is sovereign in its own sphere. Faith and reason work together to produce a unified knowledge that is richer and more profound than would be possible if each were strictly separated from the other.

If we place the writings of Augustine, Boethius and Anselm into one perspective, we have the basic exemplification of the Augustinian tradition. Its outlook and doctrines, though frequently debated and revised, have provided the context for subsequent thought and discussion. As such they have served as a decisive formative influence on Western civilization. Central to the education of the first millennium, the Augustinian tradition has defined the manner in which the impact of classical, biblical and byzantine thought were to be received in Western Europe. In its focus on interiority coupled with action, on the interrelation of the religious and the rational, the mystical and the practical, it has shaped the distinctiveness of the development of life and thought in Western Europe. In its long-range influence, through successive meetings of East and West, it has provided a singular influence upon the whole of Western civilization.

9. AUGUSTINE: The Nature of Memory

Augustine of Hippo (A.D. 354-430) was born in Tagaste, North Africa, in what is now Algeria. He was educated in the local schools and completed his studies at Carthage. His mother, Monica, was a devout Christian, but his father, Patricius, was a pagan who converted to Christianity in about the year A.D. 371. Augustine was raised as a Christian although he had not been baptized. During his stay at Carthage he became a Manichean (a non-Christian religious sect) and took a mistress with whom he lived for about fifteen years. They had a son, Adeodatus, who died at the age of eighteen.

Augustine broke with the Manicheans when he journeyed to Rome and went through a period of skepticism. He moved to Milan where he met St. Ambrose who guided him through a great interior struggle resulting in his conversion to Christianity. Returning to North Africa, he established a religious order for men. Within a few years he himself was ordained a priest and then made Bishop of Hippo. In addition to his duties as bishop he engaged in several notable controversies with the Manicheans, the Donatists, and the Pelagians. He also produced an amazing amount of philosophical and theological literature—some 94 works, 220 letters, and nearly 400 sermons. In August, A.D. 430, he fell sick and died at the age of seventy-six while the Vandals were besieging Hippo.

Augustine was concerned with the relationship of faith and knowledge. He developed a highly sophisticated concept of the interrelationship of reason, authority and religious faith. We must have faith in our ability to know* before reason can guide us to knowledge. We must first believe in the content of religious doctrines before reason can help us understand them.

The selections below are drawn from his *Confessions, On Free Choice,* and the *City of God.*

The *Confessions* is an autobiographical document that has had a justly enduring claim on men's minds and hearts for nearly sixteen centuries.

---

* See the remarkable argument in the *City of God*, Bk. XI, Chap. 26, which antedates Descartes' *Cogito* by some 1200 years!

The particular selection presented here* is a discussion of the nature of memory, which had a great influence on subsequent thinking concerning the nature of human knowledge. Augustine differentiates memory from other human powers such as the senses and the understanding. Memory, like a bottomless container fitted out with innumerable compartments, retains the content of experience always available for recall. Human nature, Augustine observes, is a marvel equaling or surpassing the other wonders of nature, and memory is not the least of the perfections of human nature.

Not with doubting, but with assured consciousness, do I love Thee, Lord. Thou hast stricken my heart with Thy word, and I loved Thee. Yea also heaven, and earth, and all that therein is, behold, on every side they bid me love Thee; nor cease to say so unto all, that they may be without excuse. But more deeply wilt Thou have mercy on whom Thou wilt have mercy, and wilt have compassion on whom Thou hast had compassion: else in deaf ears do the heaven and the earth speak Thy praises. But what do I love, when I love Thee? not beauty of bodies, nor the fair harmony of time, nor the brightness of the light, so gladsome to our eyes, nor sweet melodies of varied songs, nor the fragrant smell of flowers, and ointments, and spices, not manna and honey, not limbs acceptable to embracements of flesh. None of these I love, when I love my God; and yet I love a kind of light, and melody, and fragrance, and meat, and embracement when I love my God, the light, melody, fragrance, meat, embracement of my inner man: where there shineth unto my soul what space cannot contain, and there soundeth what time beareth not away, and there smelleth what breathing disperseth not, and there tasteth what eating diminisheth not, and there clingeth what satiety divorceth not. This is it which I love when I love my God.

And what is this? I asked the earth, and it answered me, "I am not He"; and whatsoever are in it confessed the same. I asked the sea and the deeps, and the living creeping things, and they answered, "We are not Thy God, seek above us." I asked the moving air; and the whole air with his inhabitants answered, "Anaximenes was deceived, I am not God." I asked the heavens, sun, moon, stars, "Nor (say they) are we the God whom thou seekest." And I replied unto

* From Book 10, chapters 8-21, *The Confessions of St. Augustine,* trans. by E. B. Pusey.

all the things which encompass the door of my flesh: "Ye have told me of my God, that ye are not He; tell me something of Him." And they cried out with a loud voice, "He made us." My questioning them, was my thoughts on them: and their form of beauty gave the answer. And I turned myself unto myself, and said to myself, "Who art thou?" And I answered, "A man." And behold, in me there present themselves to me soul, and body, one without, the other within. By which of these ought I to seek my God? I had sought Him in the body from earth to heaven, so far as I could send messengers, the beams of mine eyes. But the better is the inner, for to it as presiding and judging, all the bodily messengers reported the answers of heaven and earth, and all things therein, who said, "We are not God, but He made us." These things did my inner man know by the ministry of the outer: I the inner knew them; I, the mind, through the senses of my body. I asked the whole frame of the world about my God; and it answered me, "I am not He, but He made me."

Is not this corporeal figure apparent to all whose senses are perfect? why then speaks it not the same to all? Animals small and great see it, but they cannot ask it: because no reason is set over their senses to judge on what they report. But men can ask, so that the invisible things of God are clearly seen, being understood by the things that are made; but by love of them, they are made subject unto them: and subjects cannot judge. Nor yet do the creatures answer such as ask, unless they can judge: nor yet do they change their voice (i.e., their appearance), if one man only sees, another seeing asks, so as to appear one way to this man, another way to that; but appearing the same way to both, it is dumb to this, speaks to that; yea rather it speaks to all; but they only understand, who compare its voice received from without, with the truth within. for truth saith unto me, "Neither heaven, nor earth, nor any other body is thy God." This, their very nature saith to him that seeth them: "They are a mass; a mass is less in a part thereof than in the whole." Now to thee I speak, O my soul, thou art my better part: for thou quickenest the mass of my body, giving it life, which no body can give to a body: but thy God is even unto thee the Life of thy Life.

What then do I love, when I love my God? who is He above the head of my soul? By my very soul will I ascend to Him. I will pass beyond that power whereby I am united to my body, and fill its whole frame with life. Nor can I by that power find my God; for so horse and mule that have no understanding, might find Him; seeing it is the same power, whereby even their bodies live. But another power there is, not that only whereby I animate, but that too whereby I imbue with sense my flesh, which the Lord hath framed for me: commanding the eye not to hear, and the ear not to see; but the eye, that through it I should see, and the ear, that through it I should hear; and to the other senses severally, what is to each their own peculiar seats and offices; which, being divers, I the one mind, do through them enact. I will pass beyond this power of mine also; for this also have the horse and mule, for they also perceive through the body.

I will pass then beyond this power of my nature also, rising by degrees unto Him Who made me. And I come to the fields and spacious palaces of my memory, where are the treasures of innumerable images, brought into it from things of all sorts perceived by the senses. There is stored up, whatsoever besides we think, either by enlarging or diminishing, or any other way varying those things which the sense hath come to; and whatever else hath been committed and laid up, which forgetfulness hath not yet swallowed up and buried. When I enter there, I require what I will to be brought forth, and something instantly comes; others must be longer sought after, which are fetched, as it were, out of some inner receptacle; others rush out in troops, and while one thing is desired and required, they start forth, as who should say, "Is it perchance I?" These I drive away with the hand of my heart, from the face of my remembrance; until what I wish for be unveiled, and appear in sight, out of its secret place. Other things come up readily, in unbroken order, as they are called for; those in front making way for the following; and as they make way, they are hidden from sight, ready to come when I will. All which takes place when I repeat a thing by heart.

There are all things preserved distinctly and under general heads, each having entered by its own avenue: as light, and all colours and forms of bodies by the eyes; by the ears all sorts of sounds; all smells by the avenue of the nostrils; all tastes by the mouth; and by the sensation of the whole body, what is hard or soft; hot or cold; smooth or rugged; heavy or light; either outwardly or inwardly to the body. All these doth that great harbour of the memory receive in her numberless secret and inexpressible windings, to be forthcoming, and brought out at need; each entering in by his own gate, and there laid up. Nor yet do the things themselves enter in; only the images of the things perceived are there in readiness, for thought to recall. Which images, how they are formed, who can tell, though it doth plainly appear by which sense each hath been brought in and stored up? For even while I dwell in darkness and silence, in my memory I can produce colours, if I will, and discern betwixt black and white, and what others I will: nor yet do sounds break in and disturb the image drawn in by my eyes, which I am reviewing, though they also are there, lying dormant, and laid up, as it were, apart. For these too I call for, and forthwith they appear. And though my tongue be still, and my throat mute, so can I sing as much as I will; nor do those images of colours, which notwithstanding be there, intrude themselves and interrupt, when another store is called for, which flowed in by the ears. So the other things, piled in and up by the other senses, I recall at my pleasure. Yea, I discern the breath of lilies from violets, though smelling nothing; and I prefer honey to sweet wine, smooth before rugged, at the time neither tasting nor handling, but remembering only.

These things do I within, in that vast court of my memory. For there are present with me, heaven, earth, sea, and whatever I could think on therein, besides what I have forgotten. There also meet I with myself, and recall myself, and when, where, and what I have done, and under what feelings. There be all which I remember, either on my own experience, or other's credit. Out of the same store do I myself with the past continually combine fresh and fresh likenesses of things which I have experienced, or, from what I have experienced, have believed: and thence again infer future actions, events and hopes, and all these again I reflect on, as present. "I will do this or that," say I to myself, in that great receptacle of my mind, stored with the images of things so many and so great, "and this or that will follow." "O that this or that might be!" "God avert this or that!" So speak I to myself: and when I speak, the images of all I speak of are present, out of the same treasury of memory; nor would I speak of any thereof, were the images wanting.

Great is this force of memory, excessive great, O my God; a large and boundless chamber! who ever sounded the bottom thereof? yet is this a power of mine, and belongs unto my nature; nor do I myself comprehend all that I am. Therefore is the mind too strait to contain itself. And where should that be, which it containeth not of itself?

Is it without it, and not within? how then doth it not comprehend itself? A wonderful admiration surprises me, amazement seizes me upon this. And men go abroad to admire the heights of mountains, the mighty billows of the sea, the broad tides of rivers, the compass of the ocean, and the circuits of the stars, and pass themselves by; nor wonder that when I spake of all these things, I did not see them with mine eyes, yet could not have spoken of them, unless I then actually saw the mountains, billows, rivers, stars which I had seen, and that ocean which I believe to be, inwardly in my memory, and that, with the same vast spaces between, as if I saw them abroad. Yet did not I by seeing draw them into myself, when with mine eyes I beheld them; nor are they themselves with me, but their images only. And I know by what sense of the body each was impressed upon me.

Yet not these alone does the unmeasurable capacity of my memory retain. Here also is all, learnt of the liberal sciences and as yet unforgotten; removed as it were to some inner place, which is yet no place: nor are they the images thereof, but the things themselves. For, what is literature, what the art of disputing, how many kinds of questions there be, whatsoever of these I know, in such manner exists in my memory, as that I have not taken in the image, and left out the thing, or that it should have sounded and passed away like a voice fixed on the ear by that impress, whereby it might be recalled, as if it sounded, when it no longer sounded; or as a smell while it passes and evaporates into air affects the sense of smell, whence it conveys into the memory an image of itself, which remembering, we renew, or as meat, which verily in the belly hath now no taste, and yet in the memory still in a manner tasteth; or as any thing which the body by touch perceiveth, and which when removed from us, the memory still conceives. For those things are not transmitted into the memory, but their images only are with an admirable swiftness caught up, and stored as it were in wondrous cabinets, and thence wonderfully by the act of remembering, brought forth.

But now when I hear that there be three kinds of questions, "Whether the thing be? what it is? of what kind it is?" I do indeed hold the images of the sounds of which those words be composed, and that those sounds, with a noise passed through the air, and now are not. But the things themselves which are signified by those sounds, I never reached with any sense of my body, nor ever discerned them otherwise than in my mind; yet in my memory have I laid up not their images, but themselves. Which how they entered into me, let them say if they can; for I have gone over all the avenues of my flesh, but cannot find by which they entered. For the eyes say, "if those images were coloured, we reported of them." The ears say, "If they sound, we gave knowledge of them." The nostrils say, "if they smell, they passed by us." The taste says, "unless they have a savour, ask me not." The touch says, "If it have not size, I handled it not; if I handled it not, I gave no notice of it." Whence and how entered these things into my memory? I know not how. For when I learned them, I gave not credit to another man's mind, but recognised them in mine; and approving them for true, I commended them to it, laying them up as it were, whence I might bring them forth when I willed. In my heart then they were, even before I learned them, but in my memory they were not. Where then? or wherefore, when they were spoken, did I acknowledge them, and said, "So is it, it is true," unless that they were already in the memory, but so thrown back and buried as it were in deeper recesses, that had not the suggestion of another drawn them forth I had perchance been unable to conceive of them?

Wherefore we find, that to learn these things whereof we imbibe not the images by our senses, but perceive within by themselves, without images, as they are, is nothing else, but by conception, to receive, and by marking to take heed that those things which the memory did before contain at random and unarranged, be laid up at hand as it were in that same memory where before they lay unknown, scattered and neglected, and so readily occur to the mind familiarised to them. And how many things of this kind does my memory bear which have been already found out, and as I said, placed as it were at hand, which we are said to have learned and come to know which were I for some short space of time to cease to call to mind, they are again so buried, and glide back, as it were, into the deeper recesses, that they must again, as if new, be thought out thence, for other abode they have none: but they must be drawn together again, that they may be known; that is to say, they must as it were be collected together from their dispersion: whence the word "cogitation" is derived. For cogo (collect) and cogito (re-collect) have the same relation to each other as ago and agito, facio and factito. But the mind hath appropriated to itself this word (cogitation), so that, not what is "collected" any how, but what is "re-collected," i.e., brought together, in the mind, is properly said to be cogitated, or thought upon.

The memory containeth also reasons and laws innumerable of numbers and dimensions, none of which hath any bodily sense impressed; seeing they have neither colour, nor sound, nor taste, nor smell, nor touch. I have heard the sound of the words whereby when discussed they are denoted: but the sounds are other than the things. For the sounds are other in Greek than in Latin; but the things are neither Greek, nor Latin, nor any other language. I have seen the lines of architects, the very finest, like a spider's thread; but those are still different, they are not the images of those lines which the eye of flesh showed me: he knoweth them, whosoever without any conception whatsoever of a body, recognises them within himself. I have perceived also the numbers of the things with which we number all the senses of my body; but those numbers wherewith we number are different, nor are they the images of these, and therefore they indeed are. Let him who seeth them not, deride me for saying these things, and I will pity him, while he derides me.

All these things I remember, and how I learnt them I remember. Many things also most falsely objected against them have I heard, and remember; which though they be false, yet is it not false that I remember them; and I remember also that I have discerned betwixt those truths and these falsehoods objected to them. And I perceive that the present discerning of these things is different from remembering that I oftentimes discerned them, when I often thought upon them. I both remember then to have often understood these things; and what I now discern and understand, I lay up in my memory, that hereafter I may remember that I understood it now. So then I remember also to have remembered; as if hereafter I shall call to remembrance, that I have now been able to remember these things, by the force of memory shall I call it to remembrance.

The same memory contains also the affections of my mind, not in the same manner that my mind itself contains them, when it feels them; but far otherwise, according to a power of its own. For without rejoicing I remember myself to have joyed; and without sorrow do I recollect my past sorrow. And that I once feared, I review without fear; and without desire call to mind a past desire. Sometimes, on the contrary, with joy do I remember my fore-past sorrow, and with sorrow, joy. Which is not wonderful, as to the body; for mind is one thing, body another. If I therefore with joy remember some past pain of body, it is not so wonderful. But now seeing this very memory itself is mind (for when we give a thing in charge, to be kept in memory, we say, "See that you keep it in mind"; and when we forget, we say, "It did not come to my mind," and, "It slipped out of my mind," calling the memory itself the mind); this being so, how is it that when with joy I remember my past sorrow, the mind hath joy, the memory hath sorrow; the mind upon the joyfulness which is in it, is joyful, yet the memory upon the sadness which is in it, is not sad? Does the memory perchance not belong to the mind? Who will say so? The memory then is, as it were, the belly of the mind, and joy and sadness, like sweet and bitter food; which, when committed to the memory, are as it were, passed into the belly, where they may be stowed, but cannot taste. Ridiculous it is to imagine these to be alike; and yet are they not utterly unlike.

But, behold, out of my memory I bring it, when I say there be four perturbations of the mind, desire, joy, fear, sorrow; and whatsoever I can dispute thereon, by dividing each into its subordinate species, and by defining it, in my memory find I what to say, and thence do I bring it: yet am I not disturbed by any of these perturbations, when by calling them to mind, I remember them; yea, and before I recalled and brought them back, they were there; and therefore could they, by recollection, thence be brought. Perchance, then, as meat is by chewing the cud brought up out of the belly, so by recollection these out of the memory. Why then does not the disputer, thus recollecting, taste in the mouth of his musing the sweetness of joy, or the bitterness of sorrow? Is the comparison unlike in this, because not in all respects like? For who would willingly speak thereof, if so oft as we name grief or fear, we should be compelled to be sad or fearful? And yet could we not speak of them, did we not find in our memory, not only the sounds of the names according to the images impressed by the senses of the body, but notions of the very things themselves which we never received by any avenue of the body, but which the mind itself perceiving by the experience of its own passions, committed to the memory, or the memory of itself retained, without being committed unto it.

But whether by images or no, who can readily say? Thus, I name a stone, I name the sun, the things themselves not being present to my senses, but their images to my memory. I name a bodily pain, yet it is not present with me, when nothing aches; yet unless its image were present to my memory, I should not know what to say thereof, nor in discoursing discern pain from pleasure. I name bodily health; being sound in body the thing itself is present with me; yet, unless its image also were present in my memory, I could by no means recall what the sound of this name should signify. Nor would the sick, when health were named, recognize what were spoken, unless the same image were by the force of memory retained, although the thing itself were absent from the body. I name numbers whereby we number; and not their images, but themselves are present in my memory. I name the image of the sun, and that image is present in my memory. For I recall not the image of its image, but the image itself is present to me, calling it to mind. I name memory, and I recognise what I name. And where do I recognise it, but in the memory itself? Is it also present to itself by its image, and not by itself?

10. AUGUSTINE: The Goodness of God and Moral Evil

Augustine sought to face the problem of human free will in a divinely ordered world. One side of free will is the ability to choose between alternative possible actions. Far greater, he believed, is the capacity of will to elicit an act of independent and spontaneous self-determination toward the good. This, for Augustine, is true freedom, for it is the ability to choose what one ought to choose exempt from external compulsion.

This selection* concentrates on ethical questions, within the context of one aspect of the problem of evil. If God is not the cause of moral evil, then what is? Augustine's answer is that man, by giving in to his lower drives, becomes enslaved by them. It is within the power of free will to control our lower drives so that they do not usurp the right order of things, which for man involves always placing that which is eternally valuable, good, and true before that which has only temporal value. This

* From *The Problem of Free Choice*, Book I, Chapters 3-6, 8-15, in *Ancient Christian Writers*, vol. 11, trans. Don Mark Pontifex (Westminster, Md.: The Newman Press). Used by permission.

does not in any way deny the genuine worth of temporal things; it places them in their proper perspective in the scheme of values. The work is written in the form of a dialogue between Augustine and his friend Evodius.

Augustine—Your problem is to find the cause of our wrongdoing, and therefore we must first discuss what doing wrong means. Explain your view about this. If you cannot cover the whole subject in a few short words, at least give some examples of wrongdoing, and tell me what you think.

Evodius—Adultery, murder, and sacrilege are examples. It would take too long to make a complete list, and I could not remember everything. All agree that these are wrongdoings.

A.—First tell me why you think adultery is wrong. Because the law forbids it?

E.—No, it is not wrong because the law forbids it; the law forbids it because it is wrong.

A.—If someone tried to confuse us, dwelling on the pleasures of adultery and asking why we thought it wrong and to be condemned, surely you do not think we ought to take shelter behind the authority of the law, when we desire not only to believe, but also to understand? I agree with you, and believe most firmly, and preach the belief to all peoples and nations that adultery is wrong. But now we are endeavouring to grasp firmly with the understanding what we have received on faith. Reflect, therefore, as carefully as you can, and tell me on what grounds you regard adultery as evil.

E.—I know an act to be evil, which I should not allow in the case of my own wife. Whoever does to another what he would not like done to himself, surely does wrong.

A.—If a man's passion was so strong that he offered his own wife to another, and freely allowed her to be seduced by him because he wished to have the same licence with this man's wife, do you think he would be doing no wrong?

E.—Of course, a very great wrong.

A.—He is not sinning against the principle you mentioned; he is not doing what he would not like done to himself. You must find another reason for your conviction that adultery is wrong.

E.—I think it wrong, because I have often seen men condemned for this crime.

A.—Are not men often condemned for good deeds? To save you further reference—read history as you have it on God's own excellent authority. You will soon see what a bad impression we should get of the Apostles and all the martyrs, if we thought that condemnation was a sure proof of wrongdoing; all were condemned for confessing their faith. So if everything which is condemned is evil, it was evil at that time to believe in Christ and to confess His faith. But, if everything that is condemned is not evil, you must find another reason for teaching that adultery is wrong.

E.—I do not see any answer to this.

A.—Well, possibly passion is the evil in adultery. Your trouble is that you are looking for the evil in the outward act, that we can see. I will prove that passion is the evil in adultery. If a man has no opportunity of living with another man's wife, but if it is obvious for some reason that he would like to do so, and would do so if he could, he is no less guilty than if he was caught in the act.

E.—Yes, that is perfectly clear. I see now that there is no need of a long argument to convince me that this is true of murder and sacrilege, and indeed of all sins. It is plain that nothing else than passion is the principal element in this whole matter of wrongdoing.

A.—Do you know that there is another word for passion, namely desire?

E.—Yes, I do.

A.—Do you think there is any difference between this and fear?

E.—I think there is a very great difference between them.

A.—I suppose you think this because desire seeks its object, while fear avoids it.

E.—Yes.

A.—If someone kills a man, not through desire of gain, but through fear of suffering some evil, will he still be a murderer?

E.—Yes indeed, but it does not follow that this act will be free from the motive of desire. If he kills a man through fear, he certainly desires to live without fear.

A.—Do you think it is a small good to live without fear?

E.—It is a great good, but the murderer cannot possibly gain this by his crime.

A.—I am not asking what he can gain, but what he desires. He certainly desires what is good if he desires to live without fear, and therefore the desire is free from blame. Otherwise we shall blame all who love what is good. So we must agree that we cannot point to evil desire as the dominant motive in every murder, it would be false to say that the dominance of passion constitutes the evil in every sin. If so, there might be a murder which was not a sin.

E.—If to kill a man is murder, this may happen sometimes without any sin. When a soldier kills the enemy, when a judge or an executioner kills the criminal, or when a weapon flies from a man's hand inadvertently and by accident, I do not think they sin by killing a man.

A.—I agree, but they are not usually called murderers. Answer this question. If a slave kills his master because he is afraid of being tortured, do you think he should count among those who kill a man, without actually deserving to be called murderer?

E.—I think this is quite a different case from the other. The former act lawfully or not unlawfully; the latter are sanctioned by no law.

A.—Again you appeal to authority. But you must remember that the task we have undertaken is to understand what we believe. We believe in the law, and so we must try, if we possibly can, to understand whether the law which punishes this act does not punish it wrongly.

E.—It certainly does not punish it wrongly, for it punishes a man who deliberately kills his master; this is quite unlike the other examples.

A.—Do you remember you said a few minutes ago that passion was the dominant motive in every evil act, and was the cause of its being evil?

E.—Yes, I remember.

A.—Did you not also agree that the man who desires to live without fear does not have an evil desire?

E.—I remember that too.

A.—It follows that when a master is killed by his slave through this desire, he is not killed through a desire that we can blame. Therefore we have not yet discovered why this action is evil. For we are agreed that evil deeds are always evil simply because they are done through passion, that is, through a blameworthy desire.

E.—I begin to think he is condemned wrongly. I should not have the courage to say this, if I could find any other solution.

A.—Have you persuaded yourself that such a crime ought not to be punished, before considering whether the slave wished to be freed from fear of his master in order to indulge his own passions? The desire to live without fear is common both to all good and to all evil men. But the important point is that good men seek it by turning away their love from things which they cannot possess without danger of losing them, while evil men try to remove obstacles, and settle down to enjoy these things, and consequently live a life of crime and wickedness, better called death.

E.—I am coming to my senses again. I am very glad that I know clearly now what that blameworthy desire is which we call passion. I can now see it is love of those things which each of us can lose against his will.

So now I suggest we should inquire whether passion is also the chief motive in acts of sacrilege, which we often see committed through superstition.

A.—We must not be in too much hurry. I think we ought to discuss first whether an open enemy or a secret assassin can be killed without any passion in defence of life, liberty, or honour.

E.—I cannot imagine that men act without passion when they fight for things they would be unwilling to lose. If they cannot lose them, why need they go to the length of killing a man in their defence?

A.—In that case the law is not just which authorizes a traveller to kill a robber in self-protection, or any man or woman to kill an assailant, if possible before the violence has been carried out. The law also orders a soldier to kill the enemy, and if he refuses to do so he is punished by the military authorities. Can we possibly call these laws unjust, or rather no laws at all? A law which is not just does not seem to me to be a law.

E.—I see pretty well that a law which gives its subjects permission to commit lesser crimes in order to prevent greater ones, has a good defence against an accusation of this kind. It is a much lesser evil for the assassin than for the man who defends his own life, to be killed. It is far more dreadful that an innocent person should suffer violence than that the assailant should be killed by the intended victim.

When a soldier kills the enemy he is enforcing the law, and so has no difficulty in carrying out his duty without passion. The law itself, which is issued to protect its subjects, cannot be convicted of passion. If its author issued it in obedience to God's will, that is, to fulfill eternal justice, he may have done so without any passion at all. Even if he issued it out of passion, it does not follow that the law need be carried out with passion, because a good law can be issued by a man who is not good. For example, if a man, having reached supreme power, should take a bribe from an interested party, and decree it unlawful to carry off a woman even for marriage, the law will not be evil because its author is unjust and corrupt. Therefore the law which, to protect its citizens, lays down that force shall be met with force, can be obeyed without passion, and the same may be said about all servants who are subject to any higher power rightly and properly.

But I do not see how the other men we mentioned can be without blame because the law is without blame. The law does not force them to kill, but leaves it to their own discretion, and so they are free not to kill anyone in defence of those things which they can lose against their will, and for this reason ought not to love. Some may perhaps doubt whether the soul's life is by any means taken away when the body perishes, but, if it can be taken away it is of no value, while if it cannot, there is no reason for fear. And as for chastity, everyone knows that it is rooted in the soul itself, since it is a virtue; it cannot, therefore, be taken away by the violence of an aggressor. Whatever the man who is killed was going to take away is not wholly in our power, and so I do not understand how it can be called ours. I do not, therefore, blame the law which allows such men to be killed, but I do not see how I am to defend their slayers.

A.—I find it much harder to see why you try to defend those whom no law holds guilty.

E.—No law may find them guilty, if we speak of those laws which are familiar to us and which are made by men. I rather think they may come under a stronger and entirely secret law, if everything is controlled by Divine Providence. How can they be free from sin against Divine Providence, if they are stained with human blood in defence of things which ought to be despised? So I think that that law which is issued for the government of a people rightly allows these acts, while Divine Providence punishes them. The law which governs a people concerns itself with the control of conduct sufficiently to keep the peace among a rough population, so far as this can be achieved by man. This other kind of fault has different punishments which are suited to it, and I think wisdom alone can save us from them.

A.—I thoroughly approve of this distinction of yours; although it is incomplete and imperfect, yet it is full of faith and of ideals. The law which is decreed to govern states seems to you to permit much and to leave it unpunished, though it is punished by Divine Providence. Rightly so. Because a law does not do everything, it does not follow that which it does do is to be blamed.

I propose now that we examine carefully how far evil deeds ought to be punished by that law which controls peoples in this life. Then let us examine what remains to be punished necessarily and secretly by Divine Providence.

E.—Yes, I should like to do this, provided we can reach the end of such an enquiry. I think it will go on for ever.

A.—Have some courage; use your reason with confidence in God. Whatever difficulties may threaten us, they are cleared away and all becomes smooth with God's help. So raising our thoughts to Him and seeking His help, let us examine the problem before us. First, tell me whether that law which is put forth in writing, is for the good of men living this present life.

E.—Obviously it is. Peoples and states are made up of such men.

A.—Do these peoples and states belong to that class of things which cannot perish or change? Are they altogether everlasting, or are they subject to time and change?

E.—Unquestionably they belong to the class of things subject to time and change.

A.—Then, if a people is well-disciplined and observant of social good, and such that every individual puts public before private interest, is not this people rightly granted by law authority to elect its own officials to govern its affairs, that is, the affairs of the state?

E.—Certainly.

A.—If the people gradually deteriorates and prefers private to public interest, and sells its vote for bribes, and is corrupted by ambitious politicians, and puts into power criminals with no sense of honour, would not any honest man of sufficient influence who is left be justified in depriving this people of self-government, and in putting them under the authority of a few honest men or even of one?

E.—Quite justified.

A.—Well then, although these two laws seem to contradict one another, one giving the people self-government, the other taking it away, and although the latter is issued in such a way that both cannot be in force at the same time in the same state, surely we shall not say that one of them is unjust, and ought not to be decreed?

E.—No.

A.—Then, I suggest we call that law temporal law, which, though just, can be justly changed in course of time.

E.—By all means.

A.—Will not any intelligent man regard that law as unchangeable and eternal, which is termed the law of reason? We must always obey it; it is the law through which wicked men deserve an unhappy, and good men a happy life, and through which the law we have said should be called temporal is rightly decreed and rightly changed. Can it ever be unjust that the wicked should be unhappy and the good happy, or that a well-disciplined people should be self-governing, while an ill-disciplined people should be deprived of this privilege?

E.—I see that this law is eternal and unchangeable.

A.—I think you also see that men derive all that is just and lawful in temporal law from eternal law. For if a nation is justly self-governing at one time, and justly not self-governing at another time, the justice of this temporal change is derived from that eternal principle by which it is always right for a disciplined people to be self-governing, but not a people that is undisciplined. Do you agree?

E.—I agree.

A.—Therefore, to explain shortly as far as I can the notion which is impressed on us of eternal law, it is the law by which it is just that everything should have its due order. Tell me if you disagree.

E.—I have nothing to say against this; it is true.

A.—Since there is this single law, from which all temporal laws for human government derive their various forms, I suppose it cannot itself be varied?

E.—I see that it is quite impossible. No power, no circumstances, no calamity can ever make it unjust that everything should have its due and perfect order.

A.—What I want to say is this. Whatever it is by which man is superior to beasts, whether mind or spirit or whether either of them is the correct term (we find both in Sacred Scripture), if this governs and controls all the other elements of which man is composed, then man is duly ordered. We see that we have much in common not only with beasts, but also with trees and plants, for we see that nourishment, growth, generation, health, are characteristic also of trees, which belong to the lowest grade of life. We recognise too that beasts have sight, hearing, smell, taste, touch, often more keenly than we have. Or take strength, vigour, muscular power, swift and easy movement of the body, in all of which we excel some of them, equal some, and are surpassed by some. We are certainly in a common class with the beasts; every action of animal life is concerned with seeking bodily pleasure and avoiding pain.

There are other characteristics which beasts do not seem to share, yet which are not the highest qualities of man, as for example, laughing and joking. If we judge rightly, we shall judge that this is characteristic of human nature, but of the lowest part of it. Then there is love of praise and glory, and ambition: though the beasts do not have these passions, we must not suppose that we are better than the beasts because we have them. When this craving is not subject to reason, it makes us wretched. Yet no one thinks that he ought to be preferred to someone else in wretchedness. When reason controls these motions of the soul, a man must be said to be in due order. It ought not to be called due order, or order at all, when the better is subordinated to the worse. Do you not think so?

E.—It is clear.

A.—When reason, or mind, or spirit controls the irrational motions of the soul, then that element is ruling in man which ought to rule in virtue of that law which we have found to be eternal.

E.—I understand and agree.

A.—Therefore, when a man is established and ordered in this way, do you not think he is wise?

E.—If not, I do not know who else is to be thought wise.

A.—I suppose you also know that very many men are foolish.

E.—That too is quite obvious.

A.—If folly is the opposite of wisdom, since we have found out who is wise, you now know who is foolish.

E.—Everyone can see that a man is foolish, if his mind is not in control.

A.—Then what must we say, when a man is in this state? Does he lack mind, or is the mind though present, not in control?

E.—I think, the second of these.

A.—I should like you to tell me by what evidence you are aware that a man has a mind which does not exercise its control.

E.—Please do this yourself: it is too hard a task for me.

A.—At least you can easily remember, what we said a few minutes ago, how beasts are tamed and broken in to serve men, and how men would suffer the same from beasts, as we have shown, unless they excelled them in some way. We did not trace this superiority to the body; it showed itself in the soul, and we found no other name for it but reason. Later we remembered it was called also mind and spirit. But if reason and mind are distinct, we certainly agree that only mind can use reason. Hence it follows that the man who possesses reason cannot lack mind.

E.—I remember this quite well, and accept it.

A.—Then do you think that those who tame beasts can be such only if they are wise? I call those wise who truly deserve the name, that is, who are controlled by mind, and who are disturbed by no power of passion.

E.—It is absurd to think that men who go by the name of animal tamers are like this, or even shepherds or herdsmen or charioteers, all of whom, as we see, control tame animals and when they are untamed break them in.

A.—There then you have plain evidence which makes it clear that a man has a mind, even when it is not in control. Such men as these have a mind, for they do things which could not be done without a mind. It is not in control, for they are foolish, and, as we know, the mind is in control only in wise men.

E.—It amazes me that, when we discussed this earlier on, I could not think how to answer.

But let us continue. We have discovered that human wisdom consists in the control of the human mind, and that it is also possible for the mind not to be in control.

A.—Do you think that passion is more powerful than mind, though we know that eternal law has granted mind control over passion? I certainly do not think so. There would not be due order if the weaker governed the stronger. So I think mind must have more power than desire, from the very fact that it is right and just for it to control desire.

E.—I think so too.

A.—Surely we do not hesitate to prefer every virtue to vice, so that virtue is stronger and more dominant, just as it is better and nobler?

E.—Undoubtedly.

A.—It follows that no wicked soul overcomes a soul which is armed with virtue.

E.—Quite true.

A.—I think you will not deny that any soul is better and stronger than any body.

E.—No one denies this, who sees—and it is obvious—that a living substance is better than a non-living substance, or one that gives life better than one that receives it.

A.—Much less, then, does any body whatever overcome a soul endowed with virtue.

E.—Plainly.

A.—Then surely a just soul, and a mind which keeps its proper and rightful control, cannot dethrone and subdue to passion another mind which keeps control with the same justice and virtue?

E.—Certainly not; not only because the same excellence is present in both, but also because the former will fall from justice, and become a wicked mind, if it tries to make another mind wicked, and by that very fact will be weaker.

A.—You have understood the point well. It remains for you to answer, if you can, whether anything seems more excellent to you than a rational and wise mind.

E.—I think nothing except God.

A.—That is my opinion too. But the problem is difficult, and now is not a suitable time to try and understand it thoroughly. Let us hold the conclusion firmly on faith, but not attempt a full and precise examination.

For the moment we can recognize that, whatever kind of being rightly excels a virtuous mind, cannot possibly be unjust. Therefore not even this, though it may have the power, will force mind to serve passion.

E.—Everyone would at once accept that.

A.—So we conclude that, since what is equal or superior does not make a mind the slave of passion, if it is in control and virtuous, on account of its justice, while what is inferior cannot do this on account of its weakness, as our argument has shown, therefore, nothing makes a mind give way to desire except its own will and free choice.

E.—I see that this is quite conclusive.

A.—It follows that you think such a mind justly punished for so great a sin.

E.—I cannot deny it.

A.—Well, surely that punishment should not be thought a light one, which consists in the mind being ruled by passion, being robbed of its store of virtue, being dragged hither and thither, poor and needy, now judging false for true, now defending, now attacking what before it approved, and in spite of this running off into fresh falsehood, now withholding its assent, and often frightened of clear reasoning, now despairing of finding any truth at all, and clinging closely to the darkness of its folly, now striving for the light of understanding, and again falling back through exhaustion. Meanwhile the passions rage like tyrants, and throw into confusion the whole soul and life of men with storms from every quarter, fear on one side, desire on another, on another anxiety, or false empty joy, here pain for the thing which was loved and lost, there eagerness to win what is not possessed, there grief for an injury received, here burning desire to avenge it. Wherever he turns, avarice can confine him, self-indulgence dissipate him, ambition master him, pride puff him up, envy torture him, sloth drug him, obstinacy rouse him, oppression afflict him, and the countless other feelings which crowd and exploit the power of passion. Can we then think this no punishment at all, which, as you see, all who do not cling to wisdom must necessarily suffer?

E.—In my opinion this punishment is a great one, and entirely just, if a man, being established on the heights of wisdom, should choose to come down and be the slave of passion; but I am doubtful whether there can be anyone who has wished, or wishes, to do so. We believe that man was so perfectly formed by God and established in a life of happiness, that only of his own will did he come down thence to the troubles of mortal life. Yet while I hold this firmly by faith, I have never grasped it with my understanding. If you think careful inquiry into this problem should be put off, you do so against my will.

But the problem which worries me most is why we should suffer grievous punishments of this kind, seeing that, though admittedly foolish, we have never been wise. How, then, can we be said to suffer these punishments deservedly, for having abandoned the fortress of virtue, and chosen to be slaves of passion? I should certainly not agree to your putting it off, if you can discuss this problem and explain it.

A.—You say that we have never been wise, as if it was a manifest truism. You are only thinking of the time since we were born into this life. But, since wisdom is in the soul, whether the soul lived in another life before it was joined to the body, and whether at one time it lived in a state of wisdom, is a great question, a great mystery, to be considered in its proper place. Yet this does not prevent us from clearing up, so far as possible, our present problem.

I am asking you whether we have a will.

E.—I do not know.

A.—Do you want to know?

E.—I do not even know this.

A.—Then you must ask me nothing more.

E.—Why?

A.—Because I ought not to answer your questions, unless you want to know what you ask. Also unless you wish to become wise, I ought not to discuss the subject with you. Finally, you could not be my friend, unless you wish me well. Reflect, too, whether you do not yourself will that your life may be happy.

E.—I agree it cannot be denied we have a will. Now go on, and let us see what you conclude from this.

A.—I will do so; but tell me first whether you are conscious of having a good will.

E.—What is a good will?

A.—A will by which we seek to live rightly and virtuously and to reach the height of wisdom. Now see whether you do not seek to live rightly and virtuously, or whether you do not have a strong desire to be wise, or can really venture to deny that we have a good will when we wish for these things.

E.—I do not deny any of this, and therefore I agree that I have not only a will, but now that I have a good will also.

A.—I want you to tell me how much you think this will is worth. Do you think that riches or honours or bodily pleasures or all these together bear any comparison with it?

E.—God forbid anything so stupid and wicked.

A.—Should it then be only a small joy to us that we have something in the soul, I mean this good will, in comparison with which these things I have mentioned are utterly worthless, yet to gain which we see countless men accepting every toil and danger?

E.—It ought to be a joy to us, and a very great joy indeed.

A.—Do you think that those who lack this joy suffer a small loss in being deprived of such a good?

E.—A very great loss.

A.—I think you now see that it lies in the power of our will whether we enjoy or lack this great and true good. What is so fully in the power of the will as the will itself?

When a man has a good will he has a possession which is far to be preferred before all earthly kingdoms and all bodily pleasures. But if a man does not possess it, then he lacks that which is more excellent than all good things not under our control, and which only the will of itself could give him. And so, when he judges himself wretched if he loses the glory of fame, great wealth, and any bodily goods, will you not judge him wretched, even though he abounds in all these things? For he clings to things which he can very easily lose and not possess while wishing to do so, but he lacks a good will which is beyond all comparison with these, and which, though it is so great a good, needs only to be desired in order to be possessed.

E.—That is very true.

A.—Therefore it is right and just that foolish men should be made wretched in this way, although they were never wise—obscure and mysterious though this latter point is.

E.—I agree.

A.—Now consider whether prudence seems to you to consist in the knowledge what to seek and what to avoid.

E.—I think it does.

A.—And is not fortitude that state of the soul in which we despise all misfortunes and the loss of things not resting in our power?

E.—I think so.

A.—Then do you agree that temperance is that state of soul which controls and checks desire in regard to those things which it is shameful to desire?

E.—That is certainly my view.

A.—And what else are we to say about justice than that it is the virtue by which each man is given his due?

E.—That is what I think about justice.

A.—Then the man who has a good will, the excellence of which we have discussed at such length, will love this alone, his most precious possession, will delight in this and make it his joy and pleasure, realising fully its value, and that he cannot be robbed of it against his will. Surely we cannot doubt that he will be opposed to all that conflicts with this one good?

E.—Most certainly he must be opposed to it.

A.—Can we suppose such a man is not endowed with prudence, who sees that this good should be sought for and everything avoided which conflicts with it?

E.—I think no one can see this without prudence.

A.—Quite right. But why should we not grant him fortitude? He cannot love and value highly all these things not under our control. They are loved through an evil will, and he is bound to resist an evil will as the enemy of his most precious good. Since he does not love these things, he does not grieve at their loss, but altogether despises them. We have declared and admitted that this is the work of fortitude.

E.—Yes, we must certainly grant him fortitude. I know no one who could be more truly said to have fortitude than the man who is perfectly resigned to the lack of those things of which it is not in our power to gain possession. We have concluded such a man must necessarily do this.

A.—Now consider whether we can deprive him of temperance, since this is the virtue which checks passion. What is so opposed to a good will as passion? Hence you can understand that the man who loves his good will resists his passions by every means, and fights against them. Therefore he is rightly said to have temperance.

E.—Go on: I agree.

A.—There remains justice, and I certainly do not see how such a man can lack this. If he possesses and loves to possess a good will, and resists, as I have said, what is opposed to it, he cannot wish evil to anyone. It follows that he harms no one, and this can only be the case, if he gives to everyone his due. You remember, I think, that you agreed when I said this was the concern of justice.

E.—I remember. I accepted your account of the four virtues just now, and agree that all of them are present in the man who values highly and loves his own good will.

A.—What then prevents us from admitting that the life of this man is praiseworthy?

E.—Nothing at all. The whole argument points to this, and in fact requires it.

A.—Well, can you possibly help thinking that a miserable life ought to be avoided?

E.—That is emphatically my opinion; I think it certainly ought to be avoided.

A.—And you do not think a praiseworthy life ought to be avoided?

E.—No, I think decidedly that it ought to be aimed at.

A.—Therefore a life which is praiseworthy is not miserable.

E.—That follows.

A.—So far as I can see, nothing now prevents you from agreeing that that life which is not miserable is the life of happiness.

E.—Obviously.

A.—We hold, then, that a man is happy who loves his own good will, and who despises in comparison with this whatever else is called good and can be lost, while the desire to keep it remains.

E.—Yes, our former conclusions lead to this, and we must agree.

A.—You have a clear grasp of the question. But I should like you to tell me whether to love one's own good will, and to value it as highly as we have said, is itself good will.

E.—Yes, it is.

A.—But if we are right in judging the one man happy whose will is good, shall we not be right in judging the other man unhappy whose will is bad?

E.—Quite right.

A.—Then what reason is there for doubting that, even though we were never wise before, yet by our will we deserve, and spend, a praiseworthy and happy life, and by our will a life that is shameful and unhappy?

E.—I agree that we have reached this conclusion by arguments which are certain and undeniable.

A.—Also consider another point. I think you remember our definition of a good will: it was, I believe, a will by which we seek to live rightly and virtuously.

E.—I remember.

A.—Then, if through our good will we love this good will itself, and cling to it, and prefer it before all things which we cannot be sure to keep because we want to, the result will be, as reason has shown, that these virtues will dwell in our soul. To possess them is to live rightly and virtuously. Hence it follows that whoever wishes to live rightly and virtuously, if he wishes so to wish in preference to the goods which are but passing, acquires this great possession with such ease, that to wish for it is the same as to possess what he wished.

E.—Really, I can hardly keep myself from crying out for joy, when a good so great and so easy to gain is suddenly set before me.

A.—This very joy, which is caused by winning this good, if it supports the soul calmly, quietly, and steadily, is called the happy life, unless you think the happy life is different from taking joy in goods which are true and certain.

E.—That is my opinion.

A.—Quite right. But do you think that anyone does not by every means desire and long for a happy life?

E.—Undoubtedly everyone desires it.

A.—Why then does not everyone gain it? We agreed that men deserve a happy life by their will, and also an unhappy life by their will, and deserve it in such a way as to receive it. But here a difficulty arises, and unless we scrutinise it carefully, it will tend to upset the clear reasoning we worked out before. For how does anyone of his own will endure an unhappy life, though no one at all wishes to live unhappily? Or how does a man through his own will gain a happy life, if so many are unhappy, and all wish to be happy?

Does it come about because to desire good or evil is different from deserving something through a good or bad will? For those who are happy and who ought also to be good, are not happy because they wished to live happily—the wicked also wish this—but because they wished to live rightly, which the wicked do not wish. Therefore it is not surprising that unhappy men do not get what they want, namely, a happy life. They do not also want that which accompanies it, and without which no one is worthy of it or gains it, that is to say, a life of right conduct.

For the eternal law, to the consideration of which it is now time to return, has settled this with unchangeable firmness; it has settled that merit lies in the will, while reward and punishment lie in happiness and misery. And so, when we say that men are wilfully unhappy, we do not mean that they wish to be unhappy, but that their will is such that unhappiness is the necessary result, unwilling though they are. Hence this does not contradict our former conclusion, that all wish to be happy, but not all are able so to be. Not all wish to live rightly, which is the only state of will that deserves a happy life. Have you any objections to this?

E.—No, I have none.

―――――――

But now let us see how this is connected with the problem we were going to discuss about the two laws.

A.—Very well. But first tell me about the man who loves to live rightly, and so delights in it that not only is it right for him but also pleasant and agreeable. Does he not love this law, and hold it most dear to him? For by it he sees that a happy life is given to a good will, and an unhappy life to an evil will.

E.—He loves it with all his heart and strength since he lives as he does in obedience to this law.

A.—Well, when he loves this law, does he love something which is changeable and temporal, or something which is firm and everlasting?

E.—Certainly, something which is everlasting and unchangeable.

A.—Do those who persist in their evil will, at the same time desire to be happy? Can they love that law by which such men rightly earn unhappiness?

E.—I think they cannot.

A.—Do they love nothing else?

E.—They love very many things, those things in gaining or keeping which their evil will persists.

A.—I suppose you mean wealth, honours, pleasures, physical beauty, and all the other things which they may be unable to gain though they want them, and may lose against their will.

E.—Yes, those are the things.

A.—You do not think these last for ever, do you, for you see they are subject to time and change?

E.—It would be sheer madness to think so.

A.—Then, since it is clear that some men love eternal things while others love temporal things, and since we agree that there are two laws, one eternal and the other temporal, if you have a sense of fairness, which of these men do you think should be subject to the eternal law, and which to the temporal law?

E.—Your question seems easy. I think that happy men through their love of eternal things live under the eternal law, while the temporal law is laid upon the unhappy.

A.—You judge rightly, provided you keep constantly in view what reason has very clearly shown, that those who serve the temporal law cannot escape the eternal law. Through it we have maintained that every just effect, every just change is brought about. You understand no doubt that those who cling to the eternal law with a good will do not need the temporal law.

E.—Yes, I understand.

A.—So the eternal law bids us turn away our love from temporal things, and turn it back, when purified, towards things that are eternal.

E.—Yes, it bids us do this.

A.—What else then do you think the temporal law orders but that, when men cling with their desire to those things which can be called ours for a short time, they shall possess them by that same right by which peace is maintained in human society, so far as is possible in such affairs?

The things I mean are, first, the body and what are called its goods, such as sound health, keen senses, strength, beauty, and so on, some of which are necessary for the useful arts, and therefore of more value, others of which are of less value. Then there is freedom, though indeed there is no true freedom except for those who are happy and cling to the eternal law; but here I mean that freedom by which men think they are free, when they do not have other men as their masters, and which is desired by those who wish to be released from any human masters. Then parents, brothers, wife, children, relations, connections, friends, and all who are joined to us by some bond. Or again the state itself, which is usually regarded as a parent; honours, too, and distinctions, and what is called popular favour. Lastly, money, under which single term is included everything of which we are rightful masters, and which we are regarded as having the power to sell and give away.

How this law assigns to each man his share, it would be a long and difficult matter to explain, and one plainly not necessary for our purpose. We need only notice that the power of this law to enforce itself does not extend further than to take away and confiscate as a punishment those things or a part of them. Hence it brings pressure to bear through fear, and to gain its end turns and twists the souls of the unhappy people for whose government it is fitted. For, while they fear to lose these things, they exercise in their use a certain restraint suitable to hold together such a society as can be composed of men of this kind. This law does not punish the sin which consists in loving the above objects, but the sin which consists in taking them wrongfully from other people.

So consider whether we have now finished the task you thought would be endless. We set out to inquire how far the right of punishment extended of that law by which earthly peoples and states are governed.

E.—I see we have finished the task.

A.—Do you see also that there would not be any punishment, whether wrongly inflicted, or inflicted by the sanction of the above law, unless men loved those things which can be taken away against their will?

E.—I see that too.

A.—Now, one man makes good use and another bad use of the same things. The man who makes bad use, clings to them and is attached to them by his love, that is to say, is subject to things which ought to be subject to him. He makes those things of service to himself, for the control and good management of which he himself ought to be of service. On the other hand, the man who uses them rightly shows indeed their value, but not for himself. They do not make him good or better, but rather are made good by him. Therefore he is not attached to them by love of them, and does not make them, as it were, members of his own soul—as would happen if he loved them—lest, when the time comes for their amputation, they may infect him with painful corruption. He is fully their master, ready to possess and control them when there is need, and still more ready to lose them and not possess them. This being so, surely you do not think silver or gold are to be condemned because some men are avaricious, or food because some men are greedy, or wine because some men are drunkards, or beautiful women because some men are fornicators and adulterers, and so on, especially as you see that a doctor makes a good use of heat, and a poisoner a bad use of bread?

E.—It is quite true that not the things themselves are to be blamed, but the men who make a bad use of them.

11. AUGUSTINE: The Two Cities

The City of God was begun in A.D. 412 and finished in A.D. 426, shortly before Augustine's death in 430. It follows the work *On Free Will*, written 388-395, and *The Confessions*, written 397-398. With the possible exception of *The Confessions, The City of God* is his most influential work. It is the great example of a theology of history, a framework for an account of the whole of history in the light of Christian teaching.

Augustine points to two cities as symbols of the sacred and secular orders: the City of God (the Heavenly City), and the community of all who are united by the love of God, and the Earthly City, the community of all who are united by love of earthly things, apart from God.

The book provides intellectual means for Augustine's understanding of the fall of Rome. The selections* reveal the conception of the two cities at work. They present a sketch of his thought regarding peace and discord, certainty and doubt, active and contemplative life. These topics are, of course, treated more fully in the book taken as a whole.

CHAPTER 17

WHAT PRODUCES PEACE, AND WHAT DISCORD, BETWEEN THE HEAVENLY AND EARTHLY CITIES.

But the families which do not live by faith seek their peace in the earthly advantages of this life; while the families which live by faith look for those eternal blessings which are promised, and use as pilgrims such advantages of time and of earth as do not fascinate and divert them from God, but rather aid them to endure with greater ease, and to keep down the number of those burdens of the corruptible body which weigh upon the soul. Thus the things necessary

* From *The City of God* (Book XIX, chapters 17, 18, 19), trans. Marcus Dodds.

for this mortal life are used by both kinds of men and families alike, but each has its own peculiar and widely different aim in using them. The earthly city, which does not live by faith, seeks an earthly peace, and the end it proposes, in the well-ordered concord of civic obedience and rule, is the combination of men's wills to attain the things which are helpful to this life. The heavenly city, or rather the part of it which sojourns on earth and lives by faith, makes use of this peace only because it must, until this mortal condition which necessitates it shall pass away. Consequently, so long as it lives like a captive and a stranger in the earthly city, though it has already received the promise of redemption, and the gift of the Spirit as the earnest of it, it makes no scruple to obey the laws of the earthly city, whereby the things necessary for the maintenance of this mortal life are administered; and thus, as this life is common to both cities, so there is a harmony between them in regard to what belongs to it. But, as the earthly city has had some philosophers whose doctrine is condemned by the divine teaching, and who, being deceived either by their own conjectures or by demons, supposed that many gods must be invited to take an interest in human affairs, and assigned to each a separate function and a separate department—to one the body, to another the soul; and in the body itself, to one the head, to another the neck, and each of the other members to one of the gods; and in like manner, in the soul, to one god the natural capacity was assigned, to another education, to another anger, to another lust; and so the various affairs of life were assigned—cattle to one, corn to another, wine to another, oil to another, the woods to another, money to another, navigation to another, wars and victories to another, marriages to another, births and fecundity to another, and other things to other gods: and as the celestial city, on the other hand, knew that one God only was to be worshipped, and that to Him alone was due that service which the Greeks call λατρεία, and which can be given only to a god, it has come to pass that the two cities could not have common laws of religion, and that the heavenly city has been compelled in this matter to dissent, and to become obnoxious to those who think differently, and to stand the brunt of their anger and hatred and persecutions, except in so far as the minds of their enemies have been alarmed by the multitude of the Christians and quelled by the manifest protection of God accorded to them. This heavenly city, then, while it sojourns on earth, calls citizens out of all nations, and gathers together a society of pilgrims of all languages, not scrupling about diversities in the manners, laws, and institutions whereby earthly peace is secured and maintained, but recognizing that, however various these are, they all tend to one and the same end of earthly peace. It therefore is so far from rescinding and abolishing these diversities, that it even preserves and adopts them, so long only as no hindrance to the worship of the one supreme and true God, is thus introduced. Even the heavenly city, therefore, while in its state of pilgrimage, avails itself of the peace of earth, and, so far as it can without injuring faith and godliness, desires and maintains a common agreement among men regarding the acquisition of the necessaries of life, and makes this earthly peace bear upon the peace of heaven; for this alone can be truly called and esteemed the peace of the reasonable creatures, consisting as it does in the perfectly ordered and harmonious enjoyment of God and of one another in God. When we shall have reached that peace, this mortal life shall give place to one that is eternal, and our body shall be no more this animal body which by its corruption weighs down the soul, but a spiritual body feeling no want, and in all its members subjected to the will. In its pilgrim state the heavenly city possesses this peace by faith; and by this faith it lives righteously when it refers to the attainment of that peace every good action towards God and man; for the life of the city is a social life.

CHAPTER 18

HOW DIFFERENT THE UNCERTAINTY OF THE NEW ACADEMY IS FROM THE CERTAINTY OF THE CHRISTIAN FAITH.

As regards the uncertainty about everything which Varro alleges to be the differentiating characteristic of the New Academy, the city of God thoroughly detests such doubt as madness. Regarding matters which it apprehends by the mind and reason it has most absolute certainty, although its knowledge is limited because of the corruptible body pressing down the mind, for, as the apostle says, "We know in part."[1] It believes also the evidence of the senses which the mind uses by aid of the body; for [if one who trusts his senses is some-

[1] 1 Cor. xiii. 9.

times deceived], he is more wretchedly deceived who fancies he should never trust them. It believes also the Holy Scriptures, old and new, which we call canonical, and which are the source of the faith by which the just lives[2] and by which we walk without doubting whilst we are absent from the Lord.[3] So long as this faith remains inviolate and firm, we may without blame entertain doubts regarding some things which we have neither perceived by sense nor by reason, and which have not been revealed to us by the canonical Scriptures, nor come to our knowledge through witnesses whom it is absurd to disbelieve.

CHAPTER 19

OF THE DRESS AND HABITS OF THE CHRISTIAN PEOPLE.

It is a matter of no moment in the city of God whether he who adopts the faith that brings men to God adopts it in one dress and manner of life or another, so long only as he lives in conformity with the commandments of God. And hence, when philosophers themselves become Christians, they are compelled, indeed, to abandon their erroneous doctrines, but not their dress and mode of living, which are no obstacle to religion. So that we make no account of that distinction of sects which Varro adduced in connection with the Cynic school, provided always nothing indecent or self-indulgent is retained. As to these three modes of life, the contemplative, the active, and the composite, although, so long as a man's faith is preserved, he may choose any of them without detriment to his eternal interests, yet he must never overlook the claims of truth and duty. No man has a right to lead such a life of contemplation as to forget in his own ease the service due to his neighbor; nor has any man a right to be so immersed in active life as to neglect the contemplation of God. The charm of leisure must not be indolent vacancy of mind, but the investigation or discovery of truth, that thus every man may make solid attainments without grudging that others do the same. And, in active life, it is not the honors or power of this life we should covet, since all things under the sun are vanity,

[2] Hab. ii. 4.
[3] 2 Cor. v. 6.

but we should aim at using our position and influence, if these have been honorably attained, for the welfare of those who are under us, in the way we have already explained.[4] It is to this the apostle refers when he says, "He that desireth the episcopate desireth a good work."[5] He wished to show that the episcopate is the title of a work, not of an honour. It is a Greek word, and signifies that he who governs superintends or takes care of those whom he governs: for ἐπί means *over,* and σκοπεῖν, *to see;* therefore ἐπισκοπεῖν means "to oversee." So that he who loves to govern rather than to do good is no bishop. Accordingly no one is prohibited from the search after truth, for in this leisure may most laudably be spent; but it is unseemly to covet the high position requisite for governing the people, even though that position be held and that government be administered in a seemly manner. And therefore holy leisure is longed for by the love of truth; but it is the necessity of love to undertake requisite business. If no one imposes this burden upon us, we are free to sift and contemplate truth; but if it be laid upon us, we are necessitated for love's sake to undertake it. And yet not even in this case are we obliged wholly to relinquish the sweets of contemplation; for were these to be withdrawn, the burden might prove more than we could bear.

12: BOETHIUS: The Varieties of Goodness

Boethius was born into a Roman patrician family about A.D. 480. He rose to a high official position in the reign of Theodoric, the Ostrogothic Emperor. Boethius was accused (probably without basis) of being a party to a conspiracy to commit treason. Theodoric sentenced him to death without a hearing, and he was cruelly put to death in A.D. 541.

In happier days Boethius had conceived the plan of translating all the works of Plato and Aristotle into Latin. Had Boethius completed his translation project, the whole history of medieval philosophy would have been radically different. Nevertheless, Boethius did achieve part of his goal, and it is largely through his translation that the early European thinkers came to know the relatively small portion of the aristotelian

---

[4] Ch. 6.
[5] 1 Tim. iii. 1.

corpus that was available to them. His commentaries, especially the two commentaries on the *Isagoge* of Porphyry, had a tremendous influence on subsequent philosophical development.

The influence of Boethius has been very great indeed. His translations provided an important link between the wisdom of Periclean Athens and Western European civilization. The logic that was studied during this first millennium of Christianity was the logic of Aristotle as transmitted by Boethius. The tone of education during this long period was also largely due to the influence of Boethius' writings. The common ground of education in Western Europe was the study of the seven liberal arts, divided into the *trivium* (grammar, logic, and rhetoric) and the *quadrivium* (geometry, arithmetic, astronomy, and music). Boethius was responsible for producing much of the source material in these areas and was thus influential in shaping the European mind.

The first selection from Boethius is a complete short work, *How Substances Can Be Good In Virtue of Their Existence Without Being Absolute Goods.** This little work is the third of the five *Theological Tractates*, and it answers the question posed by its title in terms of a platonic participation theory. Briefly, Boethius argues that there is only one absolute good (God) and there is a perfect identity between its being and its goodness. In all other things a distinction may be made: the being of a concrete thing is not the same as its goodness. The perfect being is good by its substance—its being, goodness, and substance are identical. All other beings are good by participation—that is, they derive their goodness by a kind of limited sharing in the goodness of the "absolute."

You ask me to disperse the obscurity of that question in my *De Hebdomadibus* which concerns how substances are good in that they exist, though they are not substantially good, and [you ask me] to show [this] a little more clearly. And you say that this should be done because the procedure of this kind of treatise is not evident to all. Yet I myself am witness to how vigorously you have already embraced this. But I reflect deeply upon my *De Hebdomadibus* for myself, and would rather keep my reflections in my memory than share them with those frivolous and capricious persons who will take nothing apart from a joke and laughter. And so you should not be opposed to the obscurities of brevity, which are not only the faithful guardian of a secret, but also have the advantage that they speak only with those who are worthy [of understanding]. Therefore, as is the practice in the mathematical and other sciences, I have set

* From *Theological Tractates* III, trans. George L. Stengren for this volume.

down terms and rules according to which I shall develop all that follows.

I. A common conception of the mind is a statement which everyone accepts as soon as it is heard. There are two kinds of these [common conceptions]. For one is so common that it is [intelligible] to all men, as for instance if you say, "If you take equals from two equals, the remainders are equal," nobody understanding that [proposition] will deny it. But the other kind is [intelligible] only to the learned, which nevertheless comes from such common conceptions of the mind, as, "Things which are incorporeal are not in a place," and the like; these [propositions] are not evident to the multitude but to the learned.

II. To be (*esse*) is different from that which is (*id quod est*); for being itself (*ipsum esse*) is not yet, but on the contrary that which is [i.e. a concrete individual] is and exists when it has the form of being.

III. A concrete individual (*quod est*) can participate in another, but being itself (*ipsum esse*) in no way participates in another. For participation comes about when something already is; but it is something when it has begun to be.

IV. That which is can have something besides itself; but being itself has no admixture of anything other than itself.

V. Only to be something is different from being something in that which is; for the former signifies substance, the latter accident.

VI. In order to exist, everything which is participates in that which is being (*esse*). And thus that which is participates in that which is being so that it may be; but it is so that it may participate in something else.

VII. Every simple thing has its being (*esse*) and its individuality (*id quod est*) as one.

VIII. In every composite, being is other than individuality.

IX. Every diversity is discordant, and likeness is to be sought; and that which seeks something else shows itself to be of the same nature as that which it seeks.

These premises are sufficient then; suitable arguments for each point will be furnished by a prudent interpreter of the argument.

Now the question is of this sort. Those things which are, are good. For the common opinion of the learned holds that everything which is tends toward the good, and everything tends toward its like.

Therefore those things which tend toward the good are themselves good. But we must ask how they are good, by participation or by substance? If by participation, they are in no way good in themselves; for what is white by participation is not white in itself by its very being. And likewise with all other qualities. If, therefore, they are good by participation, they are in no way good in themselves: hence they do not tend toward the good. But it has been agreed [that they do tend toward the good]. Therefore they are not good by participation but by substance. But those things which are good by substance are good by their very being. But they have their actuality from that which is being. Therefore their being is good; therefore the actuality of all things is good. But if being is good, those things which exist are good insofar as they exist, and for them to be is the same as to be good; therefore they are substantial goods, since they do not participate in goodness. But if in them being itself is good, since they are substantial goods, doubtless they are like the first good, and in this way they are this good itself, for nothing is like it except itself. From this it follows that all things which are, are God, and this would be wrong to say. Therefore they are not substantial goods and thus in those things it is not the case that to be is to be good. But neither do they participate in goodness; for they would in no way tend toward the good. Therefore in no respect are they good.

This sort of solution may be brought to bear on this question. There are many things which cannot be separated in actuality but which can be separated in the mind and by thought; as, for example, no one can actually separate a triangle or the rest [of the mathematical figures] from the underlying matter, but one can mentally explore the triangle and its properties separately from matter. Hence let us remove from our minds for a while the presence of the first good, the being of which is, indeed, acknowledged in the opinion of all the learned and unlearned and can be known in the religions of barbaric races. Having thus briefly put this aside, let us postulate that all things that are, are good, and let us consider how they can be good, if they did not flow from the first good. In this way I see that for them, to be is other than to be good. For let it be postulated that there is one and the same substance that is good, white, heavy, and round. Then it would be the case that its substance would be other than its roundness, other than its color, other than its goodness. For if each of these were the same as its substance, heaviness would be the same as color or the good and the good would be the same as heaviness—which is contrary to nature. Therefore, in those things to be would be other than to be something, and then they would be something good, but they would not have the good as [a constituent of] their very being (*ipsum esse*). Therefore if they are in any respect they would not be the good or from the good, and they would not be the same as the good, but for them to be would be other than to be good. But if they were nothing at all other than the good, not heavy, nor colored, nor distended by the dimension of space, nor were there any other quality in them except only that they were good, then they would seem to be not things but the principle of things, rather not they would seem, but it would seem; for there is only one of this sort that is only good and nothing else. But since they are not simple, they could not be at all unless that which is good alone willed them to be. Wherefore since their being flows from the will of the good, they are said to be good. For the first good, since it is such, is good in that it exists; but the second good is also good since it flows from that whose very being is good. But the very being of all things flows from that which is the first good and which is good in such a way that it may be rightly said that in its very being it is good. Therefore their being is good; for then it is in it [i.e., the first good].

Thus the question is resolved. For although things may be good in that they exist, yet they are not like the first good, since they are in no way things whose very being is good. But since there can be no actuality of things unless it flows from the first being, that is, the good; therefore their being is good [but] it is not like that from which it is. For [the first good] is good in that it is; for it is nothing other than the good. But [secondary good] if it were not from it [the first good], could perhaps be good, but it could not be good in that it exists. Then it might perhaps participate in the good; but since they would not have their very being from the good, they could not have the good. Therefore when in mind and thought we have taken the first good away from them, though they may be good, yet they could not be good in their very being. And since they could not actually exist unless that which is truly good had produced them, therefore their being is good, and they are not like the substantial good from which they flow. And unless they flowed from it, although they might be good, they could not be good in their very being, since they would be both other than the good and not from the good, since the first good is both being itself and the good itself, and its being is good. But those things which are white will not have to be white in that they exist, since that they exist flows from the will of God, not that they are white. For it is one thing to be, another thing to be white; and this is because He that brought it about that they are is indeed good, but not white. Therefore it is compatible with the will of the good that they be good in that they are; but it is not harmonious with the will of one that is not white that what is such that its property is to be white should be so in that it exists; for they do not flow from the will of one who is white. Therefore because one who is not white willed them to be white they are white; but they are good in that they exist because he who is good willed them to be good. According to this reasoning, then, ought all things be just because he who is just willed them to exist? Not at all. For to be good concerns essence, but to be just relates to acts. But in Him it is the same to be and to act; therefore it is the same to be good and to be just. But for us action and being are not the same; for we are not simple. Therefore, for us to be good is not the same as to be just, but for all of us our being is the same in that we exist. Therefore all things are good, but not all are just. Finally, good is indeed generic, but just is specific, and this species [just] does not descend into all. Therefore some things are indeed just, but all things are good.

13. BOETHIUS: True Happiness

The selections which follow are taken from the *Consolation of Philosophy*. This work is divided into five books.

Boethius might be called a Christian Job. Like the biblical Job, Boethius was a prosperous and important person who led a blameless, upright life, and who has suddenly been made to suffer without any apparent reason. Conscious of his innocence, he languishes in prison lamenting his misfortune, trying to write poetry to alleviate his misery, when Philosophy personified appears to him. Boethius gives an allegorical description of her as a noble and great lady. She drives away the muses of poetry so that Boethius may receive the only consolation suitable: that of philosophy. Thus the title has a twofold significance: Philosophy personified consoles him in a dialogue, and the philosophical content of the dialogue is the consolation of a man unjustly imprisoned.

After noting that great philosophers like Socrates have also been unjustly put to death, Dame Philosophy asks Boethius whether he thinks that the universe is governed by chance or by reason, thus raising the issue of divine Providence.

In Book II, she points out that he did not do anything to deserve his previous good fortune—it was, in effect, gratuitous—so it is hardly fitting that he should bewail his misfortune, since he has lost only an inferior and capricious good. True happiness does not consist in the possession of the goods of fortune or in anything external; on the contrary, true happiness should be sought within one's own nature: blessedness, knowledge, and virtue cannot be lost in the whims of fortune.

In Book III, Dame Philosophy continues to show that true happiness cannot be found in fickle and ephemeral earthly goods. The selection below from Chapters 9-11* shows the development of the positive theme that true happiness consists in the satisfaction and self-possession that come from the attainment of the highest good.

The next selection† which is from Chapter 11 of Book III and Chapter 2 of Book IV develops the concept of goodness, and gives a clever argument to show that good men are always powerful and evil men are totally lacking in any real power.

The two selections from Book V‡ deal with themes that constantly recur in the history of philosophy, and are, of course still timely: chance, divine Providence, and free will.

It should be noted that Boethius wrote this magnificent work during a relatively short period when he could hardly have been expected to have had a tranquil mind. Obviously he was also separated from his beloved family and his precious library. This makes the vast erudition that pervades the *Consolation* all the more impressive. Platonic, Aristotelian, and Augustinian principles, doctrines, and themes are woven into a consistent and harmonious development. Yet this is no mere eclectic feat—it is a brilliant creative synthesis that manifests Boethius' ability as a philosopher of significant stature.

* Selection 13, "True Happiness," trans. George L. Stengren for this volume.
† Selection 14, "The Nature and Power of Goodness," trans. George L. Stengren for this volume.
‡ Selection 15, "Chance and Free Will," trans. George L. Stengren for this volume.

[Dame Philosophy:] "Let it be enough that thus far the form of counterfeit happiness has been shown, and if you have grasped it clearly, order now requires that [I should] show what true [happiness] is."

"Certainly I see," [Boethius] said, "that one cannot gain sufficiency with riches, nor power with kingdoms, nor respect with dignities, nor fame with glory, nor joy with pleasures."

"Have you perceived the reasons why that is so?"

"I seem to have a slight glimpse of them, but I would prefer to know them more clearly from you."

"The reason is most apparent. For human error separates what is simple and undivided in nature, and changes it from the true and perfect to the false and imperfect. Do you think that which lacks nothing needs power?"

"Certainly not," I said.

"You are quite right. For if something is weak in any aspect of its power, in this it must need the help of another."

"Yes," I said.

"Therefore sufficiency and power are one and the same in nature."

"So it seems."

"Now do you think that what is of this kind ought to be scorned or rather of all things is it most worthy of respect?"

"But this," I said, "cannot be doubted."

"Then let us add respect to sufficiency and power, so that we may judge these three to be one."

"Let us add [it], if we wish to acknowledge the truth."

"But," she said, "do you think that this is obscure and unknown or [is it] most clear and well known to all? Now consider whether that which has been conceded to lack nothing, to be most powerful, [and] most worthy of honor, needs fame which it cannot give itself, and for that reason seem a bit lower."

"I cannot deny," I said, "that being what it is, it is also most famous."

"Therefore, it follows that we must acknowledge that fame does not differ from the above three."

"It follows," I said.

"And so, that which lacks nothing, which can do everything by its own powers, is it not obviously also most joyful?"

'I can't think of any way," I said, "that any sadness could afflict

such a one. And so, from what has been said, it must be granted
that [such a being] is full of joy."

"And for the same reason it follows that sufficiency, power, fame,
respect, and joy, are indeed different names, but in no way do they
differ in substance."

"That is necessarily so," I said.

"Therefore, this, which is one and simple in nature, human wickedness separates, and while one tries to obtain a part of a thing which
lacks part, he finds neither the part—there is none—nor the whole,
which he does not seek."

"How can this be?" I asked.

"He who seeks riches to avoid want," she said, "does not strive
for power, prefers to be lowly and unknown, and even avoids many
natural pleasures lest he lose the money he has gained. But in this
way he does not achieve sufficiency, whom lowliness abases, whom
obscurity conceals. But one who only desires power, wastes wealth,
despises pleasures, honor, and glory as nothing [since they are not]
power. But you see how many things are lacking to this man also.
For it happens that sometimes he lacks necessities, so that he is
tormented with anxieties, and when he cannot shake them off, he
even ceases to be what he craved most, to be powerful. One may
argue similarly of honors, glory, and pleasures. For since every one
of these is [fundamentally] the same as the rest, whoever seeks any
of them without the others, cannot even achieve the one he desires."

"What then?" I said.

"If one desired to obtain them all together, he would indeed wish
for supreme happiness. But will he find it in these things which we
have shown to be unable to deliver what they promise?"

"Hardly," I said.

"So we must by no means look for happiness in these things
which are each believed to provide parts of what is desired."

"I admit that." I said, "and nothing can be said more truly
than this."

"So you have," she said, "both the form and the causes of counterfeit happiness. Now turn the eyes of your mind to [its] contrary; for
there you will immediately see true [happiness] which we promised
[to show you]."

"Certainly," I said, "this is clear even to a blind man, and you
showed it a while ago when you tried to expose the cause of false

[happiness]. For, unless I am mistaken, that is true and perfect happiness which makes [a man] sufficient, powerful, respected, famed, and joyful. And that you may know that I have paid close attention to you, I see that, since they are all [fundamentally] one, what can truly provide one of these is full and unambiguous happiness."

"O student, you [are] fortunate [in having] this opinion, if you add this also—"

"What?" I said.

"Do you think that there is anything among these mortal and transitory things that can produce this [happy] condition?"

"Not at all," I said, "and I think that you have shown that so that nothing more could be desired.

"Hence these things seem to give mortals either likenesses of the true good or certain imperfect goods, but they cannot grant the true and perfect good."

"I agree," I said.

"Now since you know what true [happiness] is, and what falsely seems to be happiness, now all that remains is that you should know where you can seek the true."

"Indeed," I said, "that is what I have long looked for eagerly."

"But since, as in Plato's *Timaeus,* we ought to implore the divine assistance even in the least things, what do you think that we should do now, that we may deserve to find the seat of the supreme good?"

"We must," I said, "invoke the Father of all things [for] no beginning [which neglects Him] is rightly established."

"[You have spoken] correctly," she said. . .

"Therefore [she continued] since you have seen what is the form of perfect and imperfect good, now I think [we] must demonstrate in what this perfection of happiness is constituted. And in this [respect] I think it must be inquired first, whether any good such as you defined a little while ago can exist in the world, lest an empty likeness of thinking deceive us contrary to the truth of the subject. But it cannot be denied that something which is the source of all goodness exists. For everything which is said to be imperfect is called imperfect because of a lack of perfection. From this it follows that if it seems that there is something imperfect in any generic class, there must also be something that is perfect in that [same class]. And indeed, if perfection is removed, no way can be found by which it may be said that the imperfect could exist. For the beginning of the world did not arise from the defective and incomplete, but proceeding from what is whole and absolute falls into these extremes of weakness. But if, as we showed a little while ago, there is a certain imperfect happiness in fragile goods, it cannot be doubted that there is some solid and perfect [happiness also]."

"The conclusion," I said, "is most firm and most true."

"So consider," she said, "where this good dwells. The common concept of human minds proves that God is the chief good of all things. For, since nothing can be thought of that is better than God, can anyone doubt that that is good than which there is nothing better? Reason so demonstrates that God is good, that it also convinces [us] that the good in Him is perfect. For if He were not, He could not be the first of all things. For there would be something superior to Him, possessing perfect goodness, which would seem to be prior and more excellent [than God]. It is clear that all perfect things are prior to less perfect things. And so, lest reason should go on to infinity, it must be admitted that the Supreme God is most full of the highest and perfect goodness. But we have established that perfect goodness is true happiness; and so true happiness must be attributed to the Supreme God."

"I agree," I said, "and there is no way in which this can be contradicted."

"But I entreat you," she said, "see how conscientiously and inviolably you approve of what we have said, that the Supreme God is most full of the highest goodness."

"How?" I said.

"Don't presume that the Father of all things who is said to be the fulness of the highest good has either received it from without or has it naturally so that you might think that the substance of God having happiness is different from the happiness possessed. For if you think [He] received it from without, you could think that which gives [it] is more excellent than that which receives. But we most worthily acknowledge that He is the most excellent of all things. But if it [i.e., happiness] is present by nature, but it is something different in essence [from His nature], since we are speaking of God the source of things, let him who can, devise who has conjoined these different things? Finally, that which is different from anything is not the same as that by which it is understood to be different. Hence, that which is different in nature from the supreme good, is not the supreme good—which is impious to think of Him than whom it is certain that there is nothing more excellent. For nothing at all can exist whose nature is better than its source, and so I may most truly conclude that that which is the source of all things is also in its substance the highest good."

"Most rightly," I said.

"But it is conceded that the highest good is happiness."

"Yes," I said.

"Therefore," she said, "God must be acknowledged to be happiness itself."

"I cannot," I said, "refute your previous statements, and I see that this inference follows from them."

"Consider," she said, "whether the same may also be more firmly proved from this, that there cannot be two supreme goods which would be different from each other. Surely it is evident that of goods which are different, one is not what the other is; and so neither could be perfect, since each lacks the other. But it is obvious that what is not perfect cannot be the supreme [good]; therefore the highest goods cannot be different [from each other essentially] in any way. Now we have established that both happiness and God are the supreme good; hence what is the highest happiness must be the supreme divinity."

"Nothing," I said, "can be inferred more truly, or more tightly reasoned, or more worthy of God."

"On this, then," she said, "as the geometricians are accustomed to infer from demonstrated propositions something they call *porismata*[1], so I will also give you as it were a corollary. For since men are made happy by obtaining happiness, and happiness is identical with divinity, it is clear that [men] are made happy by obtaining divinity: but as [men] are made just by obtaining justice, wise by wisdom, so for a like reason it must be that those who obtain divinity become gods. Therefore everyone who is happy is a god, but the nature [of God is] only one; but nothing prevents there being many by participation."

[1] The plural of the Greek word *porisma*. As used here, it indicates that it is possible to find conditions that will make a certain problem insoluble, indeterminate, or capable of innumerable solutions. Perhaps a simpler equivalent would be "corollary," "difficulty," or "paradox."

"And this is admirable and precious," I said, "whether you prefer to call it a *porisma* or a corollary."

"But there is nothing more admirable than what reason persuades [us] should be added to these."

"What?" I asked.

"Since happiness seems to contain many things, are they all joined together as if they were distinct parts of a body of happiness, or does some one of these constitute the substance of happiness, to which the others are referred?"

"I would like you to clarify this," I said, "by mentioning its details."

"We think," she said, "that happiness is a good, don't we?"

"Yes, the highest [good], certainly," I said.

"You may," she said, "add this to them all. For happiness is judged identical with the greatest sufficiency, the same as supreme power, respect, fame, and joy. What then? Are all these—sufficiency, power, and the rest—the good as certain parts of happiness, or are they referred to good as all [inferiors are] to the head?"

"I understand," I said, "what you propose to investigate, but I desire to hear what you conclude."

"Here is the decision of this matter. If all these were parts of happiness, they would differ from one another. For this is the nature of parts, that being distinct they compose one body. But these have all been shown to be the same; and so they are hardly parts. Otherwise happiness would seem to be composed of one part, which cannot be."

"Certainly there is no doubt [about this]," I said, "but I await what remains."

"It is evident that the rest are to be referred to goodness. For sufficiency is sought because it is judged to be good, power because it is also believed to be good; the same may be inferred of respect, fame, and joy. Therefore goodness is the supreme cause of all that is desired. For what is either not good in reality or in no way resembles the good, can by no means be desired. And on the other hand, those things that are not good of their nature, yet if they seem to be, they are sought as if they were truly good. Hence the summit, center, and cause of all that may be desired is rightly thought to be goodness. Now that for the sake of which something is sought seems to be what is most desired, as [for example] if one would wish to ride, he desires not so much the movement of riding as the effect of health. Therefore, since all things are sought for the sake of good, it is not those things but rather the good itself that is desired by all. But we have conceded that to be happiness for the sake of which other things are desired; hence it also follows that happiness alone is sought. And from this it is plainly apparent that the substance of good and of happiness is one and the same."

"I do not see how anyone can disagree."

"But we have shown that God and true happiness are one and the same."

"Yes," I said.

"Therefore we may safely conclude that the substance of God consists in nothing other than the good itself."

14. BOETHIUS: The Nature and Power of Goodness*

"I agree," I said, "for it is clearly linked together with the most firm reasons."

Then she said, "How much will you value it if you come to know what the good itself is?"

"Infinitely," I said, "inasmuch as I would likewise know God also who is the good."

"I will show this most truly," she said, "if the things that were provided a little while ago be maintained."

"They will be maintained."

"Have we not proved," she said, "that the things that are sought by many are not true and perfect goods, since they differ from each other, and since each lacks [the goodness proper to] the other, cannot provide full and absolute good? But then the true good can exist only when they are united, as it were, in one form and causality, so that the same may be sufficiency, power, respect, fame, and joy. But unless they are all one and the same, do they have anything among them worth desiring?"

* See Introduction to Selection 13.

"It has been demonstrated," I said, "and it can in no way be doubted."

"Therefore, those things that are not good when they differ become good when they begin to be one, are they not made good by the achieving of unity?"

"So it seems," I said.

"But do you agree or do you deny that everything which is good is good by participation in the good?"

"So it is."

"Then you ought to agree for the same reason that the one and the good are the same; for those things are the same in substance of which there are not naturally different effects."

"I cannot deny it," I said.

"Then do you know," she said, "that everything that exists remains and subsists as long as it is one, but perishes and is destroyed as soon as it stops being one?"

"How?"

"As in living beings," she said, "so long as body and soul remain conjoined in one, it is called a living being; but when this unity of both is destroyed, it perishes and can no longer be a living being. The body, too, has a human appearance as long as it remains in one form by the conjoining of parts; but if the separated and dispersed parts of the body have dissolved [their] unity, then it ceases to be what it was. Likewise, it will no doubt be evident to any one who examines the rest [of the attributes discussed, e.g., power] that each subsists as long as it is one, but when unity ceases, it perishes."

"Considering more [details]," I said, "it seems to me that there is no alternative."

"Is there then," she said, "anything insofar as it acts naturally that abandons the desire for subsisting so that it craves destruction and dissolution?"

"If," I said, "I consider living things which have any nature to will and refuse, I find nothing that without external compulsion abandons the intention of surviving and rushes of its own accord to destruction. For every living thing strives to preserve health, and avoids harm and death. But I don't know what to think of plants and trees and nonliving things."

"But there is no reason for you to be uncertain of this too, when you consider first that plants and trees grow in places agreeable to them, where, insofar as their nature permits, they cannot quickly dry up and perish. For some spring up in fields, others on mountains, some endure swamps, others cling to rocks, for some the barren sands are fertile, and if you try to transplant them to any other places, they may begin to dry up. But nature gives to each what is congenial [to it] and strives to keep them from perishing as long as they can survive. But what [if I were to say] that all of them, as it were having plunged their lips into the earth, draw food by the roots and distribute strength throughout the inner parts and the bark? What about the fact that the softest part, such as the pulp,[1] always is hidden inside, and [protected] outside by the durability of wood, and finally the bark is exposed to the assault of the weather as better able to withstand damage? And how great is the diligence of nature, that all things are propagated by the multiplication of seed! Who does not know that all of these are, as it were, certain machines which [individually] last for a while, but also through successive generations have a kind of permanent survival? Do not the things which are thought to be inanimate also strive to attain what is harmonious with their essences? For why does lightness lift up flames, or gravity weigh down earth, except that each of these places and motions are agreeable?[2] Now that which is agreeable with anything conserves it, and that which is incompatible corrupts it. So also those things which are hard, such as stones, adhere most tenaciously to their parts so that they resist lest they be easily destroyed. And fluids, such as air and water, indeed are easily divided, but quickly flow together again, and fire avoids all division. We are not now treating of the movements of the knowing soul, but of natural tendency, such as that we digest without thinking what we have eaten, without knowing we breathe while asleep; for even in animals the love of life comes not from volitions of the soul, but from the principles of nature. For often in desperate circumstances the will embraces death, which nature shuns, and, on the other

---

[1] The word *medulla* is translated as "inner parts" above, and here as "pulp." Probably the cambium layer, which lies between the bark and the wood, is what is meant by *medulla*. Dame Philosophy's knowledge of botany is somewhat inexact.

[2] This reflects the aristotelian doctrine of "natural place" which was to be so severely attacked by seventeenth century philosophers and scientists after Galileo's famous experiments. Cf. for example, Hobbes' bitter attack on this notion in *Leviathan*, Part IV, chap. 46.

hand, the will sometimes restrains the act of propagation on which alone the continuation of mortal things depends, which nature always desires. So too, the love of oneself proceeds not from vital activity but from natural intention. For providence gave this to its creatures as the greatest cause of continuing, so that they naturally desire to continue as long as they can; and so there is not any way that you can doubt that all things which exist naturally desire continuance of existence, [and] avoid destruction."

"I acknowledge," I said, "that now I see without doubt what seemed uncertain before."

"Now," she said, "what seeks to subsist and perdure desires to be one; for if this [unity] is taken away, being itself will not remain."

"That is true," I said.

"Therefore," she said, "all things desire unity (*unum*)."

I agreed.

"But we have shown that the one is the same as the good."

"Yes, indeed."

"Therefore all things seek the good, which you may describe thus: the good is that which is desired by all."[3]

"Nothing," I said, "can be thought more true. For either all things are referred to no one [principle] and will float about without a ruler as it were devoid of one head, or if there is anything to which all things hasten, that will be the supreme good of all."

And she said: "I rejoice greatly, O student, that you have fixed in [your] mind the mark of truth. But in this you have clarified what you said you were ignorant of a little while ago."

"What?" I said.

"Which is," she said, "the end of all things. For surely it is that which is desired by all things, which because we have proven [it] to be the good, we must admit that the good is the end of all things."

Then I said: "How wonderful that you promise great things! And I don't doubt that you can bring them about; don't delay what you have kindled."

"First then," she said, "you may know that power is always present in good men, [and] evil men are deprived of any strength, indeed the one is proved by the other. For since good and evil are contraries, if it is certain that the good is powerful, the weakness of evil is clear; and if the weakness of evil is evident, the strength of

---

[3] Cf. Aristotle, *Nicomachean Ethics*, Bk. I, Chap. 1 (1094a 2-3).

good is known. But so that the credibility of our opinion may be richer, I will take both ways, confirming the propositions sometime from one aspect, sometime from the other.

"It is obvious that there are two things by which all human acts are brought about, namely will and power, and if either of these is lacking, there is nothing which can be done. For if will is lacking, no one undertakes what he does not will; but if power is absent, the will is in vain. Thus it happens that if you see anyone will to obtain what he does not obtain, you cannot doubt that he lacked the power to obtain what he willed."

"It is obvious," I said, "and it can in no way be denied."

"Will you doubt that he had the power, when you see him bring about what he wills?"

"Hardly."

"But it is agreed that anyone is powerful in what he can do, and weak in what he cannot do."

"I admit that," I said.

"Do you remember then," she said, "that it was inferred from our previous discussions that the tendency of every human will is to hasten to happiness even though it may take different routes."

"I remember," I said, "that that was also proved."

"Do you recall that happiness is the good itself in the same way that when happiness is sought, the good is desired by all?"

"I don't recall it," I said, "since I hold it fixed in [my] memory."

"Therefore all men, both good and wicked, with no different intention strive to attain to the good?"

"Yes," I said, "it follows."

"But it is certain that [men] become good by obtaining the good."

"It is certain."

"Therefore good men obtain what they desire."

"So it seems."

"But if wicked men were to obtain the good which they desire, they could not be evil."

"That is so."

"Hence since they both seek the good, but one obtains it and the other doesn't, can it be doubted that the good are indeed powerful, and the wicked are weak?"

"Anyone," I said, "who doubts [this] either cannot consider the nature of things or the conclusion of [your] reasons."

"Again," she said, "if there are two [people] to whom the same thing is proposed according to nature, and one of them accomplishes it perfectly with his natural capacity, but the other cannot manage it with his natural capacity but in some way other than is compatible with nature and does not accomplish what was proposed, but imitates the one who did it, which of these will you judge is more powerful?"

"Although I gather what you mean," I said, "still I wish to hear it more plainly."

"Will you deny," she said, "that the motion of walking is according to the nature of men?"

"No," I said.

"And do you doubt that this is the natural function of the feet?"

"There is no doubt of this either," I said.

"Therefore if someone who can walk on feet walks, another in whom this natural function of feet is absent, tries to walk by crawling on his hands, which of these can be rightly thought to be more powerful?"

"Infer the rest," I said, "for no one doubts that he who can use a natural capacity is stronger than he who cannot use it."

"But the highest good, which is proposed to the good and the wicked alike, the good seek by the natural function of the virtues, but the wicked try to obtain it through various concupiscences, which are not the natural capacity for obtaining the good. Or do you think otherwise?"

"Not at all," I said, "for it is clear what follows. For from the things which I have granted, it is necessarily the case that the good are powerful, and the wicked are weak."

"You anticipate correctly," she said, "and that, as physicians are wont to hope, is an indication of an upright and stalwart nature. But since I see that you are most ready to understand, I will pack the reasons together. For see how great is the weakness of vicious men who cannot attain to what their natural intention leads and almost compels. And what if they were without the help of this so great and almost invincible help of the guidance of nature? Consider also what a great lack of power wicked men have. For they do not seek light or trifling rewards, which they pursue and cannot obtain, but they fail in the very summit and pinnacle of things, and the poor wretches cannot achieve what they labor for night and day; in this respect the powers of good men are outstanding. For just as you

would think him most powerful in walking who could go on foot as
far as there were any place to go, so you must judge him most
powerful who achieves the goal of all that can be desired, beyond
which there is nothing. The opposite also follows from this, that it
is the same to be wicked and to be lacking in all powers. For why,
having abandoned virtue, do they follow vices? By ignorance of the
good? But what is weaker than the blindness of ignorance? Do
they know what should be followed? But [perhaps] passion (*libido*)
drives them the other way. So also intemperance [makes them] weak,
who cannot fight against vice. Or do they knowingly and voluntarily
abandon the good, and lean toward vices? But in this way they not
only abandon being powerful, but they abandon being altogether.
For those who give up the common goal of all things which exist,
abandon being too. It may indeed seem quite strange to some that
we should say that evil men, who are the majority, are not, but this
is so. Now I don't deny that evil [men] are evil; but I do deny purely
and simply that they are.

"For as you may call a cadaver a dead man, but you cannot call
it simply a man, so while I concede that the vicious are evil, I cannot
admit that they are absolutely [evil]. For 'that which is' is a thing
that retains order and adheres to its nature; but what fails to keep
order and preserve its nature also fails to be 'that which is' in its
own nature. 'But,' you may say, 'evil [men] can [do many things].'
I will not deny this, but this power of theirs proceeds not from
strength but from weakness. For they can do evil, which they could
not do if they had been able to continue in the performance of the
good. And this possibility demonstrates more evidently that they
can do nothing. For if, as we concluded a little while ago, evil is
nothing, since they can only do evil, it is clear that the wicked can
do nothing."

"That is evident."

"And so that you may understand what the force of this power
is, a little while ago we determined that there is nothing more
powerful than the supreme good."

"Yes," I said.

"But," she said, "He [i.e. the supreme good, God] can do no evil."

"No."

"Is there anyone," she said, "who thinks that men can do all
things?"

"No one except a madman."

"But men can do evil."

"I fervently wish," I said, "that they could not."

"Therefore, since he that can do only good can do all things, and those who can do evil cannot do all things, it is evident that those who can do evil are less powerful. Furthermore, we have shown that all power is to be included among the things that should be desired, and all things that ought to be desired are referred to the good as to the perfection of their nature. But the possibility of accomplishing wickedness cannot be referred to the good; therefore it should not be desired. But every power should be desired; hence it is clear that the possibility of evil is not a power. From all of these [considerations] the power of good and the undoubtable weakness of evil is apparent and it is clear that the opinion of Plato is true: that only wise men can do what they desire, and wicked men practice what they please, but they cannot do what they desire. For they do what they please, thinking that they will obtain the good through the things that delight them; but they do not obtain it, since shameful deeds do not arrive at happiness."

15. BOETHIUS: Chance and Free Will*

Having said these things, she began to turn the discussion toward treating and explaining certain other [points]. Then I said: "Your exhortation is quite correct, and your authority most worthy, but I know by experience that, as you have said, the question of providence is wrapped up with many other [problems]. Now I ask whether you think that chance is anything at all, and [if so] what it is."

"I hasten," she said then, "to fulfill my promise and show you the way to return to your country. But these other matters, although it is very useful to know them, yet they are a bit far from our purpose, and we should be afraid that [you might be] worn out by digression and be unable to finish your direct journey."

"Don't be afraid of that," I said. "For to know the things in

* See Introduction to Selection 13.

which I take great delight will refresh me, once your argument is established fully with undoubted conviction, [and] nothing of what remains may be disputed."

Then she said: "I will do as you wish," and began thus: "If anyone," she said, "defines chance as an event produced by purposeless motion and not by the connection of causes, I assert that there is no such thing as chance, and I declare that chance is just an empty word (*inanem vocem*) with no real meaning. For what place can be left for purposelessness when God puts all things into order? For 'nothing exists from nothing' is a true opinion which none of the ancients denied, although they [held] that not of the operating principle,[1] but of the material subject, postulating it as a kind of basis for speculations about nature. But if something proceeds from no causes, it will seem to have arisen from nothing. But if this is impossible, then there can be no chance of the kind we defined a moment ago."

"What then," I said, "is there nothing which can rightly be called chance or fortune? Or is there something albeit unknown to ordinary people, to which those words correspond?"

"My Aristotle," she said, "in the *Physics*[2] delineated that both briefly and truly with accurate reason."

"How?" I said.

"Whenever," she said, "something is done for the sake of some certain goal, and from some [other unknown] factors something other than what was intended happens, this is called chance: as is the case when someone digging the ground to cultivate a field finds a quantity of hidden gold. This is believed to have happened by chance, but it is not true that it is from nothing; for it has proper causes whose unforeseen and unexpected convergence seem to have produced a chance [event]. For unless the farmer had dug the ground, [and] unless another had buried his money in that place, the gold would not have been found. Therefore, these are the cause of the happy accident, which proceeds from the meeting and con-

[1] This is what is usually called the "efficient cause." The efficient cause and the "material subject" are two of the four Aristotelian causes. Cf. Aristotle, *Physics*, Book II, Chap. 3 (194b25-195a5); *Metaphysics*, Book V, Chap. 2 (1013a24-35).

[2] See Aristotle's *Physics*, Book II, Chaps. 4-6. What follows in the remainder of this selection is a concise and accurate paraphrase by Boethius of those three chapters in Aristotle's *Physics*.

fluence of causes, and not from the intention of the doer. For neither the one who buried the gold nor the one who worked the field intended that that gold should be found; but as I said, that one man buried [gold and] the other dug [it up] united and concurred. Therefore chance can be defined as an unforeseen [event arising] from the confluence of causes in those things which are done for some goal; but order makes the causes converge and blend proceeding with inevitable connection, which, descending from the fount of Providence, disposes all things in their places and times."

"I see it," I said, "and I agree that it is as you say. But in this series of causes linked together is there any freedom for our will or does the fatal chain also bind the movements of human minds themselves?"

"There is [free will]," she said, "for there can be no rational nature that is not endowed with free will. For what can naturally use reason has that judgment by which it can discern everything; of itself, therefore, it distinguishes between what should be avoided and what should be desired. Now whoever seeks, judges what ought to be desired; and whoever shuns, evaluates what ought to be avoided. Hence in those things in which reason is present, freedom of willing and refusing is present. But I don't think that this is equal in all. For the celestial and divine substances [have] a perspicacious judgment, and an uncorrupted will and efficacious power [to obtain their] wishes is present. But human souls must be more free when they keep themselves in the contemplation of the divine mind, but less [free] when they slip away toward bodies, even less, when they are ensnared with earthly entanglements. But it is the ultimate slavery when having been given over to vices, they lose possession of their own reason. For when they have cast their eyes down from the supreme light of truth to the lower and the dark, they then grope in a cloud of ignorance, they are afflicted with destructive passions. and by yielding and consenting to them they increase the slavery which they have imposed on themselves, and are in a certain sense captives of their own freedom. And yet He who from eternity sees all things with the foresight of Providence sees that, and by predestination disposes of each according to its merits."

16. ANSELM: The Existence of God

Anselm (1033-1109), born in northern Italy, entered the Benedictine Abbey of Bec in Normandy at the age of twenty-six. Within three years he was Prior of Bec, a position he held for fifteen years. During this period he wrote his two best known philosophical works, the *Monologium* (1076), and the *Proslogium* (1077-1078).

He became abbot of Bec in 1078 and served there for another fifteen years writing several other works. In 1093 a reluctant Anselm was installed as Archbishop of Canterbury and continued writing. During this period he was plagued with a turbulent Church-State conflict which was resolved temporarily in 1107.

The selection "The Existence of God" is taken from the preface and first two chapters of the *Monologium* (Soliloquy)* and presents an a-posteriori argument for the existence of God; that is, it proceeds from effect back to cause. This argument has a neoplatonic character in that it employs participation theory to prove that God exists. The degrees of goodness, being, etc., indicate that there is a perfect cause of these attributes, and individuals possessing these perfections in an imperfect manner must have them by sharing or participating in the perfect archetype. That is, whenever there are degrees of more or less goodness and the like, there must be an absolute to which they are compared. In the platonic tradition, the existence of relative qualities, such as beauty, imply the existence of an absolutely perfect Beauty, in which the limited being shares, and which is the cause of the presence of that quality in the limited being.

Anselm presented the original statement of "The Ontological Argument" for the existence of God in the *Proslogium* (Discourse).† Judging by the influence, interest and controversy that it has aroused from Anselm's day to our own, its importance is apparent. It is an a-priori argument derived, as the word "ontological" indicates, from the concept of Being itself.

The ontological argument proceeds from an analysis of the idea of God to the assertion of His existence. This a-priori argument has been attacked for making an illicit transition from a concept to a factual claim. The first such attack came from Gaunilon, a contemporary of Anselm,

---

* Trans. Sidney Norton Deane, 1903.

† Trans. M. J. Charlesworth (Oxford: Clarendon Press, 1965). Used by permission.

and Anselm replied to him with further clarification of his argument. Other attacks on the validity of the Anselmian argument and its derivatives, e.g. the arguments of Thomas Aquinas and Immanual Kant, are for the most part similar to Gaunilon's. Despite these attacks it has remained a focus of controversy through Western philosophic history and has been defended by thinkers as diverse as Descartes in the seventeenth century and Hegel in the nineteenth century.

In the second chapter of his *Proslogium* Anselm begins his famous proof. Significantly, Anselm addresses God, and asks him to enrich belief with understanding. Further Anselm says that we *believe* that God is that than which nothing greater can be conceived. If God does *not* actually exist, then something greater *can* be conceived (i.e., something which has the attribute of actual existence), but this is a contradiction.

In the third chapter Anselm puts the argument in terms of necessity and contingency. Anything other than God, he observes, can be conceived not to exist, i.e., as contingent. The concept of God is radically different—actual existence is a necessary and intrinsic feature of the essence of God.

The fourth chapter explains that there are two ways to "say in the heart" or conceive something. One way is simply to understand the word signifying it. The other way is to apprehend the very entity signified. One can conceive of God in the first way without simultaneously affirming His existence. But no one who conceives God *as He is* can conceive of God as not existing, although he may say so.

PREFACE

In this book Anselm discusses, under the form of a meditation the Being of God, basing his argument not on the authority of Scripture, but on the force of reason.

Certain brethren have often and earnestly entreated me to put in writing some thoughts that I had offered them in familiar conversation, regarding meditation on the Being of God, and on some other topics connected with this subject, under the form of a meditation on these themes. It is in accordance with their wish, rather than with my ability, that they have prescribed such a form for the writing of this meditation; in order that nothing in Scripture should be urged on the authority of Scripture itself, but that whatever the conclusion of independent investigation should declare to be true, should, with common proofs and with a simple argument, be briefly enforced by the cogency of reason, and plainly expounded in the light of truth. It was their wish also, that I should not disdain to meet such simple and almost foolish objections as occur to me.

This task I have long refused to undertake. And, reflecting on the matter, I have tried on many grounds to excuse myself; for the more they wanted this work to be adaptable to practical use, the more was what they enjoined on me difficult of execution. Overcome at last, however, both by the modest importunity of their entreaties and by the not contemptible sincerity of their zeal; and reluctant as I was because of the difficulty of my task and the weakness of my talent, I entered upon the work they asked for. But it is with pleasure inspired by their affection that, so far as I was able, I have prosecuted this work within the limits they set.

I was led to this undertaking in the hope that whatever I might accomplish would soon be overwhelmed with contempt, as by men disgusted with some worthless thing. For I know that in this book I have not so much satisfied those who entreated me, as put an end to the entreaties that followed me so urgently. Yet, somehow it fell out, contrary to my hope, that not only the brethren mentioned above, but several others, by making copies for their own use, condemned this writing to long remembrance. And, after frequent consideration, I have not been able to find that I have made in it any statement which is inconsistent with the writings of the Catholic Fathers, or especially with those of St. Augustine. Wherefore, if it shall appear to any man that I have offered in this work any thought that is either too novel or discordant with the truth, I ask him not to denounce me at once as one who boldly seizes upon new ideas, or as a maintainer of falsehood; but let him first read diligently Augustine's books on the Trinity, and then judge my treatise in the light of those.

But it is my prayer and earnest entreaty, that if any shall wish to copy this work, he shall be careful to place this preface at the beginning of the book, before the body of the meditation itself. For I believe that one will be much helped in understanding the matter of this book, if he has taken note of the intention, and the method according to which it is discussed. It is my opinion, too, that one who has first seen this preface will not pronounce a rash judgment, if he shall find offered here any thought that is contrary to his own belief.

CHAPTER I

There is a being which is best, and greatest, and highest of all existing beings.

If any man, either from ignorance or unbelief, has no knowledge of the existence of one Nature which is the highest of all existing beings, which is also sufficient to itself in its eternal blessedness, and which confers upon and effects in all other beings, through its omnipotent goodness, the very fact of their existence, and the fact that in any way their existence is good; and if he has no knowledge of many other things, which we necessarily believe regarding God and his creatures, he still believes that he can at least convince himself of these truths in great part, even if his mental powers are very ordinary, by the force of reason alone.

And, although he could do this in many ways, I shall adopt one which I consider easiest for such a man. For, since all desire to enjoy only those things which they suppose to be good, it is natural that this man should, at some time, turn his mind's eye to the examination of that cause by which these things are good, which he does not desire, except as he judges them to be good. So that, as reason leads the way and follows up these considerations, he advances rationally to those truths of which, without reason, he has no knowledge. And if, in this discussion, I use any argument which no greater authority adduces, I wish it to be received in this way: although, on the grounds that I shall see fit to adopt, the conclusion is reached as if necessarily, yet it is not, for this reason said to be absolutely necessary, but merely that it can appear so for the time being.

It is easy, then, for one to say to himself: Since there are goods so innumerable, whose great diversity we experience by the bodily senses, and discern by our mental faculties, must we not believe that there is some one thing, through which all goods whatever are good? Or are they good, one through one thing, and another through another? To be sure, it is most certain and clear, for all who are willing to see, that whatsoever things are said to possess any attribute in such a way that in mutual comparison they may be said to possess it in greater, or less, or equal degree, are said to possess it by virtue of some fact, which is not understood to be one thing in one case and another in another, but to be the same in different cases, whether it is regarded as existing in these cases in equal or unequal degree. For, whatsoever things are said to be *just,* when compared one with another, whether equally, or more, or less, cannot be understood as just, except through the quality of *justness,* which is not one thing in one instance, and another in another.

Since it is certain, then, that all goods, if mutually compared, would prove either equally or unequally good, necessarily they are all good by virtue of something which is conceived of as the same in different goods, although sometimes they seem to be called good, the one by virtue of one thing, the other by virtue of another. For, apparently it is by virtue of one quality, that a horse is called *good,* because he is strong, and by virtue of another, that he is called *good,* because he is swift. For, though he seems to be called good by virtue of his strength, and good by virtue of his swiftness, yet swiftness and strength do not appear to be the same thing.

But if a horse, because he is strong and swift, is therefore good, how is it that a strong, swift robber is bad? Rather, then, just as a strong, swift robber is bad, because he is harmful, so a strong, swift horse is good, because he is useful. And, indeed, nothing is ordinarily regarded as good, except either for some utility—as, for instance, safety is called good, and those things which promote safety—or for some honorable character—as, for instance, beauty is reckoned to be good, and what promotes beauty.

But, since the reasoning which we have observed is in no wise refutable, necessarily, again, all things, whether useful or honorable, if they are truly good, are good through that same being through which all goods exist, whatever that being is. But who can doubt this very being, through which all goods exist, to be a great good? This must be, then, a good through itself, since every other good is through it.

It follows, therefore, that all other goods are good through another being than that which they themselves are, and this being alone is good through itself. Hence, this alone is supremely good, which is alone good through itself. For it is supreme, in that it so surpasses other beings, that it is neither equalled nor excelled. But that which is supremely good is also supremely great. There is, therefore, some one being which is supremely good, and supremely great, that is, the highest of all existing beings.

CHAPTER II

The same subject continued.

But, just as it has been proved that there is a being that is supremely good, since all goods are good through a single being, which is good through itself; so it is necessarily inferred that there is something supremely great, which is great through itself. But I do not mean physically great, as a material object is great, but that which, the greater it is, is the better or the more worthy—wisdom, for instance. And since there can be nothing supremely great except what is supremely good, there must be a being that is greatest and best, i.e., the highest of all existing beings.

17. ANSELM: The Ontological Argument*

That God truly exists (CHAPTER II)

Well then, Lord, You who give understanding to faith, grant me that I may understand, as much as You see fit, that You exist as we believe You to exist, and that You are what we believe You to be. Now we believe that You are something than which nothing greater can be thought. Or can it be that a thing of such a nature does not exist, since "the Fool has said in his heart, there is no God" [Ps. xiii. I, lii. I]? But surely, when this same Fool hears what I am speaking about, namely, "something-than-which-nothing-greater-can-be-thought", he understands what he hears, and what he understands is in his mind, even if he does not understand that it actually exists. For it is one thing for an object to exist in the mind, and another thing to understand that an object actually exists. Thus, when a painter plans beforehand what he is going to execute, he has [the picture] in his mind, but he does not yet think that it actually exists because he has not yet executed it. However, when he has actually painted it, then he both has it in his mind and understands that it exists because he has now made it. Even the Fool, then is forced to agree that something-than-which-nothing-greater-can-be-thought exists in the mind, since he understands this when he hears

* See Introduction to Selection 16.

it, and whatever is understood is in the mind. And surely that-than-which-a-greater-cannot-be-thought cannot exist in the mind alone. For if it exists solely in the mind even, it can be thought to exist in reality also, which is greater. If then that-than-which-a-greater-cannot-be-thought exists in the mind alone, this same that-than-which-a-greater-*cannot*-be-thought is that-than-which-a-greater-*can*-be-thought. But this is obviously impossible. Therefore there is absolutely no doubt that something-than-which-a-greater-cannot-be-thought exists both in the mind and in reality.

That God cannot be thought not to exist (CHAPTER III)

And certainly this being so truly exists that it cannot be even thought not to exist. For something can be thought to exist that cannot be thought not to exist, and this is greater than that which can be thought not to exist. Hence, if that-than-which-a-greater-cannot-be-thought can be thought not to exist, then that-than-which-a-greater-cannot-be-thought is not the same as that-than-which-a-greater-cannot-be-thought, which is absurd. Something-than-which-a-greater-cannot-be-thought exists so truly then, that it cannot be even thought not to exist.

And You, Lord our God, are this being. You exist so truly, Lord my God, that You cannot even be thought not to exist. And this is as it should be, for if some intelligence could think of something better than You, the creature would be above its creator and would judge its creator—and that is completely absurd. In fact, everything else there is, except You alone, can be thought of as not existing. You alone, then, of all things most truly exist and therefore of all things possess existence to the highest degree; for anything else does not exist as truly, and so possesses existence to a lesser degree. Why then did "the Fool say in his heart, there is no God" [Ps. xiii. i, lii. i] when it is so evident to any rational mind that You of all things exist to the highest degree? Why indeed, unless because he was stupid and a fool?

How "the Fool said in his heart" what cannot be thought

(CHAPTER IV)

How indeed has he "said in his heart" what he could not think; or how could he not think what he "said in his heart", since to "say in one's heart" and to "think" are the same? But if he really (indeed, since he really) both thought because he "said in his heart" and did not "say in his heart" because he could not think, there is not only one sense in which something is "said in one's heart" or thought. For in one sense a thing is thought when the word signifying it is thought; in another sense when the very object which the thing is is understood. In the first sense, then, God can be thought not to exist, but not at all in the second sense. No one, indeed, understanding what God is can think that God does not exist, even though he may say these words in his heart either without any [objective] signification or with some peculiar signification. For God is that-than-which-nothing-greater-can-be-thought. Whoever really understands this understands clearly that this same being so exists that not even in thought can it not exist. Thus whoever understands that God exists in such a way cannot think of Him as not existing.

I give thanks, good Lord, I give thanks to You, since what I believed before through Your free gift I now so understand through Your illumination, that if I did not want to *believe* that You existed, I should nevertheless be unable not to *understand* it.

III.

---

*Secular and
Separatist Traditions*

ALTHOUGH the long period of the first twelve centuries is widely thought of in terms of the large traditions of developing Christianty, or as an uneven continuation of classical antiquity, it is important to note some of the other dimensions of thought and life. Among these were the "secular" traditions in intellectual life, exemplified in various ways by John Scotus Erigena, David of Dinant and Amaury of Bène. The "separatist" or "heretical" religious traditions were best known in the Western Cathar or Albigensian movement.

In addition, the traditions of the warrior and of chivalry, illustrated in celebrated epics, marked the beginnings of vernacular literature. The traditions of courtly love, seen in the songs of the troubadours, represent a further development. These strands were significant in determining the course of life and thought in the period. They have some special relevance for the understanding of later periods, as in the case of prefigurations of the period of the Protestant separations and of the contemporary period of broad secularization.

John Scotus Erigena (A.D. 810-877) was successively condemned by the religious authorities of the West. His efforts to provide in depth an intellectual answer to questions which originated in religious life provided in the eyes of men of the period both an intellectual advance and a religious reversal. The neoplatonic tradition inherited from classical antiquity provided adaptable modes of thought. These in the hands of Gregory of Nyssa and Augustine were seen as a creative employment of the ancient intellectuality for the communication of the teachings of the religious community. It was thought that Erigena had sacrificed religious teaching to the needs of a certain mode of neoplatonic thought. Here we have a special illustration of the problem of the adjustment of the works of natural reason and religious teaching.

The repeated condemnations of the teachings of John Scotus Erigena—in A.D. 855, 859, 1225, 1241, 1684—are in many ways astonishing. Erigena's stated intention in his great work, *On the Division of Nature,* was to render faithful interpretation of Christian teaching, as found in the Scriptures.

His work incorporated a whole host of accepted religious teaching authorities, repeatedly including Dionysius the Areopagite and Gregory of Nyssa. The work of Erigena, coming as it did in the ninth century, from one born in Ireland and a teacher in the French court, is truly incredible in the vastness and newness of its awareness of the intellectual and religious world of the Christian East. The consistency and the excellence of Erigena's intellectuality were undoubted.

Why, then, do we find condemnations so repeatedly and firmly applied by religious leaders? The question does not regard the religious rightness or accuracy of the condemnations, much less judgment as to their effect on the subsequent development of intellectual life. The question does regard the condemnations as significant manifestations of persistent attitudes within the body of Christian leadership. Subsequent condemnations, among many others, were to affect Amaury of Bène and David of Dinant in 1210, and, later in the thirteenth century, Siger of Brabant in 1277. The concern behind the sum of the condemnations may be interpreted as insistence that secular learning, however beneficent, not be the ultimate criterion or judge of the method and content of religious teaching. From this perspective, it seems that the intended intellectual service of religious teaching, whether in buttressing its truth or in interpreting its meaning or in purifying its content through secular learning, must be determined with respect to subject-matter, principles, methods, conclusions, and purposes by successive judgments at each point from the original sources of religion itself. What we have called the tradition of the secular seemed, in a great variety of ways, to have made the situation otherwise.

The separatist tradition is, perhaps, best discussed through reference to concrete example. The Albigensian movement in the twelfth century which was centered in the region of Toulouse in southern France was one of the most prominent of many dissenting groups. The movement was not an appeal primarily to some kind of philosophy or of social reform, but embodied some essentially different religious teachings. The movement derived, according to some authorities, from the early centuries' teachings of the Manicheans and Gnostics, and from the heretical tenth century movement of the Bogomils in Bulgaria, which in time reached Byzantium and was driven from it in 1110 and 1140. The Albigensians in southern France were subject to ruthless religious war from 1208 to 1229, and were to lose the final vestiges of their power in 1244.

The precise teachings of the Albigensians are difficult to reconstruct, due to their own policy of secrecy and to the burning of their books by their religious and political opponents. As far as reconstruction of their positions goes, it seems that they founded communities to replace the traditional Christian Church, taught a dualistic account of the world wherein matter was evil and the body a prison of the spirit whose true home was apart from it. At least for an elite, they required a thorough-going deprecation of sexuality. In these doctrines lies a basis for rounded criticism of feudal society and of its religious establishment.

Though the Albigensian centers were destroyed in the Crusades launched from the north of France, it seems that the continuation of their influence in indirect ways has been extraordinary. The founding of the Dominican Order in the thirteenth century was in some measure in response to their teaching. The Albigensians provided further background for a tradition of separation in the West, a tradition which was to influence the development of both religious and anti-religious movements in subsequent centuries.

Secular and separatist traditions were to find other supports within medieval life, as at times in the cult of the warrior and in the cult of courtly love. Often we come upon these developments only after they have been integrated within the general stream of Christian influences. It remains that the warrior and the troubador represent further dimensions of the rich variety present within the civilization of the period. We know this side of medieval life best through its songs of valor and its songs of love.

The special place of honor held by the warrior leaders in the life of barbarian tribes, whether those who conquered and settled as the Franks, or perennial marauders as the Vikings, was to provide the basis for a whole line of development within Western Christianity. The reception of the barbarian warrior and his needs was no less of a problem for the new civilization than was the reception of the intellectual heritage of ancient Greece or the governmental and legal heritage of ancient Rome. The warrior was in time to become a Christian knight, or even a member of a religious order of Christian knights. In the present time there would seem to be special need to reflect historically on problems of defense and war and aggression, especially in their relation to the acceptance and rejection of religious thought.

The troubador and the tradition of courtly love hold a special position within the civilization of the West. The story of love, no less than the story of war, was to be transformed in important ways within the new civilization, yet the tradition of courtly love was itself to influence in a positive way the orientation of civilization as a whole. The warrior and the courtier were at times to be fused in the imaginative writing of the period.

The Song of Roland, a French poem of the eleventh century, tells of Charlemagne and his eighth century war against Islamic forces in Spain. Pope Urban II was to appeal to the example of this King of the Franks in seeking support for the First Crusade against the forces of Islam in the East. *The Song of Roland,* great as a poem and as a celebration of the Christian warrior and his virtues, records a meeting of East and West in the person of the founder of the Holy Roman Empire. The story in this case was to be far more influential than the history which it treats with poetic fancy.

The Poem of the Cid, a Spanish epic composed about 1140, is the story of the valor of Rodrigo Diaz of Bivar, 1043-1099. The quarrels and the alliances of Christian and Moslem principalities within Spain, the interventions of Moslem power from Africa, dynastic and personal feuds, all enter the complex background of the heroic knight.

The warrior's ideals personified by the Cid are a key to the moral values which stood out in popular imagination—sense of honor, piety, magnanimity. The remarkable intermingling of Christian and Islamic peoples and politics, in peace and war, in alliances and in political unities, dramatize the pluralism and the relative anarchy within feudal Spain. For hundreds of years the story of this national hero was to continue to reflect, and to form, the ideas of a people. Moral ideas and religious attachments and political arrangements are there together. Like *The Song of Roland, The Poem of the Cid* portrays the violence of hazardous times, the presence of Islam, the weakness of political organization, the formation of moral ideas in conjunction with the peculiar circumstances of feudal life, the vigor of people who were in the process of making Europe.

Aucassin and Nicolette belongs to the tradition of the songs of love, a vital alternative to the earlier tradition of the warrior epics. These songs of love bear similarity to those of the *Arabian Nights*. The tradition of such songs and of the wandering troubadors is related in some instances to the religious and social influence of the Albigensian strongholds in the south of France.

The simplicity and beauty of the love exemplified in *Aucassin and Nicolette* stands in contrast to the passion often expressed in other songs, passion never to be fulfilled in carnal love. Songs of love and songs of war tell the story, perhaps better than any record of events, of the operating thoughts, hopes and values of the people in these centuries.

The secular traditions in intellectual life, the separatist traditions in religious life, the cults of the warrior and of courtly love—all these were at times to come together. In a consideration of the period which gives special emphasis to the place of ideas, it is important to note not only the intellectual issues in the abstract, but the religious and social contexts which frequently give to the ideas themselves their special orientation and dynamism.

18. ERIGENA: The Return of All Things to Their Source

John Scotus Erigena (A.D. 810-877) is best known as the author of *On the Division of Nature*. He was born in Ireland. In A.D. 845 he went to the court of the French king, Charles the Bald, where (from about A.D. 850) he was master of the palace school. In 855 some of his theological writings were condemned by the Synod of Valence. He seems to have left France after A.D. 870 to return to England, where, it is said, he suffered violence and died in A.D. 877.

The selection* is taken from Book II of Erigena's most important work, *On the Division of Nature*. By "nature" Erigena means the most general category of all things. "Nature" is the name given to all things that are and are not. This ultimate generic class is divided into four species or forms:

1. That which creates and is not created; i.e., God.
2. That which creates and is created; i.e., the divine Ideas as archetypes or exemplars (platonic forms).
3. That which is created and does not create; i.e., the created universe.
4. That which neither creates nor is created; i.e., God as the end or goal of creation.

By "division," then, Erigena means the procession of all things from their primal source in God. In the present selection, Erigena shows the fulfillment of this process in what he calls "analysis." For Erigena "analysis" is the reintegration of all things through a return to their goal, or final cause, which is also their source. In this way he shows that the first and fourth divisions of nature are actually identical and only conceptually distinct. This difficult work as a whole, and this passage in particular, is reminiscent of the *Enneads* of Plotinus (A.D. 205-270).

1. [Professor] Since in the previous book [we discussed] the general division of the whole of Nature, not as genus into forms or

---

* Translated especially for this volume by George L. Stengren from *Migne*, PL 122:523D-531C.

of the whole into parts—for God is not the genus of the creature, nor [is] the creature a species of God, just as the creature is not the genus of God, nor is God a species of creature. The principle is the same in [terms of] the whole and parts: because God is not the whole of the creature, and the creature [is] not part of God, as the creature is not the whole of God, nor is God part of the creature: although [in defense of] the above theory [we may say that] according to Gregory the Theologian[1] "we may be part of God," we who share human nature, "since in Him we live and move, and are," [*Acts* 17:28.] and God is metaphorically called both genus and whole, both species and part. For everything which is in Him and from Him, can be piously and reasonably said about Him—but by an intelligible contemplation of the universe—by "universe" I mean God and creature. We spoke briefly [before], now let us go over the same division of nature more thoroughly if it seems [desirable to you].

[Student] Indeed it seems [desirable to me] and quite necessary. For unless it is explored by a more thorough investigation of reason, it will seem to have been only touched upon, but not settled in detail.

[Professor] And so it was, in my opinion, with the fourfold division of the whole of nature (mentioned above) into that form or species, if the first cause of all things, which surpasses every form and species, was correctly called form or species, inasmuch as it is the formless principle of all forms and species, which creates and is not created. Now we call God the formless principle lest anyone think that He should be included in the number of forms, when He is the cause of all forms. Truly, everything that is formed seeks Him, since He is in Himself infinite and more than infinite; for He is the infinity of all infinities. Therefore, that which is not structured or defined by any form, because it is known by no intellect, is more reasonably said to be formless than formed, because, as has often been said, we can speak more truly of God by negation than by affirmation.[2] The second [division of nature was] into that which both creates and is

[1] Gregory Nazianzen (A.D. 329-390) was an Eastern Christian writer, one of the Greek Fathers in Asia Minor. Together with Basil the Great and Gregory of Nyssa, he is one of the three great Cappadocians.

[2] [This is sometimes known as "Negative Theology" because it holds that the only true statements about God are negative ones, e.g. "God is not corporeal." This approach is found in Maimonides and St. Thomas Aquinas, to mention only two in addition to Erigena. Ed.]

[itself] created. The third [division] follows, what is created and does not create. Finally the fourth [division of nature], what neither creates nor is created.

[Student] That is soundly divided.

[P] Since therefore the oppositions of the previously mentioned forms of nature have already been spoken about in [our] earlier discussion—for we considered how a third results: indeed the first pair stand diametrically opposed to each other; for, as we said, the created and the non-creating are opposed to the creating and the non-created. Likewise, the second form is differently related to the fourth; for the created and creating is opposed to that which is neither created nor creating. But we say that nature as a whole has forms, because in a certain way our intelligence is formed from it, when it tries to treat of this itself. For, of itself, nature as a totality does not receive forms everywhere. Indeed, it is not inappropriate that we say that it is contained in God and creature, and in this way, insofar as [nature] is a creator, it does not receive any form in itself, but surpasses the multiformity of nature formed from it. Right now I think [we] ought to reflect on their likeness and difference.

[S] The order of things demands nothing else.

[P] The second form is like the first in that it creates, but it differs from it [the first] in that it is created. For the first creates and is not created, but the second both creates and is created. The third is like the second in that it is created, but it differs from it in that it creates nothing. For the second both creates and is created, but the third is created and does not create. The third is like the fourth in that it does not create, but dissimilar in that it is created. For the third is created and does not create, but the fourth neither creates nor is created. Likewise the fourth is like the first, because it is not created but seems to differ because it does not create. Indeed the first creates and is not created, but the fourth neither creates nor is created. And since oppositions and similarities and differences have been spoken of, I see that I should speak briefly about their return and collection in that discipline which the philosophers call *analutikén*.[3]

---

[3] [The translator has merely transliterated the Greek characters of Erigena's text into the Roman alphabet. Such transliterated words will be found in italics in this passage (526 A-C). The transliteration of the Greek letters *omega* and *eta* will be marked long to differentiate them from *omicron* and *epsilon*. Ed.]

[S] Order demands this too. For there is no rational division, whether of essence into genera, or of genus into forms and numbers, or of the whole into parts (which is properly called a logical division), or of the universe into those things which true reason contemplates in it, which cannot return again through those same steps through which the division was first multiplied, until it arrives at that one remaining inseparably in itself, from which that division received its origin. But first explain a little about the etymology of that name, which is *analutiké,* for it is not fully clear to me, [and] I see that it is necessary.

[P] *Analutiké* is derived from the verb *analúō,* that is, "I resolve" or "I return"; for *aná* is translated "back" [L. *re*-], and *lúō* as "set free" [L. *solvo*]. Thence also the name *análusis* arises, which similarly is turned into "resolution" or "return." But *análusis* is properly said as the explanation of questions proposed; whereas *analutiké* [is used] of the return of the division of forms to the source of the same division. For every division, which is called *Mérismos* by the Greeks, seems as it were a downward descending from a certain defined one to infinite numbers, that is, from the most general to the most specific. But every reintegration, as beginning again from the most specific, and ascending up to the most general, is called *analutiké.* It is, therefore, a return and resolution of individuals into forms, of forms into genera, of genera into *ousías,*[4] of essences into wisdom and prudence, from which all division arises, and in which it terminates.

[S] Enough has been said about the etymology of *analutikēi*; proceed to the rest.

2. [P] Then let there be an analysis, that is, an integrating return, of the four forms mentioned above, by combining pairs into one. Now the first and fourth [divisions of nature] are one, since they are understood of God alone; for He is the source of all things, and they are preserved [in existence] by Him, and He is the goal of all things, and they seek Him that they may rest in Him eternally and

---

[4] [The Greek word *ousía* is a noun formed from the present participle of the Greek verb "to be"—*èinai*. It is very difficult to translate into any exact Latin or English equivalent that would convey all the shades of meaning of the Greek term. Some of the words that have been used are: "essence," "substance," and "entity." In various contexts one or another of these English words may be close to the meaning of *ousía,* which in Greek means something like "concrete individual beingness," but this is awkward and only an approximation. In the present passage it probably means "essence." Ed.]

immutably. If, indeed, the cause of all things is said to create, because the totality of those things, which have been created after it and from it, proceed from it by a certain wonderful and divine multiplication into genera and species and numbers and also into differences and the other [details], which are considered in established nature. But since, when they come to the end [of their allotted time], all things will return to the same cause from which they proceed, therefore it is called the goal of all things, and it is said [to be that which] neither creates nor is created.

[527A-531A has been omitted]

[531B]
[P] For [man] is composed of the two universal parts of established nature by a certain wonderful union of the sensible and the intelligible, that is, conjoined from the extremities of the whole of creation. Indeed, nothing in the nature of things is lower than the body, and nothing higher than the intellect, as St. Augustine says in his book *On the True Religion,* "Between our mind, by which we know the Father Himself, and the truth, through which we know Him, there is no created intermediary." From these words of the Holy Father it may be understood that even after the fall [i.e., through Adam] human nature did not lose its fundamental dignity but still has it. For the master did not say there was no created intermediary, but "there is no intermediary." Therefore not even in our weaknesses do we desert God interiorly, nor are we deserted by Him, when between our mind and Him no nature intervenes. Indeed leprosy of the soul or body does not take away the keenness of the mind by which we know Him, and in which the image of the Creator is especially constituted. Do you see, therefore, how the division of all substances is terminated in human nature?

[S] I see [it] clearly, and having been persuaded by the above reasons, I greatly marvel at the dignity of our nature among all the things that have been made, when I perceive in it, as it were, a certain wonderful composition of all created substances."

19. THE SONG OF ROLAND: The Pride of Valor

*The Song of Roland** (late eleventh century) is an epic poem in the Old French which recounts a disastrous military expedition by Charlemagne against the Moors in Spain. The events described took place in A.D. 778, and the poem is based on an oral tradition that was far removed in time and place from the original by the time the poem was composed.

The poem describes an ambush that took place as half of Charlemagne's army was going through a pass in the western Pyrennees. Charlemagne's forces were led by the young hero, Roland, who, in the legendary tradition of the epic, wields a mighty and marvelous sword named Durendal. The selection recounts the death scene of Roland.

Charlemagne arrives, is temporarily overcome with suitably epic grief, and then leaving guards over the bodies of the fallen heroes rides off in pursuit of the fleeing Saracens. The second half of the poem describes this pursuit, culminating in single combat between Charlemagne and the leader of the Saracens, the Emir Baligant. Charlemagne is grievously wounded, but, urged on by the angel Gabriel, he dispatches Baligant with one blow and leads his victorious forces back to France.

171

Now Roland feels his sight grow dim and weak;
With his last strength he struggles to his feet;
All the red blood has faded from his cheeks.
A grey stone stands before him at his knee:
Ten strokes thereon he strikes, with rage and grief;
It grides[1], but yet nor breaks nor chips the steel.
"Ah!" cries the Count, "St. Mary succour me!
Alack the day, Durendal[2], good and keen!
Now I am dying, I cannot fend for thee.
How many battles I've won with you in field!

---

* *The Song of Roland*, trans. Dorothy L. Sayres, copyright executors of Dorothy L. Sayres, 1957; sections 171-175. Used by permission.

[1] grides; to grate, or make a harsh sound. Ed.

[2] Durendal; the name of Roland's sword. Ed.

With you I've conquered so many goodly fiefs[3]
That Carlon[4] holds, the lord with the white beard![5]
Let none e'er wield you that from the foe would flee—
You that were wielded so long by a good liege![6]
The like of you blest France shall never see."

172

Count Roland smites the sardin[7] stone amain.
The steel grides loud, but neither breaks nor bates.[8]
Now when he sees that it will nowise break
Thus to himself he maketh his complaint:
"Ah, DurenJal! so bright, so brave, so gay!
How dost thou glitter and shine in the sun's rays!
When Charles was keeping the vales of Moriane,
God by an angel sent to him and ordained
He should bestow thee on some count-capitayne.
On me he girt thee, the noble Charlemayn.
With this I won him Anjou and all Bretayn,
With this I won him Poitou, and conquered Maine;
With this I won him Normandy's fair terrain,
And with it won Provence and Acquitaine,
And Lombardy and all the land Romayne,
Bavaria too, and the whole Flemish state,
And Burgundy and all Apulia gained;
Constantinople in the King's hand I laid;
In Saxony he speaks and is obeyed;
With this I won Scotland, [Ireland and Wales,]
And England, where he set up his domain;
What lands and countries I've conquered by its aid,

[3] fief; a reward given by a lord to his subjects for services, usually in the form of land. Thus Roland claims to have conquered territory which Charlemagne could award to his retinue. Ed.

[4] Carlon; Charlemagne. Ed.

[5] the lord with the white beard; Charlemagne is invested with patriarchal antiquity in the epic. Actually, at the time of the events described he was between thirty-six and thirty-eight years old. Ed.

[6] liege; a knight, or lord, to whom others owe allegiance and service and who is himself subject to higher authority, as Roland was subject to Charlemagne. Ed.

[7] sardin; red, either blood-red as a ruby, or brownish red as chalcedony. Ed.

[8] bates; to be blunted. Ed.

For Charles to keep whose beard is white as may!
Now am I grieved and troubled for my blade;
Should Paynims[9] get it, 'twere worse than all death's pains.
Dear God forbid it should put France to shame!"

173

Count Roland smites upon the marble stone;
I cannot tell you how he hewed it and smote;
Yet the blade breaks not nor splinters, though it groans;
Upward to heaven it rebounds from the blow.
When the Count sees it never will be broke,
Then to himself right softly he makes moan:
"Ah, Durendal, fair, hallowed, and devote,
What store of relics lie in thy hilt of gold!
St Peter's tooth, St Basil's blood, it holds,
Hair of my lord St Denis, there enclosed,
Likewise a piece of Blessed Mary's robe;
To Paynim hands 'twere sin to let you go;
You should be served by Christian men alone,
Ne'er may you fall to any coward soul!
Many wide lands I conquered by your strokes
For Charles to keep whose beard is white as snow,
Whereby right rich and mighty is his throne."

174

Now Roland feels death press upon him hard;
It's creeping down from his head to his heart.
Under a pine-tree he hastens him apart,
There stretches him face down on the green grass,
And lays beneath him his sword and Olifant.
He's turned his head to where the Paynims are,
And this he doth for the French and for Charles,
Since fain is he that they should say, brave heart,
That he has died a conquerer at the last.
He beats his breast full many a time and fast,
Gives, with his glove, his sins into God's charge.

AOI

---

[9] Paynim; pagan: ignorance about Islamic beliefs had not dissipated and Moslems were called pagans. Ed.

175

Now Roland feels his time is at an end;
On the steep hill-side, toward Spain he's turned his head,
And with one hand he beats upon his breast;
Saith: *"Mea culpa*; Thy mercy, Lord, I beg
For all the sins, both the great and the less,
That e'er I did since first I drew my breath
Unto this day when I'm struck down by death."
His right-hand glove he unto God extends;
Angels from Heaven now to his side descend.

AOI

20. THE POEM OF THE CID: The Warrior Hero

The Poem of the Cid (A.D. 1140) is a Spanish vernacular epic which tells of the heroic deeds and afflictions borne by one Rodrigo (Ruy) Díaz de Bivar, known as "The Cid."

The Cid was never defeated in battle, even against vastly more numerous forces. He is presented as a noble leader, generous even to his defeated enemies. He is a folk hero, the embodiment of the virtues most esteemed in feudal Spain. Though lowborn, he shows himself through integrity, loyalty, and valor to be superior to those who were noble merely by birth.

The selection presented here is an excerpt from the first *cantar*.* It tells of the Cid's exile from Castile and of how he supported himself and his followers by military conquest.

With tearful eyes he turned to gaze upon the wreck behind:
His rifled coffers, bursten gates, all open to the wind:
Nor mantle left, nor robe of fur; stript bare his castle hall:
Nor hawk nor falcon in the mew, the perches empty all.
Then forth in sorrow went my Cid, and a deep sigh sighed he;
Yet with a measured voice, and calm, my Cid spake loftily—
"I thank thee God our Father, thou that dwellest upon high,
I suffer cruel wrong to-day, but of mine enemy."

* *The Poem of the Cid*, trans. John Ormsby.

As they came riding from Bivar[1] the crow was on the right,
By Burgos gate, upon the left, the crow was there in sight.[2]
My Cid he shrugged his shoulders and he lifted up his head:
"Good tidings! Alvar Fanez;[3] we are banished men!" he said.
With sixty lances in his train my Cid rode up the town,
The burghers and their dames from all the windows looking down;
And there were tears in every eye, and on each lip one word:
"A worthy vassal—would to God he served a worthy lord!"
Fain would they shelter him, but none durst yield to his desire.
Great was the fear through Burgos town of King Alfonso's ire.
Sealed with his royal seal hath come his letter to forbid
All men to offer harbourage or succour to my Cid.
And he that dared to disobey, well did he know the cost—
His goods, his eyes, stood forfeited, his soul and body lost.
A hard and grievous word was that to men of Christian race;
And, since they might not greet my Cid, they hid them from his face.
He rode to his own mansion gates;[4] shut firm and fast they were,
Such the king's rigour, save by force, he might not enter there;
And loudly though his henchmen call, within no sound is heard,
No answer to their call; my Cid up to the threshold spurred,
His foot from out the stirrup raised and on the door smote hard:
It yielded not beneath the stroke, 'twas stout and strongly barred:
But from a chamber window high a damsel's voice implored:
"O thou that in a happy hour didst gird thee with the sword,
It is the order of the king; we dare not, O my lord!
Sealed with his royal seal hath come his letter to forbid
The Burgos folk to open door, or shelter thee, my Cid.

---

[1] Bivar, now a small hamlet about three miles to the north of Burgos, on the Santander road. A few stones near the river are said to mark the site of the Cid's castle.

[2] The Cid's belief in augury is more than once alluded to in the poem, and he is taunted with it in a letter from the Count of Barcelona quoted in the *Gesta*. It seems, however, to have been common in Spain at the time, for in the *Cento Novelle Antiche* Messer Imberal del Balzo is described as much given to augury "a guisa spagnuola."

[3] Albricia (Arabic, Al-baschara), a fee claimed by the bringer of news. Alvar Fanez (or Fernandez), son of Fernan Lainez, was the Cid's cousin, and next to him the most distinguished warrior of the time in Moorish warfare; and as such is celebrated in the old poem on the taking of Almería.

[4] The Cid's town house (su posada) was in the Calle Alta near the Arco de San Martin. The site is marked by three pillars of modern date.

Our goods, our homes, our very eyes, in this are all at stake;
And small the gain to thee, though we meet ruin for thy sake.
Go, and God prosper thee in all that thou dost undertake."
So spake the little damsel, and she hurried from the place.
Then knew my Cid no hope was left of King Alfonso's grace.

And turning away he spurred on through Burgos to Santa Maria, and passing through the gate he halted beside the Arlanzon, and my Cid Ruy Diaz, he who girt on the sword in a good hour, with a goodly company around him, pitched his tent there in the Glera,[5] as if he were on a mountain-side, since there was no house open to him. Moreover, he was forbidden to buy food of any sort in Burgos, nor durst any man sell him a farthing's-worth. But Martin Antolinez, the worthy Burgalese, brought them bread and wine of his own, and my Cid and his men were refreshed. And said Martin Antolinez, "Campeador, born in a good hour, we must go forth this night, for I shall be held to account, and earn the wrath of King Alfonso, because I have served you. But if I escape safe with you, sooner or later the king will be glad to have me for a friend; if not, I care not a fig for what I leave behind." Said my Cid, "Martin Antolinez, a stout lance art thou; if I live I will repay thee double; but my gold and silver are spent; money have I none, and I need it for my troop, and have it I must; for nothing is obtained for nothing. With your help I will make two chests, and we will fill them with sand, so that they be heavy, and they shall be covered with red leather and studded with gilt nails,[6] and thou shalt go to Rachel and Vidas, and say that I cannot carry with me my treasure, for it is very weighty, and that I would pawn it for what may be reasonable. I call God and all his Saints to witness, that I cannot help this, and do it against my will." And Martin Antolinez without delay passed through Burgos and entered the castle and sought out Rachel and Vidas. And Rachel and Vidas were together, counting their wealth and profits. In friendly fashion Martin Antolinez came to them: "Rachel and Vidas, my dear friends, give me your hands that ye will not discover me to Christian or to Moor. I am come to make you rich for ever with no risk of loss. The Campeador has levied much tribute, and has carried away great and rich treasure, on account of which he has been accused. He has two chests full of fine gold. These he cannot carry with him unseen, and he would leave them in your hands if ye will lend him what money may be reasonable, and put the chests in your place of safety,[7]

---

[5] The Glera is the gravelly plain to the east of Burgos, through which the Arlanzon river flows.

[6] One of these chests, long since stripped of its red leather and gilt nails, is still seen or, to use a safer word shown, in the sacristy of Burgos Cathedral.

[7] Literally, "in your safe"—"en vuestro salvo."

swearing and pledging yourselves both that ye will not look into them for this year to come." Rachel and Vidas consulted together. "We must seek profit by every means. We know well he has wealth: what rich treasure he took when he entered the lands of the Moors. He who has money sleeps not without care. We will take these chests and put them where they shall not be seen; but tell us what will content the Cid, and what interest will he give us for the year?" Said Martin Antolinez in friendly fashion, "My Cid desires what is reasonable, and asks little for leaving his treasure in your hands. Needy men are gathering to him from all sides. He requires six hundred marks." Said Rachel and Vidas, "We will give them willingly." Said Martin, "Night is coming on, and my Cid is pressed: we would that ye give us the marks." "But," said Rachel and Vidas, "business is not done thus; but by first taking and then giving." "Good," said Martin Antolinez, "let us all three to the Campeador, and we will help you to carry the chests and put them in your place of safety, so that neither Moor nor Christian may know." With that they betook themselves to the tent of the Campeador, and they kissed his hands, and my Cid said smiling, "Don Rachel and Vidas, ye have forgotten me. I am exiled now, and under the wrath of the king, but ye will have somewhat of my substance, and while ye live ye shall never suffer loss." Then Martin Antolinez set forth the agreement that they should give him six hundred marks on those chests, and keep them safely till the end of the year, and pledge themselves by oath not to look into them meanwhile; else that they should be forsworn, and that my Cid should not give them a farthing of the interest. Then said Martin Antolinez, "Take up the chests and carry them away, and I will go with you to bring back the marks, for my Cid has to march before the cock crows." You might see how glad they were when they came to move the chests. They were not able to hoist them on their shoulders, strong as they were. And in the palace they spread a carpet, and over it a sheet of white linen, whereon they paid down three hundred marks in silver and other three hundred in gold. And Don Martin counted them, taking them without weighing, and with them he loaded five squires he had with him. This done, he said, "Now, Don Rachel and Vidas, that the chests are in your hands, I who have brought you this gain have fairly earned breeches." And Rachel and Vidas said between themselves, "Let us give him a good gift, for it was he who sought us out." "You deserve something," they said, "and we will give you wherewithal you may get breeches and a fur robe and a fair mantle; we will give you thirty marks; you have earned them, and it is reasonable, and you will testify to what we have agreed." Don Martin received the marks with thanks and took his leave, glad to quit this house; and passed through Burgos and across the Arlanzon, and came to the tent of the Cid, who received him with open arms. "Campeador," he said, "I bring good tidings. You have gained six hundred marks and I thirty. Now bid them strike the tents and let us go at once. At San Pedro de Cardeña[8] ere the cock crow we shall see your high-born lady, and we will take rest and then quit the kingdom, for the day of grace draws to a close." With that the tents were struck, and my Cid and his band mounted and rode forth. When the good Campeador reached San Pedro, the Abbot Don Sancho was chanting matins at daybreak, and Doña Ximena and her five ladies were praying to St. Peter and the Creator to aid my Cid the Campeador. With great joy they received him of the good hour, and said the Cid, "Sir Abbot, as I am going forth from the land, I give you fifty marks, and if I live they shall be doubled. I do not wish to cause expense to the monastery. And here for Doña Ximena I give you a hundred marks, that you maintain her and her daughters and ladies for this year; and if this should not suffice, let them want for nothing, I charge you. For one mark that you spend I will give four to the monastery." Ximena sank on her knees, weeping, and kissing his hands. "Campeador, born in a good hour, by wicked tale-bearers art thou driven from the land. For the love of the blessed Mary gives us counsel." And he took his daughters in his arms. "Ximena," said he, "wife whom I love as my soul, I have to go, and ye must remain behind; but please God and the blessed Mary I shall yet bestow these my daughters in marriage, if fortune does not desert me, and some days of life are left to me." Meanwhile, through Castile it was noised abroad that my Cid the Campeador was quitting the land. And some left houses and others honours, and that day on the bridge of Arlanzon a hundred and fifteen cavaliers assembled, asking for my Cid. Martin Antolinez joined them, and they went to San Pedro. And when my Cid was aware of it, he rode forth to meet them, and said: "I pray God that to you, who have left houses and heritages for me, I may be able to restore doubled what you have lost. To-morrow, when the cocks crow, the good Abbot will ring to matins in San Pedro, and, mass said, we will mount; for the day of grace is nearly at an end, and we have far to go." The night passed and morning came, and with the first cocks they prepared to mount, while the bells were ringing to matins. And my Cid and his wife entered the church, and Ximena threw herself on the steps before the altar, praying fervently to God to protect my Cid Campeador from evil.

The prayer was said, the mass was sung, they mounted to depart;
My Cid a moment stayed to press Ximena to his heart:
Ximena kissed his hand, as one distraught with grief was she:
He looked upon his daughters: "These to God I leave," said he;

[8] The monastery of San Pedro de Cardeña stands about six miles south-east of Burgos. It contains the tomb, but not the bones, of the Cid and Ximena.

"Unto our Lady and to God, Father of all below;
He knows if we shall meet again:—and now, sirs, let us go."
As when the finger-nail from out the flesh is torn away,
Even so sharp to him and them the parting pang that day.
Then to his saddle sprang my Cid, and forth his vassals led;
But ever as he rode, to those behind he turned his head.
Minaya with small favour this so tender yearning viewed.
"Thou in the good hour born!" he cried, "where is thy fortitude?
Our thoughts should now be for our road, and thine are wandering;
Out of this sorrow of to-day to-morrow joy will spring.
God who hath given souls to us will give us guidance too."
To Abbott Sancho then they turn, and charge him to be true,
And serve Ximena loyally and her young daughters twain,
Themselves and all their following, the ladies of their train.
And well the Abbot knew the charge would bring his house much
    gain.
"Should any come to join our band, if to our trail they hold,
They'll find us," said Minaya, "in the waste or on the wold."
With that they give their steeds the rein and on their way they ride;
The day of grace is well-nigh sped; no longer may they bide.
And thus an exile from the land the loyal Champion went:
Over against Spinar de Can[9] that night he pitched his tent:
The good town San Estéban[10] next upon the left they sight:
The Moorish towers of Ahilon[11] rise far upon their right:
Then quitting Alcobilla, of Castilian towns the last,
And the highway of Quinea, they on rafts[12] the Duero passed.

At Higeruela my Cid halted, while men came to him from all sides.
And as he laid him down after supper a sweet vision visited him in his
sleep. The angel Gabriel came to him in a dream, saying, "Mount, Cid,
brave Campeador. Never mounted knight in so good a case: whilst thou
livest thou shalt prosper."

The next day—it was the last of the day of grace—they halted at the

---

[9] Spinar de Can—probably now Espinosa.

[10] San Estéban de Gormaz and Alcubilla, towns on the right bank of the
Duero.

[11] Ahilon—now Ayllon.

[12] 'On rafts'—'sobre navas de palos.' But near this spot is a place called
'Navapalos' on Coello's map, which may be a reminiscence of the Cid's passage
of the river at this point; or, on the other hand, may be the name of a place
where even in the Cid's time there was a rude raft ferry.

Sierra de Miedes,[13] and there the Campeador mustered his men, and besides men on foot he counted three hundred pennoned lances. By night they crossed the Sierra and went down the Loma and descended upon Castejon on the Henares. And my Cid, by the advice of Alvar Fanez, placed himself in ambush with a hundred of his company, while he despatched Alvar Fanez, and Alvar Alvarez, and Alvar Salvadores, and Galin Garcia, with two hundred, on a foray towards Hita and Guadalajara as far as Alcala.[14] Dawn broke and the sun rose—God! how splendid he showed!—And the men of Castejon arose and opened their gates, and sallied forth to their labours and their fields, leaving the gates open and but few people in Castejon. Then the Campeador issued from the ambush and rushed upon Castejon. And those that held the gate were panic-stricken and left it undefended, and Ruy Diaz entered by the gate with naked sword in hand, and slew eleven of those he encountered, and won Castejon with its gold and silver. The fifth part of the spoil fell to my Cid, but it could not be sold here, nor did he care to have captive men or women in his company. So he spoke with those of Castejon, and he sent to Hita and Guadalajara to know for how much this fifth part would be bought. And the Moors appraised it at three thousand marks of silver. And my Cid was pleased with the offer, and on the third day the money was paid. And my Cid agreed with his company not to remain in the castle, as King Alfonso was near; and they departed rich from the castle they had taken, the Moorish men and women blessing them; and with the utmost speed they went up the Henares and across the Alcarias by the caves of Anquita and the plain of Torancio and Fariza and Cetina. Great was the spoil my Cid took as he went: little did the Moors know what daring they had. Next my Cid passed by Alhama[15] down the valley to Bubierca and Ateca and planted himself over against Alcocer[16] upon a round hill, lofty and strong, near to the Salon, so that they could not

[13] The Sierra de Miedes is an eastern continuation of the Guadarrama range, which divides Old from New Castile.

[14] Guadalajara was really taken from the Moors by Alvar Fanez about this time, and in grateful memory preserves his mounted effigy on the town-hall, but when he took it he was in the service of Alfonso, not under the Cid. "Alcalá" is Alcalá de Henares, afterwards the birthplace of Cervantes.

[15] Alhama, now a popular watering-place, "the Bath" or "Baden" of Aragon: not to be confounded with the more famous Alhama of the ballads, near Granada. The Cid's line of march corresponds exactly with the line of the Madrid and Saragossa railway.

[16] Generally confounded with the Alcocer south of the Tagus, about seventy miles distant. The name, which is simply another form of Alcázar, the castle, has disappeared from the locality here referred to; but there can be no doubt that the Alcocer of the poem was a Moorish stronghold on the site of the existing Castle of Ateca on the River Jalon or Salon (the Salo of Martial), about seven miles above Calatayud.

cut him off from the water, for it was his purpose to take Alcocer. And he levied tribute upon the people of Alcocer and Ateca and Terrel.[17] There my Cid abode fifteen weeks, but when he saw that Alcocer would not surrender he devised a stratagem. He left one tent pitched, and took the others and marched his men down the Salon in their armour, with their swords at their sides. When they of Alcocer saw it, God! how they exulted. "Bread and barley have failed my Cid, and he retreats like one defeated, leaving a tent behind him. Let us haste and seize the spoil before they of Terrel take it." So they sallied out of Alcocer, great and small, so eager to seize the prey, that they thought of nothing else, leaving the gates open and no one to guard them. When the good Campeador saw a wide space between them and the Castle, he ordered the standard to be turned and gave his horse the spur, crying, "Strike home, gentlemen, without faltering: by God's grace, the spoil is ours!" and wheeled upon them in the middle of the plain. God! how great was the joy of that morning! My Cid and Alvar Fanez on their good steeds charged forwards, and got between them and the Castle, and my Cid's vassals fell upon them without mercy, and in a small space slew three hundred Moors. Those who were in advance made for the Castle, and sword in hand seized the gate, and soon the remainder came up, for the rout was complete; and in this manner, look you, my Cid won Alcocer. Pero Bermuez, who bore the standard, planted it on the highest part; and said my Cid: "Thanks be to the God of Heaven and all his Saints, now shall we have better lodgings for both man and horse. As for the Moors, we cannot sell them, and we shall gain nothing by cutting off their heads. Let us drive them in, for we have the mastery, and take possession of their houses and make them serve us." A heavy blow it was to them of Ateca; nor did it please them of Terrel or of Calatayud. They sent word to the king of Valencia, how one whom they call my Cid Ruy Diaz of Bivar, banished in anger by King Alfonso, had posted himself over against Alcocer, and taken the Castle. "Give help," they said, "or thou wilt lose Ateca and Terrel and Calatayud, which cannot escape; and it will go hard with all the Salon-side, and along the Siloca too."[18] And when King Tamin heard it, he despatched three thousand Moors, saying, "Take him alive and bring him to me, for he must render account for entering my lands." And they marched by Segorbe and Celfa, and came to Calatayud, great numbers joining them as they went, and under the two kings, named Fariz and Galve, they came and surrounded the good Cid in Alcocer, and took up

[17] Written "Teruel" in the MS., the transcriber having apparently confounded it with Teruel on the Guadalaviar. The place meant is now Terrer, a village about three miles from Calatayud.

[18] Siloca, now the Jiloca, an affluent of the Jalon above Calatayud.

positions and pitched tents. And day and night the Moorish scouts
patrolled around, and mighty was their host. And my Cid's men were cut
off from the water. And they wished to go forth to battle, but he strictly
forbade them; so for three weeks complete they were besieged, and at the
beginning of the fourth, my Cid turned to take counsel with his men.

"From water they have cut us off, our bread is running low;
If we would steal away by night, they will not let us go;
Against us there are fearful odds if we make choice to fight;
What would ye do now, gentlemen, in this our present plight?"
Minaya was the first to speak: said the stout cavalier,
"Forth from Castile the Gentle thrust, we are but exiles here;
Unless we grapple with the Moor bread he will never yield;
A good six hundred men or more we have to take the field;
In God's name let us falter not, nor countenance delay,
But sally forth and strike a blow upon to-morrow's day."
"Like thee the counsel," said my Cid; "thou speakest to my mind;
And ready to support thy word thy hand we ever find."
Then all the Moors that bide within the walls he bids to go
Forth from the gates, lest they, perchance, his purpose come to know.
In making their defences good they spend the day and night,
And at the rising of the sun they arm them for the fight.
Then said my Cid: "Let all go forth, all that are in our band;
Save only two of those on foot, beside the gate to stand.
Here they will bury us if death we meet on yonder plain,
But if we win our battle there, rich booty shall we gain.
And thou Pero Bermuez, this my standard thou shalt hold;
It is a trust that fits thee well, for thou art stout and bold;
But see that thou advance it not unless I give command."
Bermuez took the standard and he kissed the Champion's hand.
Then bursting through the Castle gates upon the plain they show;
Back on their lines in panic fall the watchmen of the foe.
And hurrying to and fro the Moors are arming all around,
While Moorish drums go rolling like to split the very ground;
And in hot haste they mass their troops behind their standards twain,
Two mighty bands of men-at-arms—to count them it were vain.
And now their line comes sweeping on, advancing to the fray,
Sure of my Cid and all his band to make an easy prey.
"Now steady, comrades," said my Cid; "our ground we have to stand;
Let no man stir beyond the ranks until I give command."

Bermuez fretted at the word, delay he could not brook;
He spurred his charger to the front, aloft the banner shook:
"O loyal Cid Campeador, God give thee aid! I go
To plant thy ensign in among the thickest of the foe;
And ye who serve it, be it yours our standard to restore."
"Not so—as thou dost love me, stay!" called the Campeador.
Came Pero's answer: "Their attack I cannot, will not stay."
He gave his horse the spur and dashed against the Moors' array.
To win the standard eager all the Moors await the shock:
Amid a rain of blows he stands unshaken as a rock.
Then cried my Cid—"In charity, on to the rescue—ho!"
With bucklers braced before their breasts, with lances pointing low,
With stooping crests and heads bent down above the saddle bow,
All firm of hand and high of heart they roll upon the foe.
And he that in a good hour was born, his clarion voice rings out,
And clear above the clang of arms is heard his battle shout,
"Among them, gentlemen! Strike home, for the love of charity!
The Champion of Bivar is here—Ruy Diaz—I am he!"
Then bearing where Bermuez still maintains unequal fight,
Three hundred lances down they come, their pennons flickering white;
Down go three hundred Moors to earth, a man to every blow;
And when they wheel, three hundred more, as charging back they go.
It was a sight to see the lances rise and fall that day;
The shivered shields and riven mail, to see how thick they lay;
The pennons that went in snow-white come out a gory red;
The horses running riderless, the riders lying dead;
While Moors call on Mohammed, and "St. James!" the Christians cry,
And sixty score of Moors and more in narrow compass lie.
Above his gilded saddle-bow there played the Champion's sword;
And Minaya Alvar Fanez, Zurita's gallant lord;[19]
And Martin Antolinez the worthy Burgalese;
And Muño Gustioz his squire—all to the front were these.
And there was Martin Muñoz, he who ruled in Mont Mayor;
And there was Alvar Alvarez, and Alvar Salvador;
And the good Galin Garcia, stout lance of Aragon;
And Feliz Muñoz, nephew of my Cid the Champion:

---

[19] I follow the reading given in Pidal and Janer's edition, "que Çorita mandó." Sanchez printed "que corta mandó," which M. Damas Hinard translates "donne l'ordre de couper"—a rather needless order at the time. According to Salazar de Mendoza (*Dignidades de Castilla*) Alvar Fanez was in fact Lord of Zurita.

Well did they quit themselves that day, all these and many more,
In rescue of the standard for my Cid Campeador.
But Minaya Alvar Fanez—the Moors have slain his steed;
And crowding on the Christians come to aid him in his need;
His lance lies shivered, sword in hand he showers blows around,
As, giving back, he, inch by inch, on foot contests the ground.
He saw it, the Campeador, Ruy Diaz of Castile:
Athwart him on a goodly steed there came an Alguacil;
With one strong stroke of his right hand he cleft the Moor in twain;
And plucked him from the saddle, and flung him on the plain.
"Now mount, Minaya, mount," quoth he, "for thou art my right arm;
I have much need of thee to-day, thou must not come to harm;
The Moors maintain a front as yet, unbroken still they stand."
Mounted again Minaya goes against them sword in hand.
With strength renewed he wields his blade as his way doth wend,
Cleaving a path like one who means to make a speedy end.
And he that in a good hour was born at Fariz deals three blows;
Two glance aside, but full and fair the third one home it goes;
Forth spurting flies the blood; the streams down the king's hauberk
    run;
He turns the rein to quit the plain—that stroke the field hath won.
And Martin Antolinez, he at Galve dealt a stroke;
Through the carbuncles[20] of the casque the sword descending broke,
And cleaving down right to the crown, in twain the helmet shore;
Well wot ye, sirs, that Galve had no lust to stay for more.
And now are both king Galve and Fariz in retreat;
Great is the day for Christendom, great is the Moors' defeat! . . .

21. AUCASSIN AND NICOLETTE:
In Praise of Love

Aucassin and Nicolette gives us an insight into the medieval minstrel's
art. The story tells of the love of Aucassin, the son of Count Garin of
Beaucaire, and Nicolette, the beautiful ward of the Viscount of Beaucaire.

[20] The carbuncle was a favourite gem with mediæval warriors for the
ornamentation of helmets and shields. In the Chanson de Roland it is mentioned more than once, for instance, "L'elme li freint ù li carbuncle luisent."
civ.

The narrative is concerned with the perils which beset their enduring love. The idealization of womanhood was a familiar theme in medieval literature. Here we see it without any evident religious connection. This story typifies certain customs and manners of the Middle Ages, but contains several vignettes that reveal a less idealized side of medieval life. Although this poem* is from the thirteenth century, it is a unique example

'Tis of Auccasin and Nicolete.

Who would list to the good lay
Gladness of the captive grey?
'Tis how two young lovers met,
Aucassin and Nicolete,
Of the pains the lover bore
And the sorrows he outwore,
For the goodness and the grace,
Of his love, so fair of face.

Sweet the song, the story sweet,
There is no man hearkens it,
No man living 'neath the sun,
So outwearied, so foredone,
Sick and woful, worn and sad,
But is healed, but is glad
      'Tis so sweet.

So say they, speak they, tell they the Tale:

How the Count Bougars de Valence made war on Count Garin de Biaucaire, war so great, and so marvellous, and so mortal that never a day dawned, but alway he was there, by the gates and walls, and barriers of the town with a hundred knights, and ten thousand men at arms, horsemen and footmen: so burned he the Count's land, and spoiled his country, and slew his men. Now the Count Garin de Biaucaire was old and frail, and his good days were gone over. No heir had he, neither son nor daughter, save one young man only; such an one as I shall tell you. Aucassin was the name of the of the poetry of the troubadors which developed in the earlier period. damoiseau: fair was he, goodly, and great, and featly fashioned of his body, and limbs. His hair was yellow, in little curls, his eyes blue and laughing, his face beautiful and shapely, his nose high and well

* This selection is from the translation by T. B. Mosher.

set, and so richly seen was he in all things good, that in him was none evil at all. But so suddenly overtaken was he of Love, who is a great master, that he would not, of his will, be dubbed knight, nor take arms, nor follow tourneys, nor do whatsoever him beseemed. Therefore his father and mother said to him;

"Son, go take thine arms, mount thy horse, and hold thy land, and help thy men, for if they see thee among them more stoutly will they keep in battle their lives and lands, and thine, and mine."

"Father," said Aucassin, "I marvel that you will be speaking. Never may God give me aught of my desire if I be made knight, or mount my horse, or face stour and battle wherein knights smite and are smitten again, unless thou give me Nicolete, my true love, that I love so well."

"Son," said the father, "this may not be. Let Nicolete go, a slave girl she is, out of a strange land, and the captain of this town bought her of the Saracens, and carried her hither, and hath reared her and let christen the maid, and took her for his daughter in God, and one day will find a young man for her, to win her bread honourably. Herein hast thou naught to make or mend, but if a wife thou wilt have, I will give thee the daughter of a King, or a Count. There is no man so rich in France, but if thou desire his daughter, thou shalt have her."

"Faith! my father," said Aucassin, "tell me where is the place so high in all the world, that Nicolete, my sweet lady and love, would not grace it well? If she were Empress of Constantinople or of Germany, or Queen of France or England, it were little enough for her; so gentle is she and courteous, and debonaire, and compact of all good qualities." . . .

When the Count Garin de Biaucaire knew that he would not avail to withdraw Aucassin his son from the love of Nicolete, he went to the Captain of the city, who was his man, and spake to him saying:

"Sir Count; away with Nicolete thy daughter in God; cursed be the land whence she was brought into this country, for by reason of her do I lose Aucassin, that will neither be dubbed knight, nor do aught of the things that fall to him to be done. And wit ye well," he said, "that if I might have her at my will, I would burn her in a fire, and yourself might well be sore adread."

"Sir," said the Captain, "this is grievous to me that he comes and goes and hath speech with her. I had bought the maiden at mine own charges, and nourished her, and baptised, and made her my daughter in God. Yea, I would have given her to a young man that should win her bread honourably. With this had Aucassin thy son naught to make or mend. But, sith it is thy will and thy pleasure, I will send her into that land, and that country where never will he see her with his eyes."

"Have a heed to thyself," said the Count Garin, "thence might great evil come on thee."

So parted they each from other. Now the Captain was a right rich man: so had he a rich palace with a garden in face of it; in an upper chamber thereof he let place Nicolete, with one old woman to keep her company, and in that chamber put bread and meat and wine and such things as were needful. Then he let seal the door, that none might come in or go forth, save that there was one window, over against the garden, and strait enough, where through came to them a little air. . . .

Nicolete was in prison, as ye have heard soothly, in the chamber. And the noise and bruit of it went through all the country and all the land, how that Nicolete was lost. Some said she had fled the country, and some that the Count Garin de Biaucaire had let slay her. Whosoever had joy thereof, Aucassin had none, so he went to the Captain of the town and spake to him, saying:

"Sir Captain, what hast thou made of Nicolete, my sweet lady and love, the thing that best I love in all the world? Hast thou carried her off or ravished her away from me? Know well that if I die of it, the price shall be demanded of thee, and that will be well done, for it shall be even as if thou hadst slain me with thy two hands, for thou hadst taken from me the thing that in this world I love the best."

"Fair Sir," said the Captain, "let these things be. Nicolete is a captive that I did bring from a strange country. Yea, I bought her at my own charges of the Saracens, and I bred her up and baptised her, and made her my daughter in God. And I have cherished her, and one of these days I would have given her a young man, to win her bread honourably. With this hast thou naught to make, but do thou take the daughter of a King or Count. Nay more, what wouldst thou deem thee to have gained, hadst thou made her thy leman, and taken her to thy bed? Plentiful lack of comfort hadst thou got thereby, for in Hell would thy soul have lain while the world endures, and into Paradise wouldst thou have entered never."

"In Paradise what have I to win? Therein I seek not to enter, but only to have Nicolete my sweet lady that I love so well. For into Paradise go none but such folk as I shall tell thee now: Thither go these same old priests, and halt old men and maimed, who all day and night cower continually before the altars and in the crypts; and such folk as wear old amices and old clouted frocks, and naked folk and shoeless, and covered with sores, perishing of hunger and thirst, and of cold, and of little ease. These be they that go into Paradise, with them have I naught to make. But into Hell would I fain go; for into Hell fare the goodly clerks, and goodly knights that fall in tourneys and great wars, and stout men at arms, and all men noble. With these would I liefly go. And thither pass the sweet ladies and courteous that have two lovers, or three, and their lords also thereto. Thither goes the gold, and the silver, and cloth of vair, and cloth of gris, and harpers, and makers, and the prince of this world. With these I would gladly go, let me but have with me, Nicolete, my sweetest lady."

"Certes," quoth the Captain, "in vain wilt thou speak thereof, for never shalt thou see her; and if thou hadst word with her, and thy father knew it, he would let burn in a fire both her and me, and thyself might well be sore adread."

"That is even what irketh me," quoth Aucassin. So he went from the Captain sorrowing. . . .

While Auccasin was in the chamber sorrowing for Nicolete his love, even then the Count Bougars de Valence, that had his war to wage, forgat it no whit, but had called up his horsemen and his footmen, so made he for the castle to storm it. And the cry of battle arose, and the din, and knights and men at arms busked them, and ran to walls and gates to hold the keep. And the towns-folk mounted to the battlements, and cast down bolts, and pikes. Then while the assault was great, and even at its height, the Count Garin de Biaucaire came into the chamber where Aucassin was making lament, sorrowing for Nicolete, his sweet lady that he loved so well.

"Ha! son," quoth he, "how caitiff art thou, and cowardly, that canst see men assail thy goodliest castle and strongest. Know thou that if thou lose it, thou losest all. Son, go to, take arms, and mount thy horse, and defend thy land, and help thy men, and fare into the stour. Thou needst not smite nor be smitten. If they do but see thee among them, better will they guard their substance, and their lives, and thy land and mine. And thou art so great, and hardy of thy hands, that well mightst thou do this thing, and to do it is thy devoir."

"Father," said Aucassin, "what is this thou sayest now? God grant me never aught of my desire, if I be dubbed knight, or mount steed, or go into the stour where knights do smite and are smitten, if thou givest me not Nicolete, my sweet lady, whom I love so well."

"Son," quoth his father, "this may never be: rather would I be quite disinherited and lose all that is mine, than that thou shouldst have her to thy wife, or to love *par amours."*

So he turned him about. But when Aucassin saw him going he called to him again, saying,

"Father, go to now, I will make with thee fair covenant."

"What covenant, fair son?"

"I will take up arms, and go into the stour, on this covenant, that, if God bring me back sound and safe, thou wilt let me see Nicolete my sweet lady, even so long that I may have of her two words or three, and one kiss."

"That will I grant," said his father.

At this was Aucassin glad. . . .

Aucassin was armed and mounted as ye have heard tell. God! how goodly sat the shield on his shoulder, the helm on his head, and the baldric on his left haunch! And the damoiseau was tall, fair, featly fashioned, and hardy of his hands, and the horse whereon he rode swift and keen, and straight had he spurred him forth of the gate. Now believe ye not that his mind was on kine, nor cattle of the booty, nor thought he how he might strike a knight, nor be stricken again: nor no such thing. Nay, no memory had Aucassin of aught of these; rather he so dreamed of Nicolete, his sweet lady, that he dropped his reins, forgetting all there was to do, and his horse that had felt the spur, bore him into the press and hurled among the foe, and they laid hands on him all about, and took him captive, and seized away his spear and shield, and straightway they led him off a prisoner, and were even now discoursing of what death he should die.

And when Aucassin heard them,

"Ha! God," said he, "sweet Saviour. Be these my deadly enemies that have taken me, and will soon cut off my head? And once my head is off, no more shall I speak with Nicolete, my sweet lady that I love so well. Natheless have I here a good sword, and sit a good horse unwearied. If now I keep not my head for her sake, God help her never, if she love me more!"

The damoiseau was tall and strong, and the horse whereon he sat was right eager. And he laid hand to sword, and fell a-smiting to right and left, and smote through helm and *nasal,* and arm and clenched hand, making a murder about him, like a wild boar when hounds fall on him in the forest, even till he struck down ten knights, and seven he hurt, and straightway he hurled out of the press, and rode back again at full speed, sword in hand. The Count Bougars de Valence heard say they were about hanging Aucassin, his enemy, so he came into that place, and Aucassin was ware of him, and gat his sword into his hand, and lashed at his helm with such a stroke that he drave it down on his head, and he being stunned, fell grovelling. And Aucassin laid hands on him, and caught him by the *nasal* of his helmet, and gave him to his father.

"Father," quoth Aucassin, "lo here is your mortal foe, who hath so warred on you with all malengin. Full twenty years did this war endure, and might not be ended by man."

"Fair son," said his father, "thy feats of youth shouldst thou do, and not seek after folly."

"Father," saith Aucassin, "sermon me no sermons, but fulfil my covenant."

"Ha! what covenant, fair son?"

"What, father, hast thou forgotten it? By mine own head, whosoever forgets, will I not forget it, so much it hath me at heart. Didst thou not covenant with me when I took up arms, and went into the stour, that if God brought me back safe and sound, thou wouldst let me see Nicolete, my sweet lady, even so long that I may have of her two words or three, and one kiss? So didst thou covenant, and my mind is that thou keep thy word."

"I!" quoth the father, "God forsake me when I keep this covenant. Nay, if she were here, I would let burn her in the fire, and thyself shouldst be sore adread."

"Is this thy last word?" quoth Aucassin.

"So help me God," quoth his father, "yea!"

"Certes," quoth Aucassin, "this is a sorry thing meseems when a man of thine age lies."

"Count of Valence," quoth Aucassin, "I took thee?"

"In sooth, Sir, didst thou," saith the Count.

"Give me thy hand," saith Aucassin.

"Sir, with good will."

So he set his hand in the other's.

"Now givest thou me thy word," saith Aucassin, "that never whiles thou art living man wilt thou avail to do my father dishonour, or harm him in body, or in goods, but do it thou wilt?"

"Sir, in God's name," saith he, "mock me not, but put me to my ransom; ye cannot ask of me gold nor silver, horses nor palfreys, *vair* nor *gris,* hawks nor hounds, but I will give you them."

"What?" quoth Aucassin. "Ha, knowest thou not it was I that took thee?"

"Yea, sir," quoth the Count Bougars.

"God help me never, but I will make thy head fly from thy shoulders, if thou makest not troth," said Aucassin.

"In God's name," said he, "I make what promise thou wilt."

So they did the oath, and Aucassin let mount him on a horse, and took another and so led him back till he was in all safety. . . .

Aucassin was cast into prison as ye have heard tell, and Nicolete, of her part, was in the chamber. Now it was summer time, the month of May, when days are warm, and long, and clear, and the night still and serene. Nicolete lay one night on her bed, and saw the moon shine clear through a window, yea, and heard the nightingale sing in the garden, so she minded her of Aucassin her lover whom she loved so well. Then fell she to thoughts of Count Garin de Biaucaire, that hated her to the death; therefore deemed she that there she would no longer abide, for that, if she were told of, and the Count knew whereas she lay, an ill death would he make her die. Now she knew that the old woman slept who held her company. Then she arose, and clad her in a mantle of silk she had by her, very goodly, and took napkins, and sheets of the bed, and knotted one to the other, and made therewith a cord as long as she might, so knitted it to a pillar in the window, and let herself slip down into the garden, then caught up her raiment in both hands, behind and before, and kilted up her kirtle, because of the dew that she saw laying deep on the grass, and so went her way down through the garden.

Her locks were yellow and curled, her eyes blue and smiling, her face featly fashioned, the nose high and fairly set, the lips more red than cherry or rose in time of summer, her teeth white and small;

her breasts so firm that they bore up the folds of her bodice as they had been two apples; so slim she was in the waist that your two hands might have clipped her, and the daisy flowers that brake beneath her as she went tip-toe, and that bent above her instep, seemed black against her feet, so white was the maiden. She came to the postern gate, and unbarred it, and went out through the streets of Biaucaire, keeping always on the shadowy side, for the moon was shining right clear, and so wandered she till she came to the tower where her lover lay. The tower was flanked with buttresses, and she cowered under one of them, wrapped in her mantle. Then thrust she her head through a crevice of the tower that was old and worn, and so heard she Aucassin wailing within, and making dole and lament for the sweet lady he loved so well. And when she had listened to him she began to say; . . .

When Aucassin heard Nicolete say that she would pass into a far country, he was all in wrath.

"Fair sweet friend," quoth he, "thou shalt not go, for then wouldst thou be my death. And the first man that saw thee and had the might withal, would take thee straightway into his bed to be his leman. And once thou camest into a man's bed, and that bed not mine, wit ye well that I would not tarry till I had found a knife to pierce my heart and slay myself. Nay, verily, wait so long I would not: but would hurl myself on it so soon as I could find a wall, or a black stone, thereon would I dash my head so mightily, that the eyes would start, and my brain burst. Rather would I die even such a death, than know thou hadst lain in a man's bed, and that bed not mine."

"Aucassin," she said, "I trow thou lovest me not as much as thou sayest, but I love thee more than thou lovest me."

"Ah, fair sweet friend," said Aucassin, "it may not be that thou shouldst love me even as I love thee. Woman may not love man as man loves woman, for a woman's love lies in the glance of her eye, and the bud of her breast, and her foot's tip-toe, but the love of man is in his heart planted, whence it can never issue forth and pass away."

Now while Aucassin and Nicolete held this parley together, the town's guards came down a street, with swords drawn beneath their cloaks, for the Count Garin had charged them that if they could take her they should slay her. But the sentinel that was on the tower saw them coming, and heard them speaking of Nicolete as they went, and threatening to slay her.

"God!" quoth he, "this were great pity to slay so fair a maid! Right great charity it were if I could say aught to her, and they perceive it not, and she should be on her guard against them, for if they slay her, then were Aucassin, my damoiseau, dead, and that were great pity." . . .

"Ha!" quoth Nicolete, "be the soul of thy father and the soul of thy mother in the rest of Paradise, so fairly and so courteously hast thou spoken me! Please God, I will be right ware of them, God keep me out of their hands."

So she shrank under her mantle into the shadow of the pillar till they had passed by, and then took she farewell of Aucassin, and so fared till she came unto the castle wall. Now that wall was wasted and broken, and some deal mended, so she clomb thereon till she came between wall and fosse, and so looked down, and saw that the fosse was deep and steep, whereat she was sore adread.

"Ah God," saith she, "sweet Saviour! If I let myself fall hence, I shall break my neck, and if here I abide, to-morrow they will take me, and burn me in a fire. Yet liefer would I perish here than that to-morrow the folk should stare on me for a gazing-stock."

Then she crossed herself, and so let herself slip into the fosse, and when she had come to the bottom, her fair feet, and fair hands that had not custom thereof, were bruised and frayed, and the blood springing from a dozen places, yet felt she no pain nor hurt, by reason of the great dread wherein she went. But if she were in cumber to win there, in worse was she to win out. But she deemed that there to abide was of none avail, and she found a pike sharpened, that they of the city had thrown out to keep the hold. Therewith made she one stepping place after another, till, with much travail, she climbed the wall. Now the forest lay within two crossbow shots, and the forest was of thirty leagues this way and that. Therein also were wild beasts, and beasts serpentine, and she feared that if she entered there they would slay her. But anon she deemed that if men found her there they would hale her back into the town to burn her. . . .

Nicolete made great moan, as ye have heard; then commended she herself to God, and anon fared till she came unto the forest. But to go deep in it she dared not, by reason of the wild beasts, and beasts serpentine. Anon crept she into a little thicket, where sleep came upon her, and she slept till prime next day, when the shepherds issued forth from the town and drove their bestial between wood and water. Anon came they all into one place by a fair fountain which was on the fringe of the forest, thereby spread they a mantle, and thereon set bread. So while they were eating, Nicolete wakened, with the sound of the singing birds, and the shepherds, and she went unto them, saying, "Fair boys, our Lord keep you!"

"God bless thee," quoth he that had more words to his tongue than the rest.

"Fair boys," quoth she, "know ye Aucassin, the son of Count Garin de Biaucaire?"

"Yea, well we know him."

"So may God help you, fair boys," quoth she, "tell him there is a beast in this forest and bid him come chase it, and if he can take it, he would not give one limb thereof for a hundred marks of gold, nay, nor for five hundred, nor for any ransom."

Then looked they on her, and saw her so fair that they were all astonied.

"Will I tell him thereof?" quoth he that had more words to his tongue than the rest; "foul fall him who speaks of the thing or tells him the tidings. These are but visions ye tell of, for there is no beast so great in this forest, stag, nor lion, nor boar, that one of his limbs is worth more than two deniers, or three at the most, and ye speak of such great ransom. Foul fall him that believes your word, and him that telleth Aucassin. Ye be a Fairy, and we have none liking for your company, nay, hold on your road."

"Nay, fair boys," quoth she, "nay, ye will do my bidding. For this beast is so mighty of medicine that thereby will Aucassin be healed of his torment. And lo! I have five sols in my purse, take them, and tell him: for within three days must he come hunting it hither, and if within three days he find it not, never will he be healed of his torment."

"My faith," quoth he, "the money will we take, and if he come hither we will tell him, but seek him we will not."

"In God's name," quoth she; and so took farewell of the shepherds, and went her way. . . .

Nicolete built her lodge of boughs, as ye have heard, right fair and feteously, and wove it well, within and without, of flowers and leaves. So lay she hard by the lodge in a deep coppice to know what Aucassin will do. And the cry and the bruit went abroad through all the country and all the land, that Nicolete was lost. Some told that she had fled, and some that the Count Garin had let slay her. Whosoever had joy thereof, no joy had Aucassin. And the Count Garin, his father, had taken him out of prison, and had sent for the knights of that land, and the ladies, and let make a right great feast, for the comforting of Aucassin his son. Now at the high time of the feast, was Aucassin leaning from a gallery, all woful and discomforted. Whatsoever men might devise of mirth, Aucassin had no joy thereof, nor no desire, for he saw not her that he loved. Then a knight looked on him, and came to him, and said:

"Aucassin, of that sickness of thine have I been sick, and good counsel will I give thee, if thou wilt hearken to me—"

"Sir," said Aucassin, "gramercy, good counsel would I fain hear."

"Mount thy horse," quoth he, "and go take thy pastime in yonder forest, there wilt thou see the good flowers and grass, and hear the sweet birds sing. Perchance thou shalt hear some word, whereby thou shalt be the better."

"Sir," quoth Aucassin, "gramercy, that will I do."

He passed out of the hall, and went down the stairs, and came to the stable where his horse was. He let saddle and bridle him, and mounted, and rode forth from the castle, and wandered till he came to the forest, so rode till he came to the fountain and found the shepherds at point of noon. And they had a mantle stretched on the grass, and were eating bread, and making great joy. . . .

When Aucassin heard the shepherds, anon he bethought him of Nicolete, his sweet lady he loved so well, and he deemed that she had passed thereby; then set he spurs to his horse, and so came to the shepherds.

"Fair boys, God be with you."

"God bless you," quoth he that had more words to his tongue than the rest.

"Fair boys," quoth Aucassin, "say the song again that anon ye sang."

"Say it we will not," quoth he that had more words to his tongue than the rest, "foul fall him who will sing it again for you, fair sir!"

"Fair boys," quoth Aucassin, "know ye me not?"

"Yea, we know well that you are Aucassin, our damoiseau, natheless we be not your men, but the Count's."

"Fair boys, yet sing it again, I pray you."

"Hearken! by the Holy Heart," quoth he, "wherefore should I

sing for you, if it likes me not? Lo, there is no such rich man in this country, saving the body of Garin the Count, that dare drive forth my oxen, or my cows, or my sheep, if he finds them in his fields, or his corn, lest he lose his eyes for it and wherefore should I sing for you, if it likes me not?"

"God be your aid, fair boys, sing it ye will, and take ye these ten sols I have here in a purse."

"Sir, the money will we take, but never a note will I sing, for I have given my oath, but I will tell thee a plain tale, if thou wilt."

"By God," saith Aucassin, "I love a plain tale better than naught."

"Sir, we were in this place, a little time agone, between prime and tierce, and were eating our bread by this fountain, even as now we do, and a maid came past, the fairest thing in the world, whereby we deemed that she should be a fay, and all the wood shone round about her. Anon she gave us of that she had, whereby we made covenant with her, that if ye came hither we would bid you hunt in this forest, wherein is such a beast that, an ye might take him, ye would not give one limb of him for five hundred marks of silver, nor for no ransom; for this beast is so mighty of medicine, that, an ye could take him, ye should be healed of your torment, and within three days must ye take him, and if ye take him not then, never will ye look on him. So chase ye the beast, an ye will, or an ye will let be, for my promise have I kept with her."

"Fair boys," quoth Aucassin, "ye have said enough. God grant me to find this quarry." . . .

Aucassin fared through the forest from path to path after Nicolete, and his horse bare him furiously. Think ye not that the thorns him spared, nor the briars, nay, not so, but tare his raiment, that scarce a knot might be tied with the soundest part thereof, and the blood sprang from his arms, and flanks, and legs, in forty places, or thirty, so that behind the Childe men might follow on the track of his blood in the grass. But so much he went in thoughts of Nicolete, his lady sweet, that he felt no pain nor torment, and all the day hurled through the forest in this fashion nor heard no word of her. And when he saw Vespers draw nigh, he began to weep for that he found her not. All down an old road, and grassgrown he fared, when anon, looking along the way before him, he saw such an one as I shall tell you. Tall was he, and great of growth, laidly and marvellous to look upon: his head huge, and black as charcoal, and more than the breadth of a hand between his two eyes, and great cheeks, and a big nose and broad, big nostrils and ugly, and thick lips redder than a collop, and great teeth yellow and ugly, and he was shod with hosen and shoon of bull's hide, bound with cords of bark over the knee, and all about him a great cloak two-fold, and he leaned on a grievous cudgel, and Aucassin came unto him, and was afraid when he beheld him.

"Fair brother, God aid thee."

"God bless you," quoth he.

"As God he helpeth thee, what makest thou here?"

"What is that to thee?"

"Nay, naught, naught," saith Aucassin, "I ask but out of courtesy."

"But for whom weepest thou," quoth he, "and makest such heavy lament? Certes, were I as rich a man as thou, the whole world should not make me weep."

"Ha, know ye me?" saith Aucassin.

"Yea, I know well that ye be Aucassin, the son of the Count, and if ye tell me for why ye weep, then will I tell you what I make here."

"Certes," quoth Aucassin, "I will tell you right gladly. Hither came I this morning to hunt in this forest; and with me a white hound, the fairest in the world; him have I lost, and for him I weep."

"By the Heart our Lord bare in his breast," quoth he, "are ye weeping for a stinking hound? Foul fall him that holds thee high henceforth! for there is no such rich man in the land, but if thy father asked it of him, he would give thee ten, or fifteen, or twenty, and be the gladder for it. But *I* have cause to weep and make dole."

"Wherefore so, brother?"

"Sir, I will tell thee. I was hireling to a rich vilain, and drove his plough; four oxen had he. But three days since came on me great misadventure, whereby I lost the best of mine oxen, Roger, the best of my team. Him go I seeking, and have neither eaten nor drunken these three days, nor may I go to the town, lest they cast me into prison, seeing that I have not wherewithal to pay. Out of all the wealth of the world have I no more than ye see on my body. A poor mother bare me, that had no more but one wretched bed; this have they taken from under her, and she lies in the very straw. This ails me more than mine own case, for wealth comes and goes; if now I have lost, another tide will I gain, and will pay for mine ox whenas

I may; never for that will I weep. But you weep for a stinking hound. Foul fall whoso thinks well of thee!"

"Certes thou art a good comforter, brother, blessed be thou! And of what price was thine ox?"

"Sir, they ask me twenty sols for him, whereof I cannot abate one doit."

"Nay, then," quoth Aucassin, "take these twenty sols I have in my purse, and pay for thine ox."

"Sir," saith he, "gramercy. And God give thee to find that thou seekest."

So they parted each from other, and Aucassin rode on: the night was fair and still, and so long he went that he came to the lodge of boughs, that Nicolete had builded and woven within and without, over and under, with flowers, and it was the fairest lodge that might be seen. When Aucassin was ware of it, he stopped suddenly, and the light of the moon fell therein.

"God!" quoth Aucassin, "here was Nicolete, my sweet lady, and this lodge builded she with her fair hands. For the sweetness of it, and for love of her, will I alight, and rest here this night long."

He drew forth his foot from the stirrup to alight, and the steed was great and tall. He dreamed so much on Nicolete his right sweet lady, that he slipped on a stone, and drave his shoulder out of his place. Then knew he that he was hurt sore, natheless he bore him with what force he might, and fastened with the other hand the mare's son to a thorn. Then turned he on his side, and crept backwise into the lodge of boughs. And he looked through a gap in the lodge and saw the stars in heaven, and one that was brighter than the rest; so began he to say: . . .

When Nicolete heard Aucassin, right so came she unto him, for she was not far away. She passed within the lodge, and threw her arms about his neck, and clipped and kissed him.

"Fair sweet friend, welcome be thou."

"And thou, fair sweet love, be thou welcome."

So either kissed and clipped the other, and fair joy was them between.

"Ha! sweet love," quoth Aucassin, "but now was I sore hurt, and my shoulder wried, but I take no force of it, nor have no hurt therefrom since I have thee."

Right so felt she his shoulder and found it was wried from its place. And she so handled it with her white hands, and so wrought in her surgery, that by God's will who loveth lovers, it went back into its place. Then took she flowers, and fresh grass, and leaves green, and bound these herbs on the hurt with a strip of her smock, and he was all healed.

"Aucassin," saith she, "fair sweet love, take counsel what thou wilt do. If thy father let search this forest to-morrow, and men find me here, they will slay me, come to thee what will."

"Certes, fair sweet love, therefore should I sorrow heavily, but, an if I may, never shall they take thee."

Anon gat he on his horse, and his lady before him, kissing and clipping her, and so rode they at adventure. . . .

Aucassin lighted down and his love, as ye have heard sing. He held his horse by the bridle, and his lady by the hands; so went they along the sea shore, and on the sea they saw a ship, and he called unto the sailors, and they came to him. Then held he such speech with them, that he and his lady were brought aboard that ship, and when they were on the high sea, behold a mighty wind and tyrannous arose, marvellous and great, and drave them from land to land, till they came unto a strange country, and won the haven of the castle of Torelore. Then asked they what this land might be, and men told them that it was the country of the King of Torelore. Then he asked what manner of man was he, and was there war afoot, and men said,

"Yea, and mighty!"

Therewith took he farewell of the merchants, and they commended him to God. Anon Aucassin mounted his horse, with his sword girt, and his lady before him, and rode at adventure till he was come to the castle. Then asked he where the King was, and they said that he was in childbed.

"Then where is his wife?"

And they told him she was with the host, and had led with her all the force of that country.

Now when Aucassin heard that saying, he made great marvel, and came into the castle, and lighted down, he and his lady, and his lady held his horse. Right so went he up into the castle, with his sword girt, and fared hither and thither till he came to the chamber where the King was lying. . . .

When Aucassin heard the King speak on this wise, he took all the sheets that covered him, and threw them all abroad about the chamber. Then saw he behind him a cudgel, and caught it into his hand, and turned, and took the King, and beat him till he was well-nigh dead.

"Ha! fair sir," quoth the King, "what would you with me? Art thou beside thyself, that beatest me in mine own house?"

"By God's heart," quoth Aucassin, "thou ill son of an ill wench, I will slay thee if thou swear not that never shall any man in all thy land lie in of child henceforth for ever."

So he did that oath, and when he had done it,

"Sir, said Aucassin, "bring me now where thy wife is with the host."

"Sir, with good will," quoth the King.

He mounted his horse, and Aucassin gat on his own, and Nicolete abode in the Queen's chamber. Anon rode Aucassin and the King even till they came to that place where the Queen was, and lo! men were warring with baked apples, and with eggs, and with fresh cheeses, and Aucassin began to look on them, and made great marvel. . . .

When Aucassin beheld these marvels, he came to the King, and said, "Sir, be these thine enemies?"

"Yea, Sir," quoth the King.

"And will ye that I should avenge you of them?"

"Yea," quoth he, "with all my heart."

Then Aucassin put hand to sword, and hurled among them, and began to smite to the right hand and the left, and slew many of them. And when the King saw that he slew them, he caught at his bridle and said,

"Ha! fair sir, slay them not in such wise."

"How," quoth Aucassin, "will ye not that I should avenge you of them?"

"Sir," quoth the King, "overmuch already hast thou avenged me. It is nowise our custom to slay each other."

Anon turned they and fled. Then the King and Aucassin betook them again to the castle of Torelore, and the folk of that land counselled the King to put Aucassin forth, and keep Nicolete for his son's wife, for that she seemed a lady high of lineage. And Nicolete heard them, and had no joy of it, so began to say: . . .

Aucassin dwelt in the castle of Torelore, in great ease and great delight, for that he had with him Nicolete his sweet love, whom he loved so well. Now while he was in such pleasure and such delight, came a troop of Saracens by sea, and laid siege to the castle and took it by main strength. Anon took they the substance that was therein and carried off the men and maidens captives. They seized Nicolete and Aucassin, and bound Aucassin hand and foot, and cast him into one ship, and Nicolete into another. Then rose there a mighty wind over sea, and scattered the ships. Now that ship wherein was Aucassin, went wandering on the sea, till it came to the castle of Biaucaire, and the folk of the country ran together to wreck her, and there found they Aucassin, and they knew him again. So when they of Biaucaire saw their damoiseau, they made great joy of him, for Aucassin had dwelt full three years in the castle of Torelore, and his father and mother were dead. So the people took him to the castle of Biaucaire, and there were they all his men. And he held the land in peace. . . .

Now leave we Aucassin, and speak we of Nicolete. The ship wherein she was cast pertained to the King of Carthage, and he was her father, and she had twelve brothers, all princes or kings. When they beheld Nicolete, how fair she was, they did her great worship, and made much joy of her, and many times asked her who she was, for surely seemed she a lady of noble line and high parentry. But she might not tell them of her lineage, for she was but a child when men stole her away. So sailed they till they won the City of Carthage, and when Nicolete saw the walls of the castle, and the country-side, she knew that there had she been nourished and thence stolen away, being but a child. Yet was she not so young a child but that well she knew she had been daughter of the King of Carthage; and of her nurture in that city. . . .

When the King of Carthage heard Nicolete speak in this wise, he cast his arms about her neck.

"Fair sweet love," saith he, "tell me who thou art, and be not adread of me."

"Sir," said she, "I am daughter to the King of Carthage, and was taken, being then a little child, it is now fifteen years gone."

When all they of the court heard her speak thus, they knew well that she spake sooth: so made they great joy of her, and led her to the castle in great honour, as the King's daughter. And they would have given her to her lord a King of Paynim, but she had no mind to marry. There dwelt she three days or four. And she considered by what means she might seek for Aucassin. Then she got her a viol, and learned to play on it, till they would have married her on a day to a great King of Paynim, and she stole forth by night, and came to the seaport, and dwelt with a poor woman thereby. Then took she a certain herb, and therewith smeared her head and her face, till she was all brown and stained. And she let make coat, and mantle, and smock, and hose, and attired herself as if she had been a harper. So took she the viol and went to a mariner, and so wrought on him that he took her aboard his vessel. Then hoisted they sail, and fared on the high seas even till they came to the land of Provence. And Nicolete went forth and took the viol, and went playing through all that country, even till she came to the castle of Biaucaire, where Aucassin lay. . . .

When Aucassin heard Nicolete speak in this wise, he was right joyful, and drew her on one side and spoke, saying:

"Sweet fair friend, know ye nothing of this Nicolete, of whom ye have thus sung?"

"Yea, Sir, I know her for the noblest creature, and the most gentle, and the best that ever was born on ground. She is daughter to the King of Carthage that took her there where Aucassin was taken, and brought her into the city of Carthage, till he knew that verily she was his own daughter, whereon he made right great mirth. Anon wished he to give her for her lord one of the greatest kings of all Spain, but she would rather let herself be hanged or burned, than take any lord, how great soever."

"Ha, fair sweet friend," quoth the Count Aucassin, "if thou wilt go into that land again, and bid her come and speak to me, I will give thee of my substance, more than thou wouldst dare to ask or take. And know ye, that for the sake of her, I have no will to take a wife, howsoever high her lineage. So wait I for her, and never will I have a wife, but her only. And if I knew where to find her, no need would I have to seek her."

"Sir," quoth she, "if ye promise me that, I will go in quest of her for your sake, and for hers, that I love much."

So he sware to her, and anon let give her twenty livres, and she departed from him, and he wept for the sweetness of Nicolete. And when she saw him weeping, she said:

"Sir, trouble not thyself so much withal. For in a little while shall I have brought her into this city, and ye shall see her."

When Aucassin heard that, he was right glad thereof. And she departed from him, and went into the city to the house of the Captain's wife, for the Captain her father in God was dead. So she dwelt there, and told all her tale; and the Captain's wife knew her, and knew well that she was Nicolete that herself had nourished. Then she let wash and bathe her, and there rested she eight full days. Then took she an herb that was named *Eyebright* and anointed herself therewith, and was as fair as ever she had been all the days of her life. Then she clothed herself in rich robes of silk whereof the lady had great store, and then sat herself in the chamber on a silken coverlet, and called the lady and bade her go and bring Aucassin her love, and she did even so. And when she came to the Palace she found Aucassin weeping, and making lament for Nicolete his love, for that she delayed so long. And the lady spake unto him and said:

"Aucassin, sorrow no more, but come thou on with me, and I will shew thee the thing in the world that thou lovest best; even Nicolete thy dear love, who from far lands hath come to seek of thee." And Aucassin was right glad.

Here singeth one:

When Aucassin heareth now
That his lady bright of brow
Dwelleth in his own countrie,
Never man was glad as he.
To her castle doth he hie
With the lady speedily,
Passeth to the chamber high,
Findeth Nicolete thereby.
Of her true love found again
Never maid was half so fain.
Straight she leaped upon her feet:
When his love he saw at last,
Arms about her did he cast,
Kissed her often, kissed her sweet
Kissed her lips and brows and eyes.
Thus all night do they devise,
Even till the morning white.
Then Aucassin wedded her,

Made her Lady of Biaucaire.
Many years abode they there,
Many years in shade or sun,
In great gladness and delight.
Ne'er hath Aucassin regret
Nor his lady Nicolete.
Now my story all is done,
      Said and sung!

IV.

The Islamic Tradition

IT IS TO A.D. 622, the date of the flight of Mohammed from Mecca to Medina, that the vast Islamic tradition looks for its date of foundation. With that century there entered into both the eastern and western regions of the Mediterranean world a new dynamism which was to have extensive influence in religious, social and intellectual life, whether in Judaism, Christianity or in secular tradition. The specific ways of organizing social and political life in the course of the evolution of Islam, the particular character of the essential religious message and influence of the *Koran,* the important degree of separation which was to develop between Islamic theologians and philosophers, all can ultimately be appreciated in their interrelations, and in their total impact upon Western civilization.

Within the intellectual sphere two figures are most clearly visible, both for their intrinsic merit and for their influence upon the general development of intellectual life within Western civilization. These are Avicenna (Ibn Sina: 980-1037) who was born in Persia and lived in the eastern region of Islam, and Averroes (Ibn Rushd: 1126-1198) who was born in Spain and lived in the western region of Islam.

Unlike most of the major intellectual figures in this period of twelve centuries, from Philo of Alexandria in the first century to John of Salisbury in the twelfth, Avicenna and Averroes did not set out to provide an intellectual communication or explication of religious teaching, or to provide a religious view of some peculiar problems. Both intended, especially Averroes, to deal with what is available to reason and to do so in the light of reason. In the plan of work, they only incidentally cover topics of importance to religion. In fact, they exerted considerable and quite special influence on later thinkers explicitly concerned with religious issues.

Their design for separation of philosophical and scientific activity from explicit concern with religious teaching has been significant. First, the separation for a time at least may have facilitated some lines of extraordinary development within the life of reason. Second, the separation of intellectual from religious life, the ideal of many in universities today, may be looked at through historical experience and be better seen for what it is, not a simple continuation of classical antiquity, but a page taken from the history of Islam. If we were to characterize this trend within universities today, we might with reason call it Averroistic.

Avicenna's development of metaphysical teaching (especially philosophical psychology, philosophical theology and the study of being as such) took the texts of Aristotle as its points of departure. It has contributed enormously to the amplitude of metaphysical discussion, not only in the Middle Ages, in the later Augustinian tradition, but also in subsequent centuries, in such figures as Suarez and Leibniz. Avicenna's writings were welcomed in Christian circles for his doctrine of the immateriality and separateness of the individual soul. At the same time he raised new problems by his teaching that God acted creatively through necessity and that the unfolding of the universe followed a pattern of necessity. It is easy to find writers identifying various teachings of Avicenna with those of Aristotle. Others, failing as well to distinguish his philosophical achievements from those of a later date, simply identify his teachings with what they call "metaphysics" or "rationalism." The friends and foes of contemporary analytic philosophy and "metaphysics" would be helped alike in seeing the specific contributions of Avicenna. His influence is so great and so little known today.

Averroes, while not free of neoplatonic elements, was to be valued for the relative rigor with which he sought to follow not only the words but also the method and mentality of Aristotle. His insistence on the necessity of the eternity of the world, and what was taken as denial of the separate immortality of the souls of individual men, presented problems with respect to the acceptance of Aristotle both within Islam and later in the Christian West. Considered in relation to Avicenna, Averroes might today be characterized as "naturalistic." He was welcomed by some in the biblical tradition as a defender of the reality and separateness of the created world. His effort to follow the precise movement of Aristotle's communications may at times have cost him a full sense of flexibility inherent in Aristotle's method and fully considered only in his works as a whole. So closely was Averroes associated with Aristotle that he was known in the subsequent century as "the Commentator."

The relevance of the Islamic tradition to life in the seventh through twelfth centuries is rich and varied. Islam, as a principal heir to the traditions of Alexandria and Byzantium and Cappadocia and other centers of the East, recalls the period of Gregory of Nyssa and Justinian. Avicenna's metaphysical turn in particular served to reinforce for the thirteenth and later centuries what we have called "the Augustinian tradition." The secular tradition, especially in the development of courtly love, was partially the result of direct contact between Islam and regions of the Christian West. The continuation of Judaic tradition, to which we will turn, developed within the political and geographical regions of the Islamic world. Finally, the twelfth century meeting of East and the West, includes, for example, the fateful meetings of Islam and Christendom in the Crusades.

Students of Western civilization will find a greatly needed perspective in attending to the presence and influence of the Islamic tradition within Western civilization. Centuries of Moslem hegemony in vast regions of eastern Europe and in the Iberian peninsula, and the proximity of Moslem northern Africa and western Asia to the rest of Europe, have influenced past and present developments. The presence of Old Testament and New Testament teachings within the religious traditions of Islam, and the presence of Islamic intellectuality within medieval Jewish and Christian as well as secular thought, have sometimes been less noticed than the remains of classical antiquity in western Europe or of Moslem influence in India or China.

Two large questions come to mind. One concerns the intellectual decline of the Islamic world, in contrast to the advance of the Western Christian world, after the twelfth century. The other question concerns the remarkable religious dynamism and zeal which have carried the Moslem religion to vast areas and numbers in Asia and Africa even to the present day.

The intellectual life of the Islamic city of Toledo in Spain was, in the twelfth century, far in advance of the intellectual life of the Christian city of Paris. The Parisian renaissance was to lead in the thirteenth century to the avid assimilation of the learning of Toledo, and to the establishment of the great universities. In time, in the field of the greatest comparative strength of the earlier Islamic heritage, it was to lead to the intellectual achievement in the seventeenth century of the physicist Galileo and the mathematician Descartes. We may ask whether the explanation of the relative intellectual decline in Islam be in social and political conditions of the Islamic world, or in some consequences of the religious teachings of Islam, or in the ordering of its intellectual life. Such questioning suggests appreciation of the interaction of intellectual, social and religious movements, and the probable need to go beyond some customary one-dimensional version of Islamic tradition in order to comprehend its influence on our own culture.

Notably characteristic of the religious dynamism of Islam as it has developed, are its openness to societal differences, and its relative disinterest in the intellectualization of religious teaching. Islam, in its development from early beginnings in the eastern and western Mediterranean to its establishment in far reaches of Asia and Africa, is a major phenomenon of world history. With its monotheism and universalism, with its incorporation of sizable particular materials from the Old Testament and the New Testament, with its long history within the confluence of Hellenistic culture, it has borne the formative elements of Western civilization. Today, however poor in technology and in instruments of international organization, Islam might yet prove the model of means for transition from Western to World civilization.

22. ALFARABI: Happiness and Virtue

Abu Nasr al-Farabi (A.D. 870-950), generally known as Alfarabi, is thought to have been Turkish by birth; he spent much of his life in Baghdad and Aleppo. He was impressed by what he saw as the fundamental unity and harmony of the philosophies of Plato and Aristotle, despite superficial differences of language and style. He saw no real conflict between religious belief and philosophical truth. Despite essentially superficial differences, they are to be distinguished in approach and technique, not in content.

Alfarabi wished to alleviate the concern of Islamic theologians who approved of Plato but considered some of Aristotle's points of view incompatible with the tenets of Islam. Alfarabi represents an important step in the attempt to reconcile the philosophic heritage of Greece with the religious traditions of Islam. He also is significant in bringing Aristotle into the discussion which had primarily looked back to Plato and neoplatonism for philosophic inspiration.

The selection is an excerpt from Alfarabi's *The Attainment of Happiness*,* which is the first book of a trilogy, the other two parts of which are: *The Philosophy of Plato* and *The Philosophy of Aristotle*. Although Alfarabi believed that there was only one philosophy expressed in different ways by various philosophers, these three short works present three distinct accounts of philosophy without any attempt to synthesize or harmonize Plato and Aristotle. *The Attainment of Happiness* is Alfarabi's own philosophical statement.

In this selection, Alfarabi asserts that nations and individuals achieve happiness through the virtues, of which there are three kinds: theoretical, deliberative, and moral—to which must be added the practical arts. The theoretical virtues are the perfections of mind which lead to certainty about the immutable nature of things. The deliberative virtues concern the contingent, the variable, i.e., what can be brought into existence by human will under particular circumstances. The moral virtues enable a man to discern what is useful, good, and noble. The practical arts are concerned with action and production.

* From *Alfarabi's Philosophy of Plato and Aristotle*, trans. Muhsin Mahdi (New York: The Free Press, 1962.) Used by permission.

In a relatively brief text Alfarabi discusses a great many points that are of interest, or importance, to twentieth-century man. We find metaphysical, epistemological, psychological, and ethical issues discussed in the context of sociological, religious, and political concerns.

. . . As for the intelligibles that can be made to exist outside the soul by will, the accidents and states that accompany them when they come into being are willed too. Now voluntary intelligibles cannot exist unless they are accompanied with these accidents and states. Since everything whose existence is willed cannot be made to exist unless it is first known, it follows that when one plans to bring any voluntary intelligible into actual existence outside the soul, he must first know the states that must accompany it when it exists. Because voluntary intelligibles do not belong to things that are one numerically, but in their species or genus, the accidents and states that must accompany them vary constantly, increase and decrease, and fall into combinations that cannot be covered at all by invariable and unchangeable formal rules. Indeed, for some of them no rule can be established. For others rules can be established, but they are variable rules and changeable definitions. Those for which no rule at all can be established are the ones that vary constantly and over short periods. The others, for which rules can be established, are those whose states vary over long periods. Those of them that come to exist are for the most part realized by the agency of whoever wills and does them. Yet because of obstacles standing in their way —some of which are natural and others voluntary, resulting from the wills of other individuals—sometimes none of them at all is realized. Furthermore, they suffer not only *temporal* variations, so that they may exist at a certain time with accidents and states different from those that accompany them at another time before or after; their states also differ when they exist in different *places*. This is evident in natural things. e.g., Man. For when it [that is, the intelligible idea Man] assumes actual existence outside the soul, the states and accidents in it at one time are different from those it has at another time after or before. The same is the case with respect to different places. The accidents and states it has when existing in one country are different from those it has in another. Yet, throughout, the intellect perceives Man as a single intelligible idea. This holds for voluntary things as well. For instance, Moderation, Wealth, and the like are voluntary ideas perceived by the intellect.

When we decide to make them actually exist, the accidents that must accompany them at a certain time will be different from the accidents that must accompany them at another time, and the accidents they must have when they exist in one nation will be different from those they must have when existing in another. In some of them, these accidents change from hour to hour, in others from day to day, in others from month to month, in others from year to year, in others from decade to decade, and in still others they change after many decades. Therefore, whoever should will to bring any of them into actual existence outside the soul ought to know the variable accidents that must accompany it in the specific period at which he seeks to bring it into existence and in the determined place in the inhabited part of the earth. Thus he ought to know the accidents that must accompany what is willed to exist from hour to hour, from month to month, from year to year, from decade to decade, or in some other period of determinate length, in a determined locality of large or small size. And he ought to know which of these accidents are common to all nations, to some nations, or to one city over a long period, common to them over a short period, or pertain to some of them specifically and over a short period.

The accidents and states of these intelligibles vary whenever certain events occur in the inhabited part of the earth, events common to all of it, to a certain nation or city, or to a certain group within a city, or pertaining to a single man. Such events are either natural or willed.

Things of this sort are not covered by the theoretical sciences, which cover only the intelligibles that do not vary at all. Therefore another faculty and another skill is required with which to discern the voluntary intelligibles, [not as such, but] insofar as they possess these variable accidents: that is, the modes according to which they can be brought into actual existence by the will at a determined time, in a determined place, and when a determined event occurs. That is the *deliberative* faculty. It is the skill and the faculty by which one discovers and discerns the variable accidents of the intelligibles whose particular instances are made to exist by the will, when one attempts to bring them into actual existence by the will at a determined time, in a determined place, and when a determined event takes place, whether the time is long or short, whether the locality is large or small.

Things are *discovered* by the deliberative faculty only insofar as they are found to be useful for the attainment of an end and purpose. The discoverer first sets the end before himself and then investigates the means by which that end and that purpose are realized. The deliberative faculty is most perfect when it discovers what is most useful for the attainment of these ends. The ends may be truly good, may be evil, or may be only believed to be good. If the means discovered are the most useful for a virtuous end, then they are noble and fair. If the ends are evil, then the means discovered by the deliberative faculty are also evil, base, and bad. And if the ends are only believed to be good, then the means useful for attaining and achieving them are also only believed to be good. The deliberative faculty can be classified accordingly. Deliberative *virtue* is that by which one discovers what is most useful for some virtuous end. As for the deliberative faculty by which one discovers what is most useful for an evil end, it is not a deliberative *virtue* but ought to have other names. And if the deliberative faculty is used to discover what is most useful for things that are only believed to be good, then that deliberative faculty is only believed to be a deliberative virtue.

(1) There is a certain deliberative virtue that enables one to excel in the discovery of what is most useful for a virtuous end common to many nations, to a whole nation, or to a whole city, at a time when an event occurs that affects them in common. (There is no difference between saying *most useful for a virtuous end* and *most useful and most noble,* because what is both most useful and most noble necessarily serves a virtuous end, and what is most useful for a virtuous end is indeed the most noble with respect to that end.) This is *political* deliberative virtue. The events that affect them in common may persist over a long period or vary within short periods. However, *political* deliberative virtue is the deliberative virtue that discovers the most useful and most noble that is common to many nations, to a whole nation, or to a whole city, irrespective of whether what is discovered persists there for a long period or varies over a short period. When it is concerned exclusively with the discovery of the things that are common to many nations, to a whole nation, or to a whole city, and that do not vary except over many decades or over longer periods of determinate length, then it is more akin to a legislative ability.

(2) The deliberative virtue with which one discovers only what

varies over short periods. This is the faculty that manages the different classes of particular, temporary tasks in conjunction with, and at the occurrence of, the events that affect all nations, a certain nation, or a certain city. It is subordinate to the former.

(3) The faculty by which one discovers what is most useful and noble, or what is most useful for a virtuous end, relative to one group among the citizens of a city or to the members of a household. It consists of a variety of deliberative virtues, each associated with the group in question: for instance, it is *economic* deliberative virtue or *military* deliberative virtue. Each of these, in turn, is subdivided inasmuch as what it discovers (*a*) does not vary except over long periods or (*b*) varies over short periods.

(4) The deliberative virtue may be subdivided into still smaller fractions, such as the virtue by which one discovers what is most useful and noble with respect to the purpose of particular arts or with respect to particular purposes that happen to be pursued at particular times. Thus it will have as many subdivisions as there are arts and ways of life.

(5) Furthermore, this faculty can be divided also insofar as (*a*) it enables man to excel in the discovery of what is most useful and noble with respect to his own end when an event occurs that concerns him specifically, and (*b*) it is a deliberative virtue by which he discovers what is most useful and noble with respect to a virtuous end to be attained by somebody else—the latter is *consultative* deliberative virtue. These two may be united in a single man or may exist separately.

It is obvious that the one who possesses a virtue by which he discovers what is most useful and noble, and this for the sake of a virtuous end that is good (irrespective of whether what is discovered is a true good that he wishes for himself, a true good that he wishes someone else to possess, or something that is believed to be good by whomever he wishes it for), cannot possess this faculty without possessing a moral virtue. For if a man wishes the good for others, then he is either truly good or else believed to be good by those for whom he wishes the good although he is not good and virtuous. Similarly he who wishes the true good for himself has to be good and virtuous, not in his deliberation, but in his moral character and in his acts. It would seem that his virtue, moral character, and acts, have to correspond to his power of deliberation and ability to discover what is most useful and noble. Hence if he discovers by his deliberative virtue only those most useful and noble means that are of great force (such as what is most useful for a virtuous end common to a whole nation, to many nations, or to a whole city, and does not vary except over a long period), then his moral virtues ought to be of a comparable measure. Similarly, if his deliberative virtues are confined to means that are most useful for a restricted end when a specific event occurs, then this is the measure of his [moral] virtue also. Accordingly, the more perfect the authority and the greater the power of these deliberative virtues, the stronger the authority and the greater the power of the moral virtues that accompany them.

(1) Since the deliberative virtue by which one discovers what is most useful and noble with respect to the ends that do not vary except over long periods and that are common to many nations, to a whole nation, or to a whole city when an event that affects them in common occurs, has more perfect authority and greater power, the [moral] virtues that accompany it should possess the most perfect authority and the greatest power.

(2) Next follows the deliberative virtue with which one excels in the discovery of what is most useful for a common, though temporary, end, over short periods; the [moral] virtues that accompany it are of a comparable rank.

(3) Then follow the deliberative virtues confined to individual parts of the city—the warriors, the rich, and so forth; the moral virtues that have to do with these parts are of a comparable rank.

(4) Finally, one comes to the deliberative virtues related to single arts (taking into account the purposes of these arts) and to single households and single human beings within single households (with attention to what pertains to them as events follow one another hour after hour or day after day); they are accompanied by a [moral] virtue of a comparable rank.

Therefore one ought to investigate which virtue is the perfect and most powerful virtue. Is it the combination of all the virtues?; or, if one virtue (or a number of virtues) turns out to have a power equal to that of all the virtues together, what ought to be the distinctive mark of the virtue that has this power and is hence the most powerful virtue? This virtue is such that when a man decides to fulfill its functions, he cannot do so without making use of the functions of all the other virtues. If he himself does not happen to possess all of these virtues—in which case he cannot make use of the functions of particular virtues present in him when he decides to fulfill the functions of that virtue—that virtue of his will be a moral virtue in the exercise of which he exploits the acts of the virtues possessed by all others, whether they are nations, cities within a nation, groups within a city, or parts within each group. This, then, is the leading virtue that is not surpassed by any other in authority. Next follows the virtues that resemble this one in that they have a similar power with respect to single parts of the city. For instance, together with the deliberative faculty by which he discovers what is most useful and noble with respect to that which is common to warriors, the general ought to possess a moral virtue. When he decides to fulfill the functions of the latter, he exploits the virtues possessed by the warriors as warriors. His courage, for instance, ought to be such as to enable him to exploit the warriors' particular acts of courage. Similarly, the one who possesses a deliberative virtue by which he discovers what is most useful and noble for the ends of those who acquire wealth in the city ought to possess the moral virtue that enables him to exploit the particular virtues of the classes of people engaged in acquiring wealth.

The arts, too, ought to follow this pattern. The leading art that is not surpassed by any other in authority is such that when we decide to fulfill its functions, we are unable to do so without making use of the functions of all the arts. It is the art for the fulfillment of whose purpose we require all the other arts. This, then, is the leading art and the most powerful of the arts—just as the corresponding moral virtue was the most powerful of all the moral virtues. It is then followed by the rest of the arts. An art of a certain class among them is more perfect and more powerful than the rest in its class if its end can be fulfilled only by making use of the functions of the other arts in its class. Such is the status of the *particular* leading arts. For instance, the art of commanding armies is such that its purpose can be achieved only by making use of the functions of the particular arts of warfare. Similarly, the leading art of wealth in the city is such that its purpose with regard to wealth can be achieved only by exploiting the particular arts of acquiring wealth. This is the case also in every other major part of the city.

Furthermore, it is obvious that what is most useful and noble is in every case either most noble according to generally accepted opinion, most noble according to a particular religion, or truly most noble. Similarly, virtuous ends are either virtuous and good according to generally accepted opinion, virtuous and good according to a particular religion, or truly virtuous and good. No one can discover what is most noble according to the followers of a particular religion unless his moral virtues are the specific virtues of that religion. This holds for everyone else; it applies to the more powerful virtues as well as to the more particular and less powerful. Therefore the most powerful deliberative virtue and the most powerful moral virtue are inseparable from each other.

It is evident that the deliberative virtue with the highest authority can only be subordinate to the theoretical virtue; for it merely discerns the accidents of the intelligibles that, prior to having these accidents as their accompaniments, are acquired by the theoretical virtue. If it is determined that the one who possesses the deliberative virtue should discover the variable accidents and states of only those intelligibles of which he has personal insight and personal knowledge (so as not to make discoveries about things that perhaps ought not to take place), then the deliberative virtue cannot be separated from the theoretical virtue. It follows that the theoretical virtue, the leading deliberative virtue, the leading moral virtue, and the leading practical art are inseparable from each other; otherwise the latter [three] will be unsound, imperfect, and without complete authority.

But if, after the theoretical virtue has caused the intellect to perceive the moral virtues, the latter can only be made to exist if the deliberative virtue discerns them and discovers the accidents that must accompany their intelligibles so that they can be brought into existence, then the deliberative virtue is anterior to the moral virtues. If it is anterior to them, then he who possesses the deliberative virtue discovers by it only such moral virtues as exist independently of the deliberative virtues. Yet if the deliberative virtue is independent of the moral virtue, then he who has the capacity for discovering the (good) moral virtues will not himself be good, not even in a single virtue. But if he himself is not good, how then does he seek out the good or wish the true good for himself or for others? And if he does not wish the good, how is he capable of discovering it without having set it before himself as an end? Therefore, if the deliberative virtue is independent of the moral virtue, it is not possible to discover the moral virtue with it. Yet if the moral virtue is inseparable from the deliberative, and they coexist, how could the deliberative virtue discover the moral and join itself to it? For if they are inseparable, it will follow that the deliberative virtue did not discover the moral virtue; while if the deliberative virtue did discover the moral virtue, it will follow that the deliberative virtue is independent of the moral virtue. Therefore either the deliberative virtue itself is the virtue of goodness, or one should assume that the deliberative virtue is accompanied by some other virtue, different from the moral virtue that is discovered by the deliberative faculty. If that other moral virtue is formed by the will also, it follows that the deliberative virtue discovered it—thus the original doubt recurs. It follows, then, that there must be some other moral virtue—other, that is, than the one discovered by the deliberative virtue—which accompanies the deliberative virtue and enables the possessor of the deliberative virtue to wish the good and the virtuous end. *That* virtue must be *natural* and must come into being by nature, and it must be coupled with a certain deliberative virtue [that is, *cleverness*] which comes into being by nature and discovers the moral virtues formed by the will. The virtue formed by the will will then be the *human* virtue by which man, after acquiring it in the way in which he acquires voluntary things, acquires the *human* deliberative virtue.

But one ought to inquire what manner of thing that *natural* virtue is. Is it or is it not identical with this voluntary virtue? Or ought one to say that it *corresponds* to this virtue, like the states of character that exist in irrational animals?—just as it is said that courage resides in the lion, cunning in the fox, shiftiness in the bear, thievishness in the magpie, and so on. For it is possible that every man is innately so disposed that his soul has a power such that he generally moves more easily in the direction of the accomplishment of a certain virtue or of a certain state of character than in the direction of doing the opposite act. Indeed man moves first in the direction in which it is easier for him to move, provided he is not compelled to do something else. For instance, if a man is innately so disposed that he is more prone to stand his ground against dangers than to recoil before them, then all he needs is to undergo the experience a sufficient number of times and this state of character becomes voluntary. Prior to this, he possessed the corresponding *natural* state of character. If this is so in particular moral virtues that accompany particular deliberative virtues, it must also be the case with the highest moral virtues that accompany the highest deliberative virtues. If this is so, it follows that there are some men who are innately disposed to a [*natural* moral] virtue that corresponds to the highest [*human* moral] virtue and that is joined to a naturally superior deliberative power, others just below them, and so on. If this is so, then not every chance human being will possess art, moral virtue, and deliberative virtue with great power.

Therefore the prince occupies his place by nature and not merely by will. Similarly, a subordinate occupies his place primarily by nature and only secondarily by virtue of the will, which perfects his natural equipments. This being the case, the theoretical virtue, the highest deliberative virtue, the highest moral virtue, and the highest practical art are realized in those equipped for them by nature: that is, in those who possess superior natures with very great potentialities.

23. AVICENNA: The Nature of Man

Ibn Sina (A.D. 980-1037), known as Avicenna to the Latin Christians, was a Persian. We have an autobiography dictated by Avicenna to one of his pupils who was his companion for some twenty-five years. Avicenna was a philosopher; he was also a physician and adviser to Islamic rulers, a scientist, and a philologist. More than two hundred books have been attributed to him—the greatest of these a medical textbook *The Canon*—but probably only half that number are authentic.

The first selection here entitled "The Nature of Man" is from Avicenna's discussion "On the Nature of Prayer" in *Katib al-Najat (Book of Deliverance).** He postulates three souls in man: a physical soul which takes care of the vegetative functions, an animal soul which is the source of movement, imagination, and appetition (these two souls perish at

* From *Avicenna On Theology*, trans. A. J. Arberry; from series "Wisdom of the East" (London: John Murray Publishers, 1951). Used by permission.

death), and a rational soul. The rational soul is the reflective, contemplative, upward reaching soul. It is not concerned with the prosaic functions of the two lower souls, but occupies itself with beauty, truth, reason, and the divine.

The second selection from Avicenna, "The Rational Soul," is the fourth chapter of his *Commentary on Aristotle's "De Anima."* * Here Avicenna speaks of the rational soul as having two faculties, a theoretical faculty and a practical faculty. Each of these may be called intelligence, but in different ways. The practical faculty controls the human body and is somewhat analogous to the animal soul's powers of imagination, appetition, and concrete judgment. Together with the theoretical faculty it produces opinions about the practical order of action.

The theoretical and practical faculties are like two faces of the soul. The practical faculty, which is turned downward toward the body, should not be dominated by the demands of the body. The theoretical faculty faces upward toward the realm of pure intelligence, from which it receives intelligible, universal forms by which it acquires the most perfect kind of human knowledge.

When God had created the animals, after the plants, the minerals and the elements, and after the spheres, the stars, the unsubstantial spirits and the intelligences perfect in themselves; when He had completed His work of origination and creation, He desired to finish His creation with the most perfect species, even as He had begun it with the most perfect genus. He therefore distinguished Man from out of all His creatures, so that as the beginning had been with Intelligence, so too the conclusion should be. He began with the noblest of substances, Intelligence, and He concluded with the noblest of beings, the Intelligent. The high purpose of creation was Man, and nothing else.

Having realized all this, thou must know that Man is the Microcosm; and as all other beings are graded in their world, so too man is graded according to his deeds and his nobility. Some men there are whose deeds accord with those of angels; some whose acts accord with those of devils, so that they perish. For Man has not been produced out of one thing only, that he should be subject to a single set of conditions: God has compounded him of many

* From *Avicenna's Psychology (Commentary on Aristotle's "De Anima")* Book II, Chapter 4, trans. F. Rahman (Oxford: Clarendon Press). Used by permission.

things of various sorts, and temperaments of divers kinds. God divided Man's substantiality into body and soul, the former containing his grosser and the latter his subtler elements. He bestowed upon him sense and reason, both secret and manifest; then He adorned his outward and manifest part, his body, with the five senses in the amplest degree and fullest order. Next out of his inward and secret parts He chose those which were strongest and noblest. The physical element He implanted in his liver, to regulate his digestion and evacuation (or attraction and repulsion), to balance the members and replace by means of nourishment the parts lost through dissolution. The animal element He associated with his heart, connected with the faculties of appetite and anger, to accord with the congenial and oppose the uncongenial: this He made the fountain-head of the five senses, and the source of the imagination and of movement. Lastly He fashioned the human, rational soul in the brain, which He lodged in the highest situation and most appropriate station. He adorned it with thought, memory and recollection, and gave the intellectual substance power over it, that it might be as it were a commander with the faculties for soldiers; the "common-sense" served as a courier, to act as an intermediary between the brain and the senses. The senses were to be the spies of the brain, each stationed at its appropriate gate, to sally forth from time to time into their own world and pick up all that was let fall by their fellows, which they should convey to the particular messenger; the latter would then deliver it, sealed and enveloped, to the faculty of the intelligence, to discriminate and choose what accorded with it, and to reject that which was not genuine.

Man was thus equipped with these souls out of all the world, through each faculty sharing with one class or other of living beings. By virtue of the animal soul he shares with the animals; his physical soul links him with the plants; his human soul is a bond between him and the angels. Moreover each of these faculties has a special sphere, and a particular function to perform: according as one of the three prevails over the other two, the individual is defined by that prevalent sphere, and related after his perception to his own genus. Similarly each function has its own sphere, its own reward, and its own purpose.

The function of the physical soul is to eat and drink, to maintain the parts of the body, and to cleanse the body of superfluities: that is all: it has no business to compete or dispute with the function of any other. The purpose of its function is to keep the body in order and the limbs in proper balance, while supplying strength to the physique. The proper order of the body is proved by a well-oiled flesh, sturdy limbs and a strong physique; and these are acquired from eating and drinking. The reward of the physical soul's function is not to be expected in the spiritual world, and does not wait upon the resurrection, for this soul will not be raised up after death: it resembles a plant, in that when it dies it is dispersed and obliterated, never to be recalled to life.

The function of the animal soul is movement, imagination, and the defence of all the body by good management. Its necessary sphere and particular function is confined to appetite and anger; anger is a branch of appetite, since it seeks to repress, to overcome, to dominate and to tyrannize; these are the various sorts of leadership, and leadership is the fruit of appetite. The special function of the animal soul is fundamentally appetite, and incidentally anger. Its purpose is to preserve the body through the faculty of anger, and to perpetuate the species through the faculty of appetite; for the species is perpetuated always by means of generation, and generation is regulated by the faculty of appetite; while the body remains guarded from injuries by virtue of its being defended, which means to dominate the enemy, to bar the gate of harm, and to prevent the harmful effects of tyranny, and all these ideas are contained and confined within the faculty of anger. Its reward is the realization of its hopes in this lower world; it is not to be expected after death, for the animal soul dies with the body, and will not be raised up at the resurrection. It resembles all the animals, in that it is not qualified to receive the Divine Allocution, and may not therefore expect any reward. When the emanation of a thing is annihilated, it cannot be raised up after death; upon death its entire existence dies, and its happiness is past.

The function of the human, rational soul is the noblest function of all, for it is itself the noblest of spirits. Its function consists of reflecting upon things of art and meditating upon things of beauty: its gaze being turned towards the higher world, it loves not this lower abode and meaner station. Belonging as it does to the higher side of life and to the primal substances, it is not its business to eat and drink, neither does it require luxury and coition: rather its function is to wait for the revelation of truths, and to reflect with perfect intuition and unclouded wit upon the perception of subtle ideas, reading with the eye of inner vision the tablet of Divine Mystery and opposing with strenuous devices the causes of vain fancy. It is distinguished from other spirits by the possession of perfect reason and far-reaching, all-embracing thought; its ambition and striving all through life is to purify the sensual impressions and to perceive the world of intelligible truths. God has singled it out above all other spirits for the gift of the faculty of reason. Reasoning is the tongue of the angels, who have no speech or utterance; reasoning belongs to them especially, which is perception without sensing and communication without words. Man's relation to the world of Spirit is established by reasoning; speech follows after it. If a man possesses no knowledge of reasoning, he is incapable of expressing truth.

The function of the soul is therefore as we have summarized it here, in the fewest possible words. The subject can be greatly amplified, but we have abbreviated its discussion here, since our purpose in this treatise is not to give an account of the human faculties and their functions. We have therefore brought forward and established merely what we required by way of preface.

24. AVICENNA: The Rational Soul*

The human rational soul is also divisible into a practical and a theoretical faculty, both of which are equivocally called intelligence. The practical faculty is the principle of movement of the human body, which urges it to individual actions characterized by deliberation and in accordance with purposive considerations. This faculty has a certain correspondence with the animal faculties of appetence, imagination, and estimation, and a certain dual character in itself. Its relationship to the animal faculty of appetence is that certain states arise in it peculiar to man by which it is disposed to quick actions and passions such as shame, laughter, weeping, &c. Its relationship to the animal faculty of imagination and estimation

* See Introduction to Selection 23.

is that it uses that faculty to deduce plans concerning transitory things and to deduce human arts. Finally, its own dual character is that with the help of the theoretical intelligence it forms the ordinary and commonly accepted opinions concerning actions, as, for instance, that lies and tyranny are evil and other similar premises which, in books of logic, have been clearly distinguished from the purely rational ones. This faculty must govern all the other faculties of the body in accordance with the laws of another faculty which we shall mention, so that it should not submit to them but that they should be subordinated to it, lest passive dispositions arising from the body and derived from material things should develop in it. These passive dispositions are called bad morals. But far from being passive and submissive this faculty must govern the other bodily faculties so that it may have excellent morals.

It is also possible to attribute morals to the bodily faculties. But if the latter predominate they are in an active state, while the practical intelligence is in a passive one. Thus the same thing produces morals in both. But if the practical intelligence predominates, it is in an active state while the bodily faculties are in a passive one, and this is morals in the strict sense (even so there would be two dispositions or moral characters); or character is only one with two different relationships. If we examine them more closely the reason why morals are attributed to this faculty is that the human soul, as will be shown later, is a single substance which is related to two planes—the one higher and the other lower than itself. It has special faculties which establish the relationship between itself and each plane: the practical faculty which the human soul possesses in relation to the lower plane, which is the body, and its control and management; and the theoretical faculty in relation to the higher plane, from which it passively receives and acquires intelligibles. It is as if our soul has two faces: one turned towards the body, and it must not be influenced by any requirements of the bodily nature; and the other turned towards the higher principles, and it must always be ready to receive from what is There in the Higher Plane and to be influenced by it. So much for the practical faculty.

25. ALGAZEL and AVERROES:
A Debate on Causation

Algazel (1058-1111) was born in Persia. He was strongly influenced by Sufism, an ascetical and mystical movement in Islam. At the age of twenty-eight he was already a noted scholar. His profound knowledge of Islamic law, theology, and philosophy led to his appointment, at the age of thirty-four, to the Chair of Theology in the Academy at Baghdad. After only four years in this post, finding himself deeply troubled by doubts and the growth of skepticism in his attitude toward theological questions, he resigned his professorship and left Baghdad in 1095. Eleven years were spent in wandering and in practicing the Sufistic discipline. At the end of this period he achieved peace of mind in religious orthodoxy. He also felt obliged to combat heresy and religious indifference through writing and teaching.

Algazel did not attack heresy out of ignorance of what he considered heretical doctrines. His attack on philosophy was prefaced by a thorough study, *The Intentions of the Philosophers*. Through a curious historical accident, later Christian thinkers took this to be the product of a genuine adherent of Arabian aristotelianism. Algazel meant this to be an objective account of the philosophers' teaching as background for the attack he mounted in the second part of the work, *The Incoherence of the Philosophers*.

Algazel attacked the philosophers on twenty issues (sixteen in metaphysics and four in physics), beginning from his belief in the Creation and ending with his belief in the resurrection of the body. He tried to show that the Greek philosophers were inconsistent in their teachings on the eternity of the world, on man's ability to acquire natural knowledge of God, on God's knowledge of universals and singulars. He maintained that their theory of causality was false and that they could not prove the spirituality, or immortality, of the human soul.

Averroes (Ibn Ruchd: 1126-1198) was born in Cordova, which was the leading center of Islamic civilization. He had a thorough grounding in Islamic studies. At the request of the Amir (Prince) abu Yaqub, Averroes wrote his commentaries on the works of Aristotle which have had great influence on European thinking.

Averroes' first reply to Algazel was a treatise, *On the Agreement of Religion and Philosophy* (1179-1180). In this treatise Averroes defended the thesis that philosophy is required, or at least recommended, by

Islamic Law. This work was followed by the *Incoherence of the Incoherence,** his polemic against Algazel. In this work Averroes undertook a point by point refutation of the twenty theses of Algazel's *Incoherence of the Philosophers.* Averroes summarized each thesis of Algazel and then gave a detailed commentary. This intellectual debate is stimulating reading, as is evident from the portion of the seventeenth disputation (the first on "Physics") which follows.

The topic under discussion is the nature of causality. Algazel's attitude is a remarkable anticipation of the viewpoint of William of Ockham (see Volume III), Nicholas Malebranche (see Volume IV), and David Hume, whose position on causality is perhaps best known and was developed from the new seventeenth-century empiricism of John Locke (see Volume V). Algazel argued that the connection between what is believed to be a cause and what is believed to be an effect is not a necessary connection although it might seem so to us: God can create either or both without a connection between them.

Averroes considered this to be pure sophistry: to deny causality is to make knowledge impossible, so that only personal opinions would remain. But the denial of necessary knowledge involves the embarrassment that even the denial is not necessary knowledge but only opinion.

Ghazali says:

According to us the connexion between what is usually believed to be a cause and what is believed to be an effect is not a necessary connexion; each of two things has its own individuality and is not the other, and neither the affirmation nor the negation, neither the existence nor the non-existence of the one is implied in the affirmation, negation, existence, and non-existence of the other—e.g. the satisfaction of thirst does not imply drinking, nor satiety eating, nor burning contact with fire, nor light sunrise, nor decapitation death, nor recovery the drinking of medicine, nor evacuation the taking of a purgative, and so on for all the empirical connexions existing in medicine, astronomy, the sciences, and the crafts. For the connexion in these things is based on a prior power of God to create them in a successive order, though not because this connexion is necessary in itself and cannot be disjoined—on the contrary, it is in God's power to create satiety without eating, and death without decapita-

---

* From "Algazel's Denial of a logically necessary connection between cause and effect answered by Averroes." In *Averroes' Tahafut-Al-Tahafut (The Incoherence of the Incoherence),* vol. I, trans. Simon van den Bergh (London: Luzac & Company Ltd., 1955). Used by permission.

tion, and to let life persist notwithstanding the decapitation, and so on with respect to all connexions. The philosophers, however, deny this possibility and claim that that is impossible. To investigate all these innumerable connexions would take us too long, and so we shall choose one single example, namely the burning of cotton through contact with fire; for we regard it as possible that the contact might occur without the burning taking place, and also that the cotton might be changed into ashes without any contact with fire, although the philosophers deny this possibility. The discussion of this matter has three points.

The first is that our opponent claims that the agent of the burning is the fire exclusively; this is a natural, not a voluntary agent, and cannot abstain from what is in its nature when it is brought into contact with a receptive substratum. This we deny, saying: The agent of the burning is God, through His creating the black in the cotton and the disconnexion of its parts, and it is God who made the cotton burn and made it ashes either through the intermediation of angels or without intermediation. For fire is a dead body which has no action, and what is the proof that it is the agent? Indeed, the philosophers have no other proof than the observation of the occurrence of the burning, when there is contact with fire, but observation proves only a simultaneity, not a causation, and, in reality, there is no other cause but God. For there is unanimity of opinion about the fact that the union of the spirit with the perceptive and moving faculties in the sperm of animals does not originate in the natures contained in warmth, cold, moistness, and dryness, and that the father is neither the agent of the embryo through introducing the sperm into the uterus, nor the agent of its life, its sight and hearing, and all its other faculties. And although it is well known that the same faculties exist in the father, still nobody thinks that these faculties exist through him; no, their existence is produced by the First either directly or through the intermediation of the angels who are in charge of these events. Of this fact the philosophers who believe in a creator are quite convinced, but it is precisely with them that we are in dispute.

It has been shown that coexistence does not indicate causation. We shall make this still more clear through an example. Suppose that a man blind from birth, whose eyes are veiled by a membrane and who has never heard people talk of the difference between night and day, has the membrane removed from his eyes by day and sees visible things, he will surely think then that the actual perception in his eyes of the forms of visible things is caused by the opening of his eyelids, and that as long as his sight is sound and in function, the hindrance removed and the object in front of him visible, he will, without doubt, be able to see, and he will never think that he will not see, till at the moment when the sun sets and the air darkens, he will understand that it was the light of the sun which impressed the visible forms on his sight. And for what other reason do our opponents believe that in the principles of existence there are causes and influences from which the events which coincide with them proceed, than that they are constant, do not disappear, and are not moving bodies which vanish from sight? For if they disappeared or vanished we should observe the disjunction and understand then that behind our perceptions there exists a cause. And out of this there is no issue, according to the very conclusions of the philosophers themselves.

The true philosophers were therefore unanimously of the opinion that these accidents and events which occur when there is a contact of bodies, or in general a change in their positions, proceed from the bestower of forms who is an angel or a plurality of angels, so that they even said that the impression of the visible forms on the eye occurs through the bestower of forms, and that the rising of the sun, the soundness of the pupil, and the existence of the visible object are only the preparations and dispositions which enable the substratum to receive the forms; and this theory they applied to all events. And this refutes the claim of those who profess that fire is the agent of burning, bread the agent of satiety, medicine the agent of health, and so on.

I [Averroes] say:

To deny the existence of efficient causes which are observed in sensible things is sophistry, and he who defends this doctrine either denies with his tongue what is present in his mind or is carried away by a sophistical doubt which occurs to him concerning this question. For he who denies this can no longer acknowledge that every act must have an agent. The question whether these causes by themselves are sufficient to perform the acts which proceed from them, or need an external cause for the perfection of their act, whether separate or not, is not self-evident and requires much investigation and research.

And if the theologians had doubts about the efficient causes which are perceived to cause each other, because there are also effects whose cause is not perceived, this is illogical. Those things whose causes are not perceived are still unknown and must be investigated, precisely because their causes are not perceived; and since everything whose causes are not perceived is still unknown by nature and must be investigated, it follows necessarily that what is not unknown has causes which are perceived. The man who reasons like the theologians does not distinguish between what is self-evident and what is unknown, and everything Ghazali says in this passage is sophistical.

And further, what do the theologians say about the essential causes, the understanding of which alone can make a thing understood? For it is self-evident that things have essences and attributes which determine the special functions of each thing and through which the essences and names of things are differentiated. If a thing had not its specific nature, it would not have a special name nor a definition, and all things would be one—indeed, not even one, for it might be asked whether this one has one special act or one special passivity or not, and if it had a special act, then there would indeed exist special acts proceeding from special natures, but if it had no single special act, then the one would not be one. But if the nature of oneness is denied, the nature of being is denied, and the consequence of the denial of being is nothingness.

Further, are the acts which proceed from all things absolutely necessary for those in whose nature it lies to perform them, or are they only performed in most cases or in half the cases? This is a question which must be investigated, since one single action-and-passivity between two existent things occurs only through one relation out of an infinite number, and it happens often that one relation hinders another. Therefore it is not absolutely certain that fire acts when it is brought near a sensitive body, for surely it is not improbable that there should be something which stands in such a relation to the sensitive things as to hinder the action of the fire, as is asserted of talc and other things. But one need not therefore deny fire its burning power so long as fire keeps its name and definition.

Further, it is self-evident that all events have four causes, agent, form, matter, and end, and that they are necessary for the existence of the effects—especially those causes which form a part of the effect, namely that which is called by the philosophers matter, by the theologians condition and substratum, and that which is called by the philosophers form, by the theologians psychological quality. The theologians acknowledge that there exist conditions which are necessary to the conditioned, as when they say that life is a condition of knowledge; and they equally recognize that things have realities and definitions, and that these are necessary for the existence of the existent, and therefore they here judge the visible and the invisible according to one and the same scheme. And they adopt the same attitude towards the consequences of a thing's essence, namely what they call "sign", as for instance when they say that the harmony in the world indicates that its agent possesses mind and that the existence of a world having a design indicates that its agent knows this world. Now intelligence is nothing but the perception of things with their causes, and in this it distinguishes itself from all the other faculties of apprehension, and he who denies causes must deny the intellect. Logic implies the existence of causes and effects, and knowledge of these effects can only be rendered perfect through knowledge of their causes. Denial of cause implies the denial of knowledge, and denial of knowledge implies that nothing in this world can be really known, and that what is supposed to be known is nothing but opinion, that neither proof nor definition exist, and that the essential attributes which compose definitions are void. The man who denies the necessity of any item of knowledge must admit that even this, his own affirmation, is not necessary knowledge.

As to those who admit that there exists, besides necessary knowledge, knowledge which is not necessary, about which the soul forms a judgement on slight evidence and imagines it to be necessary, whereas it is not necessary, the philosophers do not deny this. And if they call such a fact "habit" this may be granted, but otherwise I do not know what they understand by the term "habit"—whether they mean that it is the habit of the agent, the habit of the existing things, or our habit to form a judgement about such things? It is, however, impossible that God should have a habit, for a habit is a custom which the agent acquires and from which a frequent repetition of his act follows, whereas God says in the Holy Book: "Thou shalt not find any alteration in the course of God, and they shall not find any change in the course of God." If they mean a habit in exist-

ing things, habit can only exist in the animated, if it exists in something else, it is really a nature, and it is not possible that a thing
should have a nature which determined it either necessarily or in
most cases. If they mean our habit of forming judgements about
things, such a habit is nothing but an act of the soul which is determined by its nature and through which the intellect becomes intellect.
The philosophers do not deny such a habit; but "habit" is an am-
biguous term, and if it is analysed it means only a hypothetical act;
as when we say "So-and-so has the habit of acting in such-and-such
a way", meaning that he will act in that way most of the time. If
this were true, everything would be the case only by supposition,
and there would be no wisdom in the world from which it might
be inferred that its agent was wise.

And, as we said, we need not doubt that some of these existents
cause each other and act through each other, and that in themselves
they do not suffice for their act, but that they are in need of an
external agent whose act is a condition of their act, and not only of
their act but even of their existence. However, about the essence of
this agent or of these agents the philosophers differ in one way, although in another they agree. They all agree in this, that the First
Agent is immaterial and that its act is the condition of the existence
and acts of existents, and that the act of their agent reaches these
existents through the intermediation of an effect of this agent,
which is different from these existents and which, according to some
of them, is exclusively the heavenly sphere, whereas others assume
besides this sphere another immaterial existent which they call the
bestower of forms.

But this is not the place to investigate these theories, and the
highest part of their inquiry is this; and if you are one of those who
desire these truths, then follow the right road which leads to them.
The reason why the philosophers differed about the origin of the
essential forms and especially of the forms of the soul is that they
could not relate them to the warm, cold, moist, and dry, which are
the causes of all natural things which come into being and pass
away, whereas the materialists related everything which does not
seem to have an apparent cause to the warm, cold, moist, and dry,
affirming that these things originated through certain mixtures of
those elements, just as colours and other accidents come into existence. And the philosophers tried to refute them.

Ghazali says:

Our second point is concerned with those who acknowledge that these events proceed from their principles, but say that the disposition to receive the forms arises from their observed and apparent causes. However, according to them also the events proceed from these principles not by deliberation and will, but by necessity and nature, as light does from the sun, and the substrata differ for their reception only through the differentiations in their disposition. For instance, a polished body receives the rays of the sun, reflects them and illuminates another spot with them, whereas an opaque body does not receive them; the air does not hinder the penetration of the sun's light, but a stone does; certain things become soft through the sun, others hard; certain things, like the garments which the fuller bleaches, become white through the sun, others like the fuller's face become black: the principle is, however, one and the same, although the effects differ through the differences of disposition in the substratum. Thus there is no hindrance or incapacity in the emanation of what emanates from the principle of existence; the insufficiency lies only in the receiving substrata. If this is true, and we assume a fire that has the quality it has, and two similar pieces of cotton in the same contact with it, how can it be imagined that only one and not the other will be burned, as there is here no voluntary act? And from this point of view they deny that Abraham could fall into the fire and not be burned notwithstanding the fact that the fire remained fire, and they affirm that this could only be possible through abstracting the warmth from the fire (through which it would, however, cease to be fire) or through changing the essence of Abraham and making him a stone or something on which fire has no influence, and neither the one nor the other is possible.

I say:

Those philosophers who say that these perceptible existents do not act on each other, and that their agent is exclusively an external principle, cannot affirm that their apparent action on each other is totally illusory, but would say that this action is limited to preparing the disposition to accept the forms from the external principle. However, I do not know any philosopher who affirms this absolutely; they assert this only of the essential forms, not of the forms of accidents. They all agree that warmth causes warmth, and that all the four qualities act likewise, but in such a way that through it the elemental fire and the warmth which proceeds from the heavenly bodies are conserved. The theory which Ghazali ascribes to the philosophers, that the separate principles act by nature, not by choice, is not held by any important philosophers; on the contrary, the philosophers affirm that that which possesses knowledge must act by choice. However, according to the philosophers, in view of the excellence which exists in the world, there can proceed out of two contraries only the better, and their choice is not made to perfect their essences—since there is no imperfection in their essence—but in order that through it those existents which have an imperfection in their nature may be perfected.

As to the objection which Ghazali ascribes to the philosophers over the miracle of Abraham, such things are only asserted by heretical Muslims. The learned among the philosophers do not permit discussion or disputation about the principles of religion, and he who does such a thing needs, according to them, a severe lesson. For whereas every science has its principles, and every student of this science must concede its principles and may not interfere with them by denying them, this is still more obligatory in the practical science of religion, for to walk on the path of the religious virtues is necessary for man's existence, according to them, not in so far as he is a man, but in so far as he has knowledge; and therefore it is necessary for every man to concede the principles of religion and invest with authority the man who lays them down. The denial and discussion of these principles denies human existence, and therefore heretics must be killed. Of religious principles it must be said that they are divine things which surpass human understanding, but must be acknowledged although their causes are unknown.

Therefore we do not find that any of the ancient philosophers discusses miracles, although they were known and had appeared all over the world, for they are the principles on which religion is based and religion is the principle of the virtues; nor did they discuss any of the things which are said to happen after death. For if a man grows up according to the religious virtues he becomes absolutely virtuous, and if time and felicity are granted to him, so that he becomes one of the deeply learned thinkers and it happens that he can explain one of the principles of religion, it is enjoined upon him that he should not divulge this explanation and should say "all these are the terms of religion and the wise", conforming himself to the Divine Words, "but those who are deeply versed in knowledge say: we believe in it, it is all from our Lord".

Ghazali says:

There are two answers to this theory. The first is to say: "We do not accept the assertion that the principles do not act in a voluntary way and that God does not act through His will, and we have already refuted their claim in treating of the question of the temporal creation of the world. If it is established that the Agent creates the burning through His will when the piece of cotton is brought in contact with the fire, He can equally well omit to create it when the contact takes place.

I say:

Ghazali, to confuse his opponent, here regards as established what his opponent refuses to admit, and says that his opponent has no proof for his refusal. He says that the First Agent causes the burning without an intermediary He might have created in order that the burning might take place through the fire. But such a claim abolishes any perception of the existence of causes and effects. No philosopher doubts that, for instance, the fire is the cause of the burning which occurs in the cotton through the fire—not, however, absolutely, but by an external principle which is the condition of the existence of fire, not to speak of its burning. The philosophers differ only about the quiddity of this principle—whether it is a separate principle, or an intermediary between the event and the separate principle besides the fire.

Ghazali says, on behalf of the philosophers:

But it may be said that such a conception involves reprehensible impossibilities. For if you deny the necessary dependence of effects or their causes and relate them to the will of their Creator, and do not allow even in the will a particular definite pattern, but regard it as possible that it may vary and change in type, then it may happen to any of us that there should be in his presence beasts of prey and flaming fires and immovable mountains and enemies equipped with arms, without his seeing them, because God had not created in him the faculty of seeing them. And a man who had left a book at home might find it on his return changed into a youth, handsome, intelligent, and efficient, or into an animal; or if he left a youth at home, he might find him turned into a dog; or he might leave ashes and find them changed into musk; or a stone changed into gold, and gold changed into stone. And if he were asked about any of these things, he would answer: "I do not know what there is at present in my house; I only know that I left a book in my house, but perhaps by now it is a horse which has soiled the library with its urine and excrement, and I left in my house a piece of bread which has perhaps changed into an apple-tree." For God is able to do all these things, and it does not belong to the necessity of a horse that it should be created from a sperm, nor is it of the necessity of a tree that it should be created from a seed; no, there is no necessity that it should be created out of anything at all. And perhaps God creates things which never existed before; indeed, when one sees a man one never saw before and is asked whether this man has been generated, one should answer hesitantly: "It may be that he was one of the fruits in the market which has been changed into a man, and that this is that man." For God can do any possible thing, and this is possible, and one cannot avoid being perplexed by it; and to this kind of fancy one may yield *ad infinitum,* but these examples will do.

But the answer is to say: If it were true that the existence of the possible implied that there could not be created in man any knowledge of the non-occurrence of a possible, all these consequences would follow necessarily. But we are not at a loss over any of the examples which you have brought forward. For God has created in us the knowledge that He will not do all these possible things, and we only profess that these things are not necessary, but that they are possible and may or may not happen, and protracted habit time after time fixes their occurrence in our minds according to the past habit in a fixed impression. Yes, it is possible that a prophet should know in such ways as the philosophers have explained that a certain man will not come tomorrow from a journey, and although his coming is possible the prophet knows that this possibility will not be realized. And often you may observe even ordinary men of whom you know that they are not aware of anything occult, and can know the intelligible only through instruction, and still it cannot be denied that nevertheless their soul and conjecturing power can acquire sufficient strength to apprehend what the prophets apprehend in so far as they know the possibility of an event, but know that it will not happen. And if God interrupts the habitual course by causing this unusual event to happen this knowledge of the habitual is at the time of the interruption removed from their hearts and He no longer creates it. There is, therefore, no objection to admitting that a thing may be possible for God, but that He had the previous knowledge that although He might have done so He would not carry it out during a certain time, and that He has created in us the knowledge that He would not do it during that time.

I say:

When the theologians admit that the opposite of everything existing is equally possible, and that it is such in regard to the Agent, and that only one of these opposites can be differentiated through the will of the Agent, there is no fixed standard for His will either constantly or for most cases, according to which things must happen. For this reason the theologians are open to all the scandalous inplications with which they are charged. For true knowledge is the knowledge of a thing as it is in reality. And if in reality there only existed, in regard both to the substratum and to the Agent, the possibility of the two opposites, there would no longer, even for the twinkling of an eye, be any permanent knowledge of anything, since we suppose such an agent to rule existents like a tyrannical prince who has the highest power, for whom nobody in his dominion can deputize, of whom no standard or custom is known to which reference might be made. Indeed, the acts of such a prince will undoubtedly be unknown by nature, and if an act of his comes into existence the continuance of its existence at any moment will be unknown by nature.

Ghazali's defence against these difficulties that God created in us the knowledge that these possibilities would be realized only at special times, such as at the time of the miracle, is not a true one. For the knowledge created in us is always in conformity with the nature of the real thing, since the definition of truth is that a thing is believed to be such as it is in reality. If therefore there is knowledge of these possibles, there must be in the real possibles a condition to which our knowledge refers, either through these possibles themselves or through the agent, or for both reasons—a condition which the theologians call habit. And since the existence of this condition which is called habit is impossible in the First Agent, this condition can only be found in the existents, and this, as we said, is what the philosophers call nature.

The same congruity exists between God's knowledge and the

existents, although God's knowledge of existents is their cause, and these existents are the consequence of God's knowledge, and therefore reality conforms to God's knowledge. If, for instance, knowledge of Zaid's coming reaches the prophet through a communication of God, the reason why the actual happening is congruous with the knowledge is nothing but the fact that the nature of the actually existent is a consequence of the eternal knowledge, for knowledge *qua* knowledge can only refer to something which has an actualized nature. The knowledge of the Creator is the reason why this nature becomes actual in the existent which is attached to it. Our ignorance of these possibles is brought about through our ignorance of the nature which determines the being or non-being of a thing. If the opposites in existents were in a condition of equilibrium, both in themselves and through their efficient causes, it would follow that they neither existed nor did not exist, or that they existed and did not exist at the same time, and one of the opposites must therefore have a preponderance in existence. And it is the knowledge of the existence of this nature which causes the actualization of one of the opposites. And the knowledge attached to this nature is either a knowledge prior to it, and this is the knowledge of which this nature is the effect, namely eternal knowledge, or the knowledge which is consequent on this nature, namely non-eternal knowledge. The attainment of the occult is nothing but the vision of this nature, and our acquisition of this knowledge not preceded by any proof is what is called in ordinary human beings a dream, and in prophets inspiration. The eternal will and eternal knowledge are the causes of this nature in existents. And this is the meaning of the divine Words: "Say that none in the heavens or on the earth know the occult but God alone." This nature is sometimes necessary and sometimes what happens in most cases. Dreams and inspiration are only, as we said, the announcement of this nature in possible things, and the sciences which claim the prognostication of future events possess only rare traces of the influences of this nature or constitution or whatever you wish to call it, namely that which is actualized in itself and to which the knowledge attaches itself.

Ghazali says:

The second answer—and in it is to be found deliverance from these reprehensible consequences—is to agree that in fire there is created a nature which burns two similar pieces of cotton which are brought into contact with it and does not differentiate between them, when they are alike in every respect. But still we regard it as possible that a prophet should be thrown into the fire and not burn, either through a change in the quality of the fire or through a change in the quality of the prophet, and that either through God or through the angels there should arise a quality in the fire which limited its heat to its own body, so that it did not go beyond it, but remained confined to it, keeping, however, to the form and reality of the fire, without its heat and influence extending beyond it; or that there should arise in the body of the person an attribute, which did not stop the body from being flesh and bone, but still defended it against the action of the fire. For we can see a man rub himself with talc and sit down in a lighted oven and not suffer from it; and if one had not seen it, one would deny it, and the denial of our opponents that it lies in God's power to confer on the fire or to the body an attribute which prevents it from being burnt is like the denial of one who has not seen the talc and its effect. For strange and marvellous things are in the power of God, many of which we have not seen, and why should we deny their possibility and regard them as impossible?

And also the bringing back to life of the dead and the changing of a stick into a serpent are possible in the following way: matter can receive any form, and therefore earth and the other elements can be changed into a plant, and a plant, when an animal eats it, can be changed into blood, then blood can be changed into sperm, and then sperm can be thrown into the womb and take the character of an animal. This, in the habitual course of nature, takes place over a long space of time, but why does our opponent declare it impossible that matter should pass through these different phases in a shorter period than is usual, and when once a shorter period is allowed there is no limit to its being shorter and shorter, so that these potencies can always become quicker in their action and eventually arrive at the stage of being a miracle of a prophet.

And if it is asked: "Does this arise through the soul of the prophet or through another principle at the instigation of the prophet?"—we answer: "Does what you acknowledge may happen through the power of the prophet's soul, like the downpour of rain or the falling of a thunderbolt or earthquakes—does that occur through him or through another principle? What we say about the facts which we have mentioned is like what you say about those facts which you regard as possible. And the best method according to both you and us is to relate these things to God, either immediately or through the intermediation of the angels. But at the time these occurrences become real, the attention of the prophet turns to such facts, and the order of the good determines its appearance to ensure the duration of the order of religion, and this gives a preponderance to the side of existence. The fact in itself is possible, and the principle in God is His magnanimity; but such a fact only emanates from Him when necessity gives a preponderance to its existence and the good determines it, and the good only determines it when a prophet needs it to establish his prophetic office for the promulgation of the good."

And all this is in accordance with the theory of the philosophers and follows from it for them, since they allow to the prophet a particular characteristic which distinguishes him from common people. There is no intellectual criterion for the extent of its possibility, but there is no need to declare it false when it rests on a good tradition and the religious law states it to be true. Now, in general, it is only the sperm which accepts the form of animals—and it receives its animal potencies only from the angels, who according to the philosophers, are the principles of existents—and only a man can be created from the sperm of a man, and only a horse from the sperm of a horse, in so far as the actualization of the sperm through the horse determines the preponderance of the analogous form of a horse over all other forms, and it accepts only the form to which in this way the preponderance is given, and therefore barley never grows from wheat or an apple from a pear. Further, we see that certain kinds of animal are only produced by spontaneous generation from earth and never are generated by procreation—e.g. worms, and some which are produced both spontaneously and by procreation like the mouse, the serpent, and the scorpion, for their generation can come also from earth. Their disposition to accept forms varies through causes unknown to us, and it is not in human power to ascertain them, since those forms do not, according to the philosophers, emanate from the angels by their good pleasure or haphazard, but in every substratum only in such a way that a form arises for whose acceptance it is specially determined through its own disposition. These dispositions differ, and their principles are, according to the philosophers, the aspects of the stars and the different relative positions of the heavenly bodies in their movements. And through this the possibility is open that there may be in the principles of these dispositions wonderful and marvellous things, so that those who understand talismans through their knowledge of the particular qualities of minerals and of the stars succeed in combining the heavenly potencies with those mineral peculiarities, and make shapes of these earthly substances, and seek a special virtue for them and produce marvellous things in the world through them. And often they drive serpents and scorpions from a country, and sometimes bugs, and they do other things which are known to belong to the science of talismans.

And since there is no fixed criterion for the principles of these dispositions, and we cannot ascertain their essence or limit them, how can we know that it is impossible that in certain bodies dispositions occur to change their phases at a quicker rhythm, so that such a body would be disposed to accept a form for the acceptance of which it was not prepared before, which is claimed to be a miracle? There is no denying this, except through a lack of understanding and an unfamiliarity with higher things and oblivion of the secrets of God in the created world and in nature. And he who has examined the many wonders of the sciences does not consider in any way impossible for God's power what is told of the wonders of the prophets.

Our opponents may say: "We agree with you that everything possible is in the power of God, and you theologians agree with us that the impossible cannot be done and that there are things whose impossibility is known and things which are known to be possible, and that there are also things about which the understanding is undecided and which it does not hold to be either impossible or possible. Now what according to you is the limit of the impossible? If the impossible includes nothing but the simultaneous affirmation and negation of the same thing, then say that of two things the one is not the other, and that the existence of the one does not demand the existence of the other. And say then that God can create will without knowledge of the thing willed, and knowledge without life, and that He can move the hand of a dead man and make him sit and write volumes with his hand and engage himself in sciences while he has his eye open and his looks are fixed on his work, although he does not see and there is no life in him and he has no power, and it is God alone who creates all these ordered actions with the moving of the dead man's hand, and the movement comes from God. But by regarding this as possible the difference between voluntary action and a reflex action like shivering is destroyed, and a judicious act will no longer indicate that the agent possesess knowledge or power. It will then be necessary that God should be able to change genera and transform the substance into an accident and knowledge into power and black into white and a voice into an odour, just as He is able to change the inorganic into an animal and a stone into gold, and it will then follow that God can also bring about other unlimited impossibilities."

The answer to this is to say that the impossible cannot be done by God, and the impossible consists in the simultaneous affirmation and negation of a thing, or the affirmation of the more particular with the negation of the more general, or the affirmation of two things with the negation of one of them, and what does not refer to this is not impossible and what is not impossible can be done. The identification of black and white is impossible, because by the affirmation of the form of black in the substratum the negation of the form of white and of the existence of white is implied; and since the negation of white is implied by the affirmation of black, the simultaneous affirmation and negation of white is impossible. And the existence of a person in two places at once is only impossible because we imply by his being in the house that he cannot be in another place, and it cannot be understood from the denial that he is in another place that he can be simultaneously both in another place and in the house. And in the same way by will is implied the seeking of something that can be known, and if we assume a seeking without knowledge there cannot be a will and we would then deny what we had implied. And it is impossible that in the inorganic knowledge should be created, because we understand by inorganic that which does not perceive, and if in the organic perception was created it would become impossible to call it inorganic in the sense in which this word is understood.

As to the transformation of one genus into another, some theologians affirm that it is in the power of God, but we say that for one thing to become another is irrational; for, if for instance, the black could be transformed into power, the black would either remain or not, and if it does not exist any more, it is not changed but simply does not exist any more and something else exists; and if it remains existent together with power, it is not changed, but something else is brought in relation to it, and if the black remains and power does not exist, then it does not change, but remains as it was before. And when we say that blood changes into sperm, we mean by it that this identical matter is divested of one form and invested with another; and it amounts to this, that one form becomes non-existent and another form comes into existence while the matter remains, and that two forms succeed one another in it. And when we say that water becomes air through being heated, we mean by it that the matter which had received the form of the water is deprived of this form and takes another, and the matter is common to them but the attribute changes. And it is the same when we say that the stick is changed into a serpent or earth into an animal. But there is no matter common to the accident and the substance, nor to black and to power, nor to the other categories, and it is impossible for this reason that they should be changed into each other.

As to God's moving the hand of a dead man, and raising this man up in the form of a living one who sits and writes, so that through the movement of his hand a well-ordered script is written, this in itself is not impossible as long as we refer events to the will of a voluntary being, and it is only to be denied because the habitual course of nature is in opposition to it. And your affirmation, philosophers, that, if this is so, the judiciousness of an act no longer indicates that the agent possesses knowledge is false, for the agent in this case is God; He determines the act and He performs it. And as to your assertion that if this is so there is no longer any difference between shivering and voluntary motion, we answer that we know this difference only because we experience in ourselves the difference between these two conditions, and we find thereby that the differentiating factor is power, and know that of the two classes of the possible the one happens at one time, the other at another; that is to say, we produce movement with the power to produce it at one time, and a movement without this power at another. Now, when we observe other movements than ours and see many well-ordered movements, we attain knowledge of the power behind them, and God creates in us all these different kinds of knowledge through the habitual course of events, through which one of the two classes of possibility becomes known, though the impossibility of the second class is not proved thereby.

I say:

When Ghazali saw that the theory that things have no particular qualities and forms from which particular acts follow, for every thing is very objectionable, and contrary to common sense, he conceded this in this last section and replaced it by the denial of two points: first that a thing can have these qualities but that they need not act on a thing in the way they usually act on it, e.g. fire can have its warmth but need not burn something that is brought near to it, even if it is usually burnt when fire is brought near to it; secondly that the particular forms have not a particular matter in every object.

The first point can be accepted by the philosophers, for because of external causes the procession of acts from agents may not be necessary, and it is not impossible that for instance fire may sometimes be brought near cotton without burning it, when something is placed with the cotton that makes it non-inflammable, as Ghazali says in his instance of talc and a living being.

As to the point that matter is one of the conditions for material things, this cannot be denied by the theologians, for, as Ghazali says, there is no difference between our simultaneous negation and affirmation of a thing and our simultaneous denial of part of it and affirmation of the whole. And since things consist of two qualities, a general and a particular—and this is what the philosophers mean by the term "definition", a definition being composed according to them of a genus and a specific difference—it is indifferent for the denial of an existent which of its two qualities is denied. For instance, since man consists of two qualities, one being a general quality, viz. animality, and the second a particular, viz. rationality, man remains man just as little when we take away his animality as when we take away his rationality, for animality is a condition of rationality and when the condition is removed the conditioned is removed equally.

On this question the theologians and the philosophers agree, except that the philosophers believe that for particular things the general qualities are just as much a condition as the particular, and this the theologians do not believe; for the philosophers, for instance, warmth and moisture are a condition of life in the transient, because they are more general than life, just as life is a condition of rationality. But the theologians do not believe this, and so you hear them say: "For us dryness and moisture are not a condition of life." For the philosophers shape, too, is one of the particular conditions of life in an organic being; if not, one of two following cases might arise: either the special shape of the animal might exist without exercising any function, or this special shape might not exist at all. For instance, for the philosophers the hand is the organ of the intellect, and by means of it man performs his rational acts, like writing and the carrying on of the other arts; now if intelligence were possible in the inorganic, it would be possible that intellect might exist without performing its function, and it would be as if warmth could exist without warming the things that are normally warmed by it. Also, according to the philosophers, every existent has a definite quantity and a definite quality, and also the time when it comes into existence and during which it persists are determined, although in all these determinations there is, according to the philosophers, a certain latitude.

Theologians and philosophers agree that the matter of existents which participate in one and the same matter sometimes accepts one of two forms and sometimes its opposite, as happens, according to them, with the forms of the four elements, fire, air, water, and earth. Only in regard to the things which have no common matter or which have different matters do they disagree whether some of them can accept the forms of others—for instance, whether something which is not known by experience to accept a certain form except through many intermediaries can also accept this ultimate form without intermediaries. For instance, the plant comes into existence through composition out of the elements; it becomes blood and sperm through being eaten by an animal and from sperm and blood comes the animal, as is said in the divine Words: "We created man from an extract of clay, then We made him a clot in a sure depository" and so on till His words "and blessed be God, the best of creators". The theologians affirm that the soul of man can inhere in earth without the intermediaries known by experience, whereas the philosophers deny this and say that, if this were possible, wisdom would consist in the creation of man without such intermediaries, and a creator who created in such a way would be the best and most powerful of creators; both parties claim that what they say is self-evident, and neither has any proof for its theory. And you, reader, consult your heart; it is your duty to believe what it announces, and this is why God—who may make us and you into men of truth and evidence—has ordained for you.

But some of the Muslims have even affirmed that there can be attributed to God the power to combine the two opposites, and their dubious proof is that the judgement of our intellect that this is impossible is something which has been impressed on the intellect, whereas if there had been impressed on it the judgement that this is possible, it would not deny this possibility, but admit it. For such people it follows as a consequence that neither intellect nor existents have a well-defined nature, and that the truth which exists in the intellect does not correspond to the existence of existing things. The theologians themselves are ashamed of such a theory, but if they held it, it would be more consistent with their point of view than the contradictions in which their opponents involve them on this point. For their opponents try to find out where the difference lies between what as a matter of fact the theologians affirm on this point and what they deny, and it is very difficult for them to make this out—indeed they do not find anything but vague words. We find, therefore, that those most expert in the art of theological discussion take refuge in denying the necessary connexion between condition and conditioned, between a thing and its definition, between a thing and its cause and between a thing and its sign. All this is full of sophistry and is without sense, and the theologian who did this was Abu-l-Ma'ali. The general argument which solves these difficulties is that existents are divided into opposites and correlates, and if the latter could be separated, the former might be united, but opposites are not united and correlates therefore cannot be separated. And this is the wisdom of God and God's course in created things, and you will never find in God's course any alteration. And it is through the perception of this wisdom that the intellect of man becomes intellect, and the existence of such wisdom in the eternal intellect is the cause of its existence in reality. The intellect therefore is not a possible entity which might have been created with other qualities, as Ibn Hazm imagined.

V.

The Development of
Judaic Tradition

I N THE first century, Philo of Alexandria pioneered the communication of Old Testament teachings in the languages of Hellenistic philosophy. In one sense his effort marked the beginning of the public reception of the Bible into the cultural world of Hellenistic learning. It was also the beginning of the acceptance of secular learning, particularly philosophical learning, as an auxiliary in the communication of religious teaching, teaching accepted independently of philosophical argumentation. Subsequent Jewish, Christian, Secular, and Islamic thought were indebted to the first century work of the Alexandrine Philo for the ground beneath the agreements and disagreements of discussion. For, even in the rejection of many of Philo's specific concerns, ideas and formulations, subsequent teachers have learned from him.

Solomon Ibn Gabirol (Avicebron, A.D. 1021-1058) and Moses ben Maimon (Maimonides, 1135-1204) continued the Judaic tradition of Philo in bringing together sacred and secular learning. Both stand out as formidable historical influences within the general world of Western thought. Both, growing up within the Islamic world with its explicit heritage and development of various strains of classical learning, provide a bridge between East and West; both strongly influenced the thirteenth century achievements of Bonaventure and Aquinas.

Ibn Gabirol, born in Málaga and educated in Saragossa, set forth in the eleventh century to deal philosophically with the root difference between created being and uncreated being, between the God of the Bible and His creatures. He attacked the problem of describing this root difference in *Source of Life,* his major work, by reference to the internal constitution of the beings themselves. The basic difference he thought could be found in the composition of parts within every created being in contrast to the perfect simplicity, or oneness, of God.

The elaboration of this philosophical argumentation which seeks to establish the· natural knowability of the fact and the nature of composition within the various sorts of creatures involves the technicalities of the doctrines of composition of "matter and form" in all creatures and of a "plurality of forms" within material things, doctrines reminiscent of the universalistic, dialectical movement of platonic thought. In connection with these teachings we might note the importance of the subsequent discussion of various kinds of composition in Aquinas' treatment of the nature of God in his *Summa Theologica*.* The centrality of the teaching of the unity of God in the Old Testament is of greater interest. However general his influence, the presence of Ibn Gabirol was felt most importantly in the tradition of Franciscan philosophers and theologians in the thirteenth century and after, in such figures as Bonaventure and Duns Scotus. These, as did Ibn Gabirol, used a vocabulary strongly reminiscent of Aristotle, while devoted in great part to method and doctrine which tend in platonic fashion to find an ultimate identity between the order of things and the order of knowledge.

Moses Maimonides in the twelfth century is the culmination, within these first twelve centuries, of the merging of sacred and secular in the Judaic tradition. Maimonides was born in 1135 in Spain, in Cordova at the height of its great cultural and political power as capital of Moslem Andalusia. In 1148 a Moslem regime notably tolerant in matters of religion and culture was replaced by a Moslem regime fanatical in its rigorism. In the subsequent years in Spain, and in the years 1160-1165 in Morocco, the young Maimonides was to pursue religious and secular learning in a world of threatening intolerance, a world which only shortly before had known great freedom and cultural achievement. After a brief visit to a Palestine desolated by the warfare of the Second Crusade, he settled in Egypt—for a while in Alexandria—from 1166 until his death in 1204. Thus, in a special way, Maimonides represents as well the confluence of East and West.

In Egypt a tolerant Moslem government was to allow the essential freedoms for his life of productive learning. In time he was to be honored as court physician. In his life and in its effects we see the confluence of Jewish, Islamic and Christian forces within the

* Cf. I, qq. 3-26.

Mediterranean world. Within the world of Islam he moved from West to East, from the Spain which was shortly to provide the Paris of the thirteenth century with its greatest intellectual impetus, to the ancient Egypt which had known Philo, and before him the origin of Judaic tradition.

Maimonides' contribution to the world of learning may be partially summed up in the following: (a) the *Mishnah Torah,* Code of Jewish Jurisprudence, a high point in Rabbinic literature; (b) the *Guide of the Perplexed,* a reconciliation of religious teaching and secular learning; (c) ten books which deal with almost every phase of the study of medicine in his time.

The Guide of the Perplexed is often referred to as of singular importance in transmitting the thought of Aristotle. In the course of doing so, it communicated many central biblical teachings in a new way, a way differing from the longer tradition of religious communications along the lines of neoplatonic and stoic thought. For Aristotle himself there was a fundamental and irreducible multiplicity and variety obtaining within the fields of knowledge, and a basic distinction between the order of things and the order of knowledge. He placed an emphasis on logic as a preparatory and instrumental study. He showed concern for sharp definition and for metaphysics as essentially a separate and final reflection on all things and all knowledge.

In the particular teachings of Aristotle, such as that on the necessary eternity of the world, there is much to perplex the believer who would hold both to the biblical teaching of a divine creation in time and to learning pursued in the light of natural reason alone. Maimonides, setting out to use Aristotle's own tools, found Aristotle's arguments for the eternity of the world only persuasive, not demonstrative. Maimonides argued that the realities in the question of the eternity or temporality of the world are such as to escape being known with certitude through human knowledge. Maimonides' interpretation of *Genesis* in favor of the creation of the world in time is alive to the various modes of speech employed in biblical writing, and his somewhat flexible interpretation here incorporates a subtlety and judgment analogous to that employed in his interpretation of Aristotle.

Further, he rejects the arguments of such as the Mutakallimūn, Moslem teachers followed by many Jews, whom he thought tried much too readily to support religious teaching with philosophical arguments. For Maimonides, religious truths are sometimes not knowable through philosophy, and philosophical teachings in favor of religion are oftentimes poor philosophically. Presumed reconciliation too often distorts religion or reason or both. Efforts toward reconciliation are called for, nevertheless, in proper questions about, for example, the existence and attributes of God, the duration of the world and the problem of evil.

For Maimonides, the projected work of the *Guide* has impressive scope and goes well beyond the requirements of specific fields of study. He saw his task as requiring that he be thoroughly familiar with the variety of interpretations of Old Testament texts, and the varieties of schools of thought in areas of secular learning. In sum, he sought to deal *critically* with whole subject-matters, and with the positions of predecessors and contemporaries, with respect to: (1) religious learning, (2) secular learning, (3) the work of relating the two. In effect, the complex of interrelations on various levels of the sacred and the secular provides the issue which his work has joined with remarkable result.

In seeking to adapt the intellectuality of Aristotle to a philosophical inquiry into the existence and attributes of God, Maimonides provided a framework for Aquinas' criticism of theological language and argumentation in the *Summa Theologica*.* Through Aquinas, Maimonides has influenced the long Dominican tradition as Ibn Gabirol has influenced through Bonaventure the long Franciscan tradition. The sharing of the whole of the Old Testament by Jews and Christians, and the sharing of the religious and intellectual traditions of the East, were to facilitate a vast presence for the thought of Ibn Gabirol and Maimonides in that later rebirth of learning which was to come in the thirteenth century. The most basic intellectual differences of Ibn Gabirol and Maimonides will reappear in new social and religious contexts, then as today.

The interrelation of religious commitment and the pursuit of learning, whether in the direct study of the Bible and the Talmud or in such philosophic efforts as have just been indicated, has been a continuing feature of the Judaic tradition. The reinforcement of religious life by way of the cultivation of the intellect, and the

* Cf. I, qq. 13, 32.

encouragement through religious zeal of intellectual achievement, both deserve considerable reflection, not only for the sake of understanding historical phenomena, but also for the sake of understanding religion and learning in themselves.

A strong interaction between religious teaching and secular learning has been a mark of high points in the central period of Western civilization, and of the Judaic tradition within this period. The interaction has been at times one of mutual support, at times one of sharp conflicts, but interaction there has been. Should the forces of society within contemporary civilization drive us to a final disregard of this twofoldness, we may do well to surmise in terms of historical experience the consequences for intellectual, social and religious life.

26. SAADYA GAON: The Nature of Doubt and Belief

Saadya Ben Joseph Al-Fayyumi (A.D. 882-942) was born in Egypt where he lived for some thirty years. In A.D. 928 he was appointed head (Gaon) of the famous Jewish academy at Sura in Babylonia, and so is called Saadya Gaon. Saadya was thoroughly imbued with the rich developments in the Jewish tradition in contrast to Philo who, although a devout Jew, was more conversant with Greek thought than with Judaic tradition.

The three Judaic philosophers of this period presented in this volume spent their lives under Islamic rule. All three wrote in Arabic. Saadya Gaon translated the Bible into Arabic. Solomon Ibn Gabirol not only wrote in Arabic but was thought to be a Moslem by medieval Christians. Maimonides became physician in the court of Saladin, the ruler in Cairo.

In A.D. 933 Saadya wrote his most important philosophical work, *The Book of Doctrine and Beliefs*, which discusses the relationship between revelation and reason. Similarly, to some Moslems he tried to clarify major problems of faith, science, and life. But he also dealt with the specifically Judaic theme of tradition.

In "The Nature of Doubt and Belief"* he recognized that doubt is a normal state of affairs in the initial stages of knowledge. True knowledge does not come easily and attaining it takes time. One must simplify by analysis the complex problem that one first encounters. This requires time, and one can have certainty and knowledge only at the end of this process of analytic discrimination. Prior to the attainment of certain knowledge one is naturally in a state of doubt.

In "The Four Roots of Knowledge"† he pointed out that three of the sources of knowledge are common to all mankind and thus require no particular religious allegiance. They are: 1) the immediate sense perception, 2) the judgment we make especially in matters of rational self-evident truths, and 3) inferences and conclusions produced by reason on

---

* "Prolegomena, II," Saadya Gaon, *Book of Doctrines and Beliefs*, trans. Alexander Altmann, in *Three Jewish Philosophers* (New York: Harper & Row Publishers Inc., 1965). Used by permission.
† "Prolegomena, III," Saadya Gaon, *op. cit.* Used by permission.

the basis of sense perceptions and rational judgment. The fourth root of knowledge is primarily available only to adherents of Judaism, and that is reliable or authentic tradition. Although the fourth source of knowledge is to some extent dependent on the first three, it has its own integrity and authenticity as a distinct source of truth.

One might ask: "How can it be reconciled with the wisdom of the Creator (be He exalted and glorified) that He allowed errors and doubts to arise in the minds of His creatures?" We may answer this question at once by saying that the very fact that they are created beings causes them to be subject to error and delusion. For according to the order of Creation they require for every work which they undertake a certain measure of time in which to complete it stage after stage. Cognition being one of their activities, it undoubtedly comes under the same rule. In its initial stage, their knowledge proceeds from a complex, vague and confused idea of things, but by their faculty of Reason they purify and clarify it in a continual process until, after a certain measure of time, their errors are removed, and a clear idea is formed without any admixture of doubt.[1] And just as every productive art is carried out by successive operations and remains incomplete if those performing it desist from it prior to its completion—such as sowing, building, weaving and the other kinds of productive work which can only be accomplished by the worker's persisting in it patiently until the end—so the work of acquiring knowledge demands that one should start from the beginning and proceed chapter after chapter until the final stage is reached. At the beginning there may be, for example, ten doubts; at the second stage they will be reduced to nine, at the third to eight, and if a man continues to reason and

---

[1] Saadya describes the process of cognition as a successive elimination of doubts. It consists of three stages: (*a*) the complex impression, which gives only a vague idea as to the nature of the object of enquiry; (*b*) the act of analysing this idea; (*c*) the acceptance of the final truth by an act of belief which is free from doubt. In his *Comm. Yes. . . . ,* Saadya speaks of the three operations of synthesis, analysis and belief which constitute the three stages in the process of cognition. He finds these three faculties expressed in the formula used by the *Sefer Yeṣirah,* "Know, reflect, preserve" (*da' we-hashōb u-neṣōr*). The faculty of synthesis presents the object in its concrete entirety; the faculty of analysis eliminates what is faulty and confirms what is correct in the impression; the faculty of belief adopts and conserves the knowledge established by the two preceding faculties. . . .

to reflect, his doubts will in this way be further reduced until, at the final stage, there will emerge in full clarity the one proposition which formed the object of his search, and which stands out clearly defined, with no error or doubt attached to it . . . Now were he to abandon his speculation when he arrived at the fifth or fourth or any other stage, the doubts which attended the preceding stages of his reflection would be removed, but there would still remain with him the doubts attached to the remaining stages in front of him. If he retains in his mind the result of his speculation up to the point which he reached, he may hope to return to this point and complete the inquiry. If he fails to retain it, he will have to start his inquiry afresh. For this reason many people have gone astray and spurned wisdom. Some of them are ignorant of the road that leads to it, others whilst taking the road fail to complete the journey and get lost, as Scripture says, "The man that strayeth out of the way of understanding shall rest in the congregation of the shades" (Prov. 21.16).

With regard to those who fail to reach the goal of wisdom the Sages of Israel have said, "With the increase in numbers of the disciples of Shammai and Hillel, who did not advance far enough in their studies, the controversies increased."[2] This utterance of theirs shows that if the disciples carry through their studies to the end, no controversy or discord arises amongst them. Let not therefore the fool in his impatience lay the blame for his own fault on the Creator (be He exalted and glorified) by saying that He implanted these doubts in him, whereas it is his own ignorance or impatience which threw him into confusion, as we have explained. Nor is it possible that any action of his can, by a single stroke, remove all doubt. For if it could, it would transcend the sphere of created beings, to which he belongs. Another person may not attach any blame for this fault of his to God,[3] but desires God to impart to him the ability to know with a knowledge that is free from doubt. Such a one asks for noth-

---

[2] *b. Sanh.* 88b; the passage is also quoted by R. Sherira Gaon in his famous *Letter* where he gives an historical account of the origin and development of Rabbinic controversies. He explains that the Hadrianic persecutions made it impossible for the disciples to complete their studies. Cf. *Iggeret de-Rabbenu Sherira Gaon*, ed. A. Hyman (London, 1910), p. 22.

[3] . . . Saadya now turns to those who, whilst not blaming God for their own fault, nevertheless, act stupidly by desiring a kind of knowledge which is peculiar to God.

ing less than to be like God. For the one who possesses immediate knowledge[4] is the Creator of the universe (be He blessed and sanctified) as we shall explain later when we come to this matter again. The knowledge of all created beings, however, is only possible through the intermediacy of causes, i.e. through inquiry and speculation, which require time as we have described. From the first until the last moment of this period of time they must remain in doubt as we have explained, and they are the praiseworthy ones who persist until they have cleansed the silver from the dross, as is said, "Take away the dross from the silver, and there cometh forth a vessel for the refiner" (Prov. 25.4); and until their churning has produced butter, as is said, "For the churning of milk bringeth forth curd" (Prov. 30.33); and until their seed sprouts and can be reaped, as is said, "Sow to yourselves according to righteousness, reap according to mercy" (Hosea 10.12); and until the fruit has ripened on their tree and turned into nourishing food, as is said, ". . . A tree of life to them that lay hold upon her" (Prov. 3.18).

Having thus dealt sufficiently with the origin of error and doubt, it is now fitting that we should explain the nature of Belief. We affirm that this is an idea arising in the soul as to what an object of knowledge really is: when the idea is clarified by speculation, Reason comprehends it, accepts it, and makes it penetrate the soul and become absorbed into it; then man believes this idea which he has attained, and he preserves it in his soul for another time or other times, as is said, "Wise men lay up knowledge" (Prov. 10.14), and as is further said, "Receive, I pray thee, instructions from His mouth, and lay up His words in thy heart" (Job 22.22).

Belief is of two kinds, true or false. True belief means believing a thing to be as it really is, the large as large, the small as small, the black as black, the white as white, the existing as existing, the non-existing as non-existing. False belief means believing a thing to be the opposite of what it really is, the large as small, the small as large, the white as black, the black as white, the existing as non-existing, and the non-existing as existing. The wise man, who deserves praise, is the one who fixes his attention on the realities of things, and adapts his belief to them. Thanks to his wisdom he relies on that which can indeed be relied on and guards against that which

[4] Lit. "Knowledge without cause," i.e. without the effort of inquiry and speculation.

must be guarded against. The fool, who is blameworthy, is the one who makes his belief the standard, and decrees that the realities of things must follow his belief. Thanks to his folly he relies on that which should be guarded against, and guards against that which can be relied on, as is said, "A wise man feareth, and departeth from evil, but the fool behaveth overbearingly, and is confident" (Prov. 14.16).

In this connection I should like to refer to certain people who cause me astonishment. Though really servants they think they have no master, and they feel confident that what they reject is false and what they affirm is correct. These people are sunk in the depths of foolishness and stand on the brink of the abyss. If they are right, let the poor man believe that his boxes and baskets are full of money, and let him see what it will profit him. Or let one believe that he is seventy years of age when he is forty, and let him see what that will benefit him. Or let him believe that he is well fed whilst he is starving or that he has drunk his fill whilst he is thirsty, or that he is well clothed whilst he is naked. Let him see in what condition he will find himself. Another one belonging to this sort of people, who has a dangerous enemy, may believe that his enemy has already died and perished, and he fears him no more. How quickly there will come upon him the evil that he apprehends not! The height of folly, however, is reached by those people who think that because they do not believe in divine authority they are free from God's commandments and prohibitions, from His promise and warning, and all that these imply. Scripture describes such people as saying, "Let us break His bonds asunder, and cast away His cords from us" (Ps. 2.3).

Some people in India try to make themselves insensitive to fire, but it still burns them whenever they touch it. Others laying claim to self-denial inure themselves to be flogged and whipped, but they nevertheless suffer pain every moment they are beaten. How much more severe will be the lot of those who brazenly defy the Creator of the universe. Apart from their ignorance, they will not escape what His wisdom had imposed on them, as is said, "He is wise in heart, and mighty in strength; who hath hardened himself against Him and prospered?" (Job 9.4).

27. SAADYA GAON: The Four Roots of Knowledge*

Having completed the inquiry with which we were first concerned, it is desirable that we should now mention the sources[1] of truth and certainty, which are the origin of all knowledge and the fountain of all cognition.[2] We shall discuss the matter so far as it has a bearing on the subject of this book. We affirm then that there exist three sources of knowledge:[3] (1) The knowledge given by sense perception;[4] (2) the knowledge given by Reason; (3) inferential knowledge.[5] We proceed now to give an explanation of each of these Roots.

By the knowledge of sense perception we understand that which a man perceives by one of the five senses, i.e. sight, hearing, smell, taste, and touch.[6] By the knowledge of Reason we understand that which is derived purely from the mind,[7] such as the approval of truth and the disapproval of falsehood. By inferential knowledge we understand a proposition which a man cannot deny without being compelled to deny at the same time some proposition obtained from Reason or sense perception. Where there is no way of denying these propositions, the previous proposition must of necessity be accepted. E.g., we are compelled to admit that man possesses a soul, although we do not perceive it by our senses, so as not to deny its obvious functions. Similarly, we are compelled to admit that the soul is endowed with Reason, although we do not perceive it by our senses, so as not to deny its (Reason's) obvious function.

We have found many people who reject these three Roots of

* See Introduction to Selection 26.
[1] Lit. "matters" (Arab. *mawādd*, from sing. *mādda*, matter), a term used by Saadya in the sense of source, origin.
[2] Having dealt with the origin of error and doubt, Saadya now turns to a discussion of the origin of their opposites, i.e. truth and certainty.
[3] An additional fourth source of knowledge, that of reliable tradition, will be mentioned further below.
[4] Lit. "the knowledge of the eye witness."
[5] Lit. "knowledge arrived at by (logical) necessity."
[6] This is the order in which the senses are enumerated by Aristotle, and following him, by most Arabic and Jewish philosophers.
[7] I.e. unaided by sense perception. Saadya refers to self-evident axioms of reason.

Knowledge. A few of them deny the first root. I shall deal with them in chapter I of this book and refute their arguments.[8] By denying the first root they (implicitly) deny the second and third as well since these are based on it. A larger group of people admit the first root, but deny the second and third. I shall deal with their view as well in chapter I and refute their arguments. Most people, however, admit the first two roots and deny the third one. The reason of this unequal distribution of views lies in the fact that the second type of knowledge is more hidden[9] than the first, and likewise the third more hidden than the second. Naturally, one is more readily inclined to deny what is hidden than what is obvious. There are also people who alternately deny a type of knowledge and approve another just as it suits them in their opposition to other people's views.[10] Each group of these affirms what their opponents reject, and claims that it is driven by inexorable logic to its own view. Some people, for instance, affirm that all things are in a state of rest, and deny that there is any movement, whereas others affirm that all things move, and deny that there is any rest.[11] Each group stigmatizes the arguments put forward by its opponents as inconclusive and erroneous. But we, the Congregation of the Believers in the Unity of God, accept the truth of all the three sources of knowledge,[12] and we add a fourth source, which we derive from the three preceding ones, and which has become a Root of Knowledge for us, namely, the truth of reliable Tradition.[13] For it is based on the knowledge of sense perception and the knowledge of Reason, as we shall explain in chapter 3 of this book.

These four Roots of Knowledge having been specified, we have now to explain in which way we may rely on them for evidence of truth.

[8] In a passage not included in this Selection.

[9] I.e. less obvious and evident.

[10] The version given above is based on the reading of the Leningrad recension.

[11] Saadya refers to the well-known controversy between Parmenides and Heraclitos, which was resumed by the Mutakallimūn.

[12] The distinction between the three sources of knowledge as stated by Saadya was also upheld by the "Faithful Brethren of Basra", but they defined Reason as that which is acquired by speculation, not as the axioms of self-evident truth.

[13] Arab. al-chabar aṣ-ṣādik. The Arabic term denotes both Kur'ān and tradition. Saadya comprises in this term the written and oral traditions of Judaism.

First with regard to the knowledge of sense perception, whenever an object makes an impression on our normal sense organ by coming into contact with it,[14] we may safely believe without any doubt that it is in reality as we perceived it, provided we are sufficiently expert not to be misled by illusions, like the people who believe that the image which appears in the mirror is an image which has been actually created there, the truth being that it is the property of polished bodies to reflect the image of an object that faces them; or like those people who regard the image of a man's stature which appears in the water reversed as real and created in that moment, not knowing that the reason for this is that the depth of the water exceeds the height of the stature. If we are careful to avoid these and similar mistakes, the belief in sense perception will prove sound, and we shall not be misled by illusions, as is said, "And they rose up early in the morning, and the sun shone upon the water, and the Moabites saw the water some way off as red as blood; and they said: This is blood" (2 Kings 3.22-3).

As to the knowledge of reason we hold that every conception formed in our mind (reason) which is free from defects is undoubtedly true knowledge, provided we know how to reason, complete the act of reasoning and guard against illusions and dreams. For there are people who affirm that the images one sees in a dream are real things which are created.[15] They are driven to this assumption in order not to have to reject the testimony of the senses. They do not know that some dreams are produced from the thoughts of yesterday which pass through the mind; of these it is said, "For a dream cometh through a multitude of business" (Eccl. 5.2); or that other dreams are due to the food they have eaten, which may have been too hot or too cold, too much or too little; in regard to these Scripture says, ". . . As when a hungry man dreameth, and, behold, he eateth . . . or as when a thirsty man dreameth, and, behold, he drinketh . . ." (Isa. 29.8); or that still other dreams are caused by the preponderance of one of the humours in the tem-

[14] Saadya holds, with Aristotle, that perception comes about when a particular element in an object comes in contact with the same element in the sense organ. Cf. *Amānāt*, p. 60 (32); Aristotle, *De sensu*, 2.

[15] Ibn Hazm reports that in the opinion of Ṣāliḥ Kubba, one of the disciples of the Muʿtazilite al-Nazzām, everything one sees in dreams conforms to reality: an inhabitant of Andalusia who sees himself in China whilst dreaming must have been actually transferred by God to China during that moment.

perament[16]—the hot and the moist create the illusion of joy and pleasure, while the dry produces the illusion of grief and sorrow; of this suffering Job[17] said, "When I say: my bed shall comfort me, my couch shall ease my complaint; then Thou scarest me with dreams, and terrifiest me through visions" (Job 7.13-14). But dreams also contain a flash of inspiration from above in the form of illuminating hints and images, as is said, "In thoughts from the visions of the night, when deep sleep falleth on men" (Job 4.13).

As to inferential knowledge the position is this: if we perceive a certain object with our senses and accept it as actually existing, but are unable to believe firmly that this object exists unless we believe that some other things co-exist with it, then it is necessary for us to believe in the existence of all those things be they a few or many. For the sense perception concerned could not have come to us without them. There may be one such inferred object or there may be two, three, four or more. Whatever the conclusion may be, it must be upheld because neither the sense perception nor any of these inferential notions can be denied.

An example of the inference of a single object is the following: if we see smoke without seeing the fire which produces the smoke, it is necessary for us to believe in the existence of the fire on account of the existence of the smoke because the one could not be accounted for without the other. Similarly, if we hear the voice of a man from behind a wall, it is necessary for us to believe in his presence there, for there could be no voice of a man unless from one who was present. An example of more than one single inference is the case when we see food being absorbed into the stomach of an animal in solid form and re-emerge in the form of waste. If we do not believe in the performance of four different functions, our sense perception could not be accounted for. These functions are performed (1) by the power of attracting nourishment into the body; (2) the power of retaining the food until it is thoroughly softened; (3) the power of digestion and assimilation; and (4) the power of expelling from the body what has become waste.[18] Since our sense perception can

---

[16] . . . The four humours correspond to the four qualities (warm, cold, dry, moist) and to the four temperaments.

[17] Lit. "the suffering man smitten with illness."

[18] A detailed description of these four faculties and their functions is given by Josef b. Yehudah, the disciple of Maimonides, in his *Sefer Mussar* (ed. W. Bacher), pp. 43-6.

only be accounted for by the performance of these four functions, it is necessary to believe that they actually take place.

The character of inferential knowledge having been explained, it is necessary for us to draw attention to certain mistakes against which one must guard, for most of the controversies between men and most of their differences in methods of argument arise from these mistakes.

(1) If someone declares that he believes in such and such a thing, because otherwise he would have to deny some sense perception, it is necessary for us to consider whether the sense perception could occur without that other thing which he believes. If this is the case, his belief is invalidated. Some people, for instance, believe that the whiteness of the Milky Way, which is testified by sense perception, is due to the fact that originally the rotation of the sun followed that course.[19] But if we examine the facts we find that other explanations are possible. The phenomenon may be caused by rising vapours or by fixed luminous particles or by an accumulation of small stars or similar causes. Thus their statement is invalidated.

(2) If someone declares that he believes in such and such a thing because, otherwise, he would have to deny some proposition furnished by Reason, it is necessary for us to consider whether this proposition would be true without the thing which he believes. In such case his belief would be invalidated. Some people, for instance, assert that there exists more than one earth. They argue that fire must occupy the centre of the universe since the most precious thing is invariably placed in the centre so as to be well guarded.[20] But in our opinion this belief[21] is equally safeguarded by our knowledge that man lives upon this earth which is the centre of the universe.[22] Thus their assertion is invalidated.

(3) If someone declares that he believes that such and such an inference must be drawn from some sense perception, but this belief

---

[19] Cf. Aristotle, *Meteorologica*, I, 8, in the name of some Pythagoreans.

[20] Cf. Aristotle, *De Caelo*, II, 13, 293a, in the name of the Pythagoreans. The assumption is that the fire is the most precious element and must therefore be surrounded by a circle of earths since "the most precious place befits the most precious thing."

[21] I.e. the proposition derived purely from the reason that the most precious thing is always placed in the centre.

[22] If we assign central importance to the human race, we must assume that the earth is placed in the centre of the universe.

of his is inconsistent with some other sense perception, we have to weigh which is the more decisive of the two sense perceptions and judge accordingly. Some people, for instance, assert that all things originated from water[23] because all living beings come from a moist substance.[24] But they ignore another testimony of their senses, namely the fact that water is fluid and flows off. It is impossible to assume that it is the basic element[25] seeing that it cannot stay by itself. If two arguments like these clash, it is proper that we should give preference to the more decisive one.

(4) If someone declares that he believes that such and such an inference must be drawn from some sense perception, but his statement involves a contradiction, it must be considered as false. Some people, for instance, assert that the good is identical with the pleasant,[26] because this is what sense perception suggests to them. But they fail to remember that to kill them affords pleasure to their enemies in much the same way as killing their enemies affords pleasure to them. Thus good and evil will be present in the same act, which is self-contradictory.

(5) If someone declares that he believes such and such a thing for such and such a reason, and, upon examining his reason, we find that it necessitates something different which he does not believe, his belief is rendered invalid.[27] Those, for instance, who affirm the pre-existence of the world, declare that they believe the universe to be without beginning in time, because they want to accept as true only what they perceive with their senses. But if they accept as true only what their senses perceive, this principle should also preclude their view that the world is without beginning in time, since it is impossible for them to perceive with their senses the timeless in its original state.

Likewise, if someone declares that he rejects such and such a thing for such and such a reason, but we find that in fact he involves himself in an even greater difficulty than the one he tried to avoid, his assertion will be invalid. Thus some of those who affirm the

23 The well-known view of Thales of Milet.

24 Arab. *'unsur*; element, origin.

25 Lit. "root."

26 The hedonistic view of the Epicureans, which dominates also Plato's earlier dialogues.

27 In other words, a belief which does not conform to the principle on which it is assumedly based is inadmissible.

Unity of God refuse to admit that God is unable to bring back yesterday, so as not to attribute to him any lack of power, but they involve themselves in an even more serious difficulty in that they attribute to Him something absurd, as will be pointed out, please God, in part of chapter 2.

In endeavouring to establish the truth of inferential knowledge we shall henceforth be on guard against these five possible forms of mistakes, namely, (1) that it does not conflict with knowledge established by sense perception; (2) that it does not conflict with knowledge established by Reason; (3) that it should not conflict with some other truths; (4) that it should not be self-contradictory, still more that it should not (5) involve a difficulty more serious than the one intended to avoid. The first and primary condition, however, is that we should carefully apply our experience[28] to our interpretation of sense perceptions and of the dictates of Reason as described. In addition, we have to persevere in the work of rational inquiry until its final completion so that altogether seven conditions have to be fulfilled in order to bring out the clear truth. If, therefore, someone who is not a member of our people comes forward with certain arguments based on inferential knowledge we have to examine his statement in the light of the above seven conditions. If it stands their test and is proved correct when weighed in their balances, it is the clear truth which we, too, have to accept.

We shall employ similar rules in dealing with the reliable Tradition, that is to say the Books of the Prophets. But this is not the place to explain the conditions peculiar to them. I have explained them at length in the Introduction to the Commentary on the Torah.

28. IBN GABIROL: Spirit in Matter

Solomon Ibn Gabirol (1021-1058) was the first Judaic philosopher in Islamic Spain. His major philosophical work, *The Source of Life*, was translated from Arabic into Latin in the twelfth century.

Like Plotinus and Erigena, Gabirol saw the universe as a series of emanations, a process of increasingly specific forms. The form of

---

[28] Which teaches us to guard against illusions and dreams.

corporeity makes a thing a physical body; a vegetative soul or form makes a thing alive, etc. A number of these forms can coexist in the same substance, and the substance is made to be a certain type of thing by the particular combination of forms present in it.

But to constitute an individual, even a unique set of forms is insufficient. According to Gabirol, matter is the universal principle of individuation, except in God. Thus there must be two kinds of matter: a spiritual, subtle matter to individuate spiritual beings such as angels and the human soul, and a gross, coarse matter to individuate physical corporeal beings. For Gabirol, then, all things other than God are composed of matter and form.

The present selection* focuses on the question of how spirit, e.g., the human soul, can be present in physical matter, e.g., the human body.

Pupil: Although the doubt regarding the union of a multitude of things in a single thing is removed, yet two other doubts have assailed me, that are not smaller than this one. It may be asked how the spiritual forms become corporeal, and how the corporeal accident arises from a spiritual substance.

Master: What we have already said in discussing this question is sufficient. But I am going to repeat it briefly. (1) I assert that whenever two contrary things unite, from their union arises a thing that is not one of them such as they were individually. Now since the simple substance is contrary to the compound substance, it is necessary that from their union there should arise another thing that is not one of them. Such is the form borne by the compound substance, for this form is not spiritual absolutely since it is borne by the corporeal matter. Similarly, it is not corporeal absolutely either, because it is more simple than the matter and can be borne sometimes, divested of matter, by the soul. (2) Furthermore, the corporeal matter is finite and contracted, and whenever a thing is finite and contracted, the form diffused on it by the substance that is before it extends over its surface and exists in it. It is therefore necessary that the form diffused by the simple substance on the corporeal matter should extend on its surface and exist in it, for the form follows the matter by taking on a contour and a figure. Thus, since the matter is in itself corporeal, it is necessary that the form diffused on it by the spiritual substance should also be spiritual.

* From *Fons Vitae,* Third Tractate, trans. Harry E. Wedeck (New York: Philosophical Library, 1962). Used by permission.

(3) Furthermore, the form regularly penetrates the matter that receives it, when the latter is ready to receive it, because the first form that comprehends all forms penetrates into the first matter and is diffused in it, as has been shown before. For if the matter is subtle, the form is diffused in it, dispersed and hidden, with the result that it escapes the senses. If, on the contrary, the matter is coarse, the form has less power to penetrate it and to be diffused through it. Then the essence of the form contracts and does not divide, so that it becomes sensible on account of its contraction: for when the essence of a thing contracts, this thing becomes corporeal and is presented to the senses: and, inversely, when the essence of a thing divides, it becomes more subtle and evades the senses. (4) The emanation of the spiritual forms on the corporeal forms and the subsequent appearance of the corporeal forms in the corporeal matter may be compared to the emanation of light on bodies and the subsequent appearance of colors.

Pupil: Show me and explain it to me.

Master: It is evident that colors are perceived by their essence and that they are not perceived by their deprivation. Now the cause of this is that light in itself is spiritual and subtle. That is why the essence, that is, its form, is invisible, unless it unites with a body that has a surface, and when it does not unite with a body that has a surface, its form is bidden and evades the senses. Thus the light diffused in the air, whose form is not perceived by the senses before it is diffused over a solid body, for example, the earth, so that the light appears and becomes perceptible. And when the form of the light appears on the surface of the body, the form of the color then appears, borne by it, since it is impossible for the form of the light to appear without the form of the color.

Here is the proof: The form of the light appears when it unites with the surface of the body. And as the surface bears in it the essence of the color, it is necessary that the light that unites with the surface should unite also with the color when it unites with the surface. And it is necessary that the color should appear with the appearance of the light. The argumentation regarding the perception of the light with the color proceeds as follows: The light of the sight unites with the light of the sun on account of its resemblance to it. Now the light of the sun unites with its color. Therefore the light of the sight unites with the color. Similarly with another mode of reasoning. The light unites with the color borne by the surface of the body. Now the light appears when it unites with the surface. Therefore the color appears when the light unites with the surface.

And with God's assistance, consider, following this reasoning, the way in which the spiritual form spreads over the corporeal matter. Compare the spiritual form that is in the simple substance to the light of the sun; compare the form diffused over the matter to the light that is on the surface of the body, and compare the color to the corporeal form that is in the corporeal matter in potentiality, for the color is in the body in potentiality. And by comparing these forms with each other, you will see that the corporeal form that is in the matter in potentiality becomes perceptible when it unites with it in the form emanating from the spirtual form on the matter. Thus the color that is in the body is in potentiality, but becomes perceptible when it unites with it the light emanating from the light of the sun on the body. And you will thus realize that the form emanating from the spiritual form on the matter appears to the sense when it unites with the corporeal form that is in the matter in potentiality, for these two forms become one only, as the light diffused on the surface of the body appears to the senses when it unites with the surface of the body, this light and the color becoming a single thing.

Pupil: Thanks to the four methods that you have enumerated, I understand how the spiritual form becomes corporeal when it unites with the corporeal matter. Show me then how it is possible for an accidental form to come from a spiritual substance.

Master: There are two possible answers to this question. One consists in saying that the corporeal form is not by itself an accident but a substance, since it completes the essence of the matter that bears it, and it is not called accident except by comparison to the matter that bears it.

The second answer consists in saying, admitting that it is an accident, that this form does not emanate from the essence of the simple substance, that is, from the matter that bears the form of this substance, but that it is drawn from its form, which is an accident of the matter that bears it, although it is a substance since it completes the essence of the simple substance. And if it is said of the form borne by the compound substance that it is a substance, it is because it emanates from the form of the simple substance, which is a substance.

Therefore since the form borne by the matter of the simple substance is a substance in itself and an accident because it is borne by the matter of the simple substance, nothing prevents the form emanating from it into the compound substance from also being a substance in itself and also an accident because it is borne by the matter of the compound substance.

Pupil: Why is the primal form called substantial and not substance, when it completes the essence of the matter, which is a substance?

Master: Because it can exist only in the matter which it subsists.

Pupil: If then the form that subsists in the compound matter is a substance, there is no accident.

Master: It cannot be declared absolutely that the form such as quantity and certain kinds of quality is an accident, for quantity is an inseparable form of the essence of the substance and it completes it, and similarly certain qualities are substantial differences, on which depends the existence of the essence of the substance in which they are. But in respect of the other categories, it cannot be said that they are substances.

29. MAIMONIDES: Proving God's Existence

Rabbi Moses ben Maimon (A.D. 1135-1204) is better known as Maimonides; his best known work, *The Guide of the Perplexed* (1190), was written in Arabic and only later translated into Hebrew. His purpose was to resolve the apparent conflict between religion and philosophy. Educated Jews had been brought up in the traditional teaching of Judaism and some also had been trained in the secular wisdom and science of Greece as transmitted through Islamic sources. They were confused or perplexed by the clash between religion and science and this led some to doubt one or the other. Maimonides wrote the *Guide* for them.

He sought to demonstrate that any conflict between science and religion is only apparent and comes from a misinterpretation of either Scripture or the writings of the philosophers. Scripture abounds in anthropomorphic expressions that should not be taken literally. That is, there are many "homonyms," metaphorical or allegorical words and passages, that should be properly interpreted. Likewise, philosophy has limitations arising out of its rational sources and procedures. The *Guide* is a complicated book, and as Maimonides himself says, it was written neither for beginners nor for popular consumption. But like Averroes, Maimonides held that for those who have the capacity for it, the study of philosophy is not prohibited, is recommended, and is even a positive religious obligation.

The selection entitled "Proving God's Existence" is taken from the beginning of the Second Part of the *Guide*.* He lists there twenty-six principles drawn from Aristotle and aristotelian commentators. He offers no argument for the truth of these principles, but refers the reader to the original sources for detailed proof. His purpose is to establish the philosophic grounds for the classical proof of the existence of God from motion. This proof follows in the next chapter of the *Guide* (selection 29b).

The second selection, "The Meaning of Wisdom," is the final chapter of the *Guide* (Third Part).† It is a fitting and inspiring conclusion to a work of wisdom that attempts a creative synthesis of the sacred and the secular.

a. [The Aristotelian Principles]

In the name of the Lord, God of the World[1]

The premises[2] needed for establishing the existence of the deity, may He be exalted, and for the demonstration that He is neither a body nor a force in a body and that He, may His name be sublime, is one, are twenty-five—all of which are demonstrated without there being a doubt as to any point concerning them. For Aristotle and the Peripatetics after him have come forward with a demonstration for every one of them. There is one premise that we will grant them, for through it the objects of our quest will be demonstrated, as I shall make clear; this premise is the eternity of the world.

1] The first premise: The existence of any infinite magnitude is impossible.

---

* From Moses Maimonides: *The Guide of the Perplexed*, trans. Shlomo Pines, Introduction to Part II and 1st chapter (Chicago: University of Chicago Press, 1963). Used by permission.

† Maimonides: *op. cit.*, Part III, Chapter 54. Used by permission.

[1] Gen. 21:33.

[2] No example prior to Maimonides of a list of twenty-five or twenty-six "premises" seems to be known.

2] The second premise: The existence of magnitudes of which the number is infinite is impossible—that is, if they exist together.[3]

3] The third premise: The existence of causes and effects of which the number is infinite is impossible, even if they are not endowed with magnitude. For instance, the assumption that one particular intellect, for example, has as its cause a second intellect, and that the cause of this second intellect is a third one, and that of the third a fourth, and so on to infinity, is likewise clearly impossible.

4] The fourth premise: Change exists in four categories: it exists in the category of substance, the changes occurring in a substance being generation and corruption. It exists in the category of quantity, namely, as growth and decrease. It exists in the category of quality, namely, as alteration. It exists in the category of place, namely, as the motion of translation. It is this change in the category of place that is more especially called motion.

5] The fifth premise: Every motion is a change and transition from potentiality to actuality.

6] The sixth premise: Of motions, some are essential and some accidental, some are violent and some are motions of a part—this being a species of accidental motion. Now essential motion is, for example, the translation of a body from one place to another. Accidental motion is, for example, when a blackness existing in this particular body is said to be translated from one place to another. Violent motion is, for example, the motion of a stone upwards through the action of something constraining it to that. Motion of a part is, for example, the motion of a nail in a ship; for when the ship is in motion, we say that the nail is likewise in motion. Similarly when any compound is in motion as a whole, its parts are likewise said to be in motion.

7] The seventh premise: Everything changeable is divisible. Hence everything movable is divisible and is necessarily a body. But everything that is indivisible is not movable; hence it will not be a body at all.

8] The eighth premise: Everything that is moved owing to accident must of necessity come to rest, inasmuch as its motion is not in virtue of its essence. Hence it cannot be moved forever in that accidental motion.

[3] Or: simultaneously.

9] The ninth premise: Every body that moves another body moves the latter only through being itself in motion when moving the other body.

10] The tenth premise: Everything that is said to be in a body is divided into two classes: either it subsists through the body, as do the accidents, or the body subsists through it, as in the case of the natural form. Both classes are to be considered as a force in the body.

11] The eleventh premise: Some of the things that subsist through body are sometimes divided through the division of the body and hence are divisible according to accident, as for instance the colors and the other forces that are distributed through the whole of the body. In a like manner some of the things that constitute a body are not divisible in any way, as for instance the soul and the intellect.

12] The twelfth premise: Every force that is found distributed through a body is finite because the body is finite.

13] The thirteenth premise: It is impossible that one of the species of motion be continuous, except local motion, and of this only that which is circular.

14] The fourteenth premise: Local motion is the primary and the first by nature among all motions; for generation and corruption are preceded by alteration, and alteration is preceded by the approach of that which alters to that which is to be altered; and there is no growth and diminution except when they are preceded by generation and corruption.

15] The fifteenth premise: Time is an accident consequent upon motion and is necessarily attached to it. Neither of them exists without the other. Motion does not exist except in time, and time cannot be conceived by the intellect except together with motion. And all that with regard to which no motion can be found, does not fall under time.

16] The sixteenth premise: In whatsoever is not a body, multiplicity cannot be cognized by the intellect, unless the thing in question is a force in a body, for then the multiplicity of the individual forces would subsist in virtue of the multiplicity of the matters or substances in which these forces are to be found.[4] Hence no multiplicity at all can be cognized by the intellect in the separate

---

[4] Literally: of their matters and substrata.

things, which are neither a body nor a force in a body, except when they are causes and effects.

17] The seventeenth premise: Everything that is in motion has of necessity a mover; and the mover either may be outside the moved object, as in the case of a stone moved by a hand, or the mover may be in the body in motion, as in the case of the body of a living being, for the latter is composed of a mover and of that which is moved. It is for this reason that when a living being dies and the mover—namely, the soul—is lacking from it, that which is moved—namely, the organic body—remains at the moment in its former state, except that it is not moved with that motion. However, inasmuch as the mover that exists in that which is moved is hidden and does not appear to the senses, it is thought of living beings that they are in motion without having a mover. Everything moved that has a mover within itself is said to be moved by itself—the meaning being that the force moving that which, in the object moved, is moving according to essence, exists in the whole of that object.

18] The eighteenth premise: Everything that passes from potentiality to actuality has something other than itself that causes it to pass, and this cause is of necessity outside that thing. For if that cause were that thing and there were no obstacle to prevent this passage, the thing would not have been for a certain time in potentia but would have always been in actu. If, however, the cause of the passage from potentiality to actuality subsisted in the thing, and if there was at the same time an obstacle to it, which was subsequently removed, there is no doubt that the factor that put an end to the obstacle is the one that caused that potentiality to pass into actuality. Understand this.

19] The nineteenth premise: Everything that has a cause for its existence is only possible with regard to existence in respect to its own essence. For it exists if its causes are present. If, however, they are not present, or if they become nonexistent, or if their relation that entails the existence of the thing in question has changed, that thing does not exist.

20] The twentieth premise: Everything that is necessarily existent in respect to its own essence has no cause for its existence in any way whatever or under any condition.

21] The twenty-first premise: Everything that is composed of two notions has necessarily that composition as the cause of its existence as it really is, and consequently is not necessarily existent in respect to its own essence, for it exists in virtue of the existence of its two parts and of their composition.

22] The twenty-second premise: Every body is necessarily composed of two things and is necessarily accompanied by accidents. The two things constituting it are its matter and its form; and the accidents accompanying it are quantity, shape, and position.

23] The twenty-third premise: It is possible for whatsoever is in potentia and in whose essence there is a certain possibility, not to exist in actu at a certain time.

24] The twenty-fourth premise: Whatsoever is something in potentia is necessarily endowed with matter, for possibility is always in matter.

25] The twenty-fifth premise: The principles of an individual compound substance are matter and form. And there is no doubt about the necessity of there being an agent, I mean to say a mover that moves the substratum so as to predispose it to receive the form. That is the proximate mover, which predisposes the matter of a certain individual. At this point it is necessary to engage in speculation with regard to motion, the mover, and the moved. However, with regard to all this, everything that it was necessary to explain has already been explained. The text of the words of Aristotle is: Matter does not move itself.[5] This therefore is the capital premise calling for an inquiry concerning the existence of the Prime Mover.

Of the twenty-five premises that I have put before you in the form of a preface, some become manifest with very little reflection and are demonstrative premises and first intelligibles or notions approaching the latter, as may be seen in the epitome we have made of their orderly exposition. Others require a number of demonstrations and premises leading up to them. However, all of them have been given demonstrations as to which no doubt is possible. With regard to some of them, this has been done in the Book of "Akroasis"[6] and its commentaries; with regard to others, in the Book of "Metaphysics" and its commentary. I have already made it known to you that the purpose of this Treatise is not to transcribe the books of the philosophers and to explain the most remote of the premises, but to mention the proximate premises that are required for our purpose.

---

[5] *Metaphysics* xii.6.1071b29-30. The quotation is accurate.
[6] Aristotle's *Physics* is meant.

I shall add to the premises mentioned before, one further premise that affirms as necessary the eternity of the world. Aristotle deemed it to be correct and the most fitting to be believed. We shall grant him this premise by way of a hypothesis[7] in order that the clarification of that which we intended to make clear should be achieved. This premise, which among them is the twenty-sixth, [consists in Aristotle's statement] that time and movement are eternal, perpetual, existing in actu.[8] Hence it follows of necessity, in his opinion, that there is a body, moving with an eternal movement, existing in actu; and this is the fifth body. For this reason, he says that the heaven is not subject to generation and corruption. For according to him, movement is not subject to generation and corruption; for he says that every movement is necessarily preceded by another movement either of the same species as itself or of other species, and that what is thought with regard to living beings—namely, that their local movement is not preceded at all by another movement—is not correct. For the cause of their movement after rest goes back finally to things calling for this local movement; these things being either an alteration of temperament necessitating a desire to seek what agrees with the living being or to flee from what disagrees with it, or an imagination, or an opinion occurring to it. Accordingly, any one of these three factors sets the living being in motion, and every one of them is necessitated by other movements. Similarly he says that in the case of everything that comes about in time, the possibility of its coming-about precedes in time its coming-about. From this there follow necessarily several points liable to validate his premise.[9] According to this premise, a finite moving object moves upon a finite distance an infinite number of times, going back over the same distance in a circle. Now this is impossible except in circular movement, as is demonstrated in the thirteenth of these premises. According to this premise, that which is infinite must necessarily exist as a succession and not simultaneously.[10]

This is the premise that Aristotle constantly wishes to establish as true. Now to me it seems that he does not affirm categorically that the arguments he puts forward in its favor constitute a demon-

---

[7] I read *taqdīr* instead of the word *taqrīr* found in the Arabic text. Graphically this emendation is very slight. It is in conformity with Ibn Tibbon's Hebrew translation.

[8] Cf. *Physics* viii.1.251b20 ff.; *Metaphysics* xii.6.1071b5 ff.

[9] Concerning the eternity of movement.

[10] Or: together.

stration. The premise in question[11] is rather, in his opinion, the most
fitting and the most probable. However, his followers and the commentators of his books claim that the premise is necessary and not
merely possible and that it has already been demonstrated. On the
other hand, every Mutalkallim desires to establish that it is impossible.
They say that there can be no mental representation of the coming-
about in succession of an infinite number of things occurring in
time. The strength of their argument is that it constitutes, in their
opinion, a first intelligible. But to me it seems that the premise in
question is possible—that is, neither necessary, as is affirmed by
the commentators of the writings of Aristotle, nor impossible, as
is claimed by the Mutakallimun. It is not the purpose now to explain
the arguments of Aristotle, or to raise our doubts concerning him,
or to explain my opinion concerning the creation of the world in
time. But the purpose at this point is to circumscribe the premises
that we need for our three problems; after first having set forth these
premises and having agreed to take them as granted, I shall set out
explaining what necessarily follows from them.

b. [The Proof Itself]

It follows necessarily from the twenty-fifth premise that there is
a mover, which has moved the matter of that which is subject to
generation and corruption so that it received form. If now it is
asked: what moved this proximate mover?—it follows of necessity
that there exists for it another mover either of its own species or of
a different species; for motion exists in four categories,[1] and sometimes these different kinds of change are called motion in a general
way, as we have mentioned in the fourth premise. Now this does
not go to infinity, as we have mentioned in the third premise. For
we have found that every movement goes back, in the last resort,
to the movement of the fifth body, and no further. It is from this
movement that every mover and predisposer in the whole lower

---

[11] The Arabic pronoun for which the words, "the premise in question," are
substituted in this translation, may alternatively refer to "the arguments" mentioned in the preceding sentence. This was Ibn Tibbon's opinion. However, the
sentences that follow appear to prove the correctness of the translation
propounded in the text.

[1] Literally: in the four categories. I.e., those enumerated in the fourth
premise.

world proceeds and derives. Now the sphere moves with a movement of translation, and this is prior to all other movements, as has been mentioned in the fourteenth premise. Similarly every movement of translation goes back, in the last resort, to the movement of the sphere. It is as if you say: this stone, which was in motion, was moved by a staff; the staff was moved by a hand; the hand by tendons; the tendons by muscles; the muscles by nerves; the nerves by natural heat; and the natural heat by the form that subsists therein, this form being undoubtedly the first mover. What obliges this mover to move could be an opinion, for instance an opinion that the stone should be brought by the blow of the staff to a hole[2] in order to stop it, so that blowing wind should not enter thereby toward the man who had this opinion.[3] Now the mover of this wind and the factor causing it to blow is the movement of the sphere. In a similar way you will find that every cause of generation and corruption goes back, in the last resort, to the movement of the sphere. Now when, in the last resort, we have gone back to this sphere, which is in motion, it follows necessarily that it must have a mover, according to what has been set forth before in the seventeenth premise. Now the mover cannot but be either in the moved or outside it, for this is a necessary division. Now if the mover is outside the sphere, it cannot but be either a body or not a body; in which latter case it should not be said to be outside the sphere, but separate from it, for what is not a body is not said to be outside a body except through an extension of the meaning of the expression. If, however, its mover is in it—I mean the mover of the sphere—it cannot but be either that the mover is a force distributed in the whole of the body of the sphere and divisible through the latter's being divided—as heat in fire—or that it is a force in the sphere that is not divisible—as are the soul and the intellect—just as has been expounded before the tenth premise. There is, accordingly, no doubt as to the mover of the sphere, being one of these four: either another body outside it, or separate from it,[4] or a force distributed in it, or an indivisible force.

Now the first supposition—namely, that the mover of the sphere

---

[2] Or: a window.

[3] Literally: to him (or: to it). It is practically certain that the man who moved the stone is referred to in the Arabic pronominal suffix.

[4] In this case the mover is supposed to be an immaterial entity.

is another body outside the sphere—is absurd, as I shall point out. For if it is a body, it must—as has been set forth in the ninth premise—be in motion when moving another body. Now in that case, this sixth body[5] likewise must be in motion when moving another body. Accordingly it would necessarily follow that it is moved by a seventh body. This in its turn must be supposed to be in motion. Accordingly it would follow necessarily that an infinite number of bodies must exist and that only in that case is the sphere in motion. Now this is absurd, as has been set forth before in the second premise.

The third possibility—namely, that the mover of the sphere is a force distributed in the latter—is likewise absurd, as I shall point out. For the sphere is a body and in consequence necessarily finite, as has been set forth before in the first premise. In consequence its force must be finite, as has been set forth in the twelfth premise. Hence this force must be divisible if the sphere is divided, as has been set forth in the eleventh premise. Hence it cannot move something for an infinite time, as we have supposed that it does in the twenty-sixth premise.

As for the fourth possibility—namely, that the mover of the sphere is an indivisible force subsisting in the sphere, as for example man's soul does in man—it is likewise absurd that this mover alone should be the cause for this perpetual motion, even if it is indivisible. The explanation of this lies in the fact that if this mover is the first mover of the sphere, it also must be in motion according to accident, as has been mentioned in the sixth premise.

I shall add here the explanation that follows. When, for example, the soul of a man, which is his form, moves him to go up from the house to an upper chamber, it is the body that is in motion according to essence, the soul being the first mover according to essence. However, the soul is in motion according to accident, for through the transporting of the body from the house to the upper chamber, the soul, which was in the house, was transported and came to be in the upper chamber. Now if the action of moving exerted by the soul would come to rest, that which was moved by it, namely, the body, also would come to rest. But then through the fact that the body would come to rest, the accidental motion, which had

[5] The sphere being considered as the fifth body, Maimonides calls it mover, should that turn out to be a body, the sixth body.

come to the soul, would be abolished. Now, everything that is moved according to accident must of necessity come to rest, as has been mentioned in the eighth premise. When, however, it comes to rest, that which is moved by it likewise comes to rest. It follows accordingly of necessity that the first mover in question necessarily must have another cause subsisting outside the whole, which is composed of a mover and of a moved. When this cause, which is the beginning of movement, is present, the first mover, which subsists in this whole, moves that in it which may be moved. When, however, it is not present, that which may be moved in the whole is at rest.[6] For this reason the bodies of animals are not perpetually in motion, even though there is in every one of them an indivisible first mover. For their mover does not move them perpetually according to essence, for the factors that incite it to cause to move are matters outside it: either quest for what agrees with that particular animal, or flight from what disagrees with it, or again an imagination or a representation in the case of those animals that have representations.[7] When acted upon by these factors, the mover causes movement. When doing this, it itself is moved accidentally. And accordingly there is no doubt about its coming to rest at a certain time, as we have mentioned. If, however, the mover of the sphere were in it in this manner, it would not be able to be in motion eternally.

Accordingly, if the motion in question is perpetual and eternal, as is stated by our adversary—and this is possible, as has been mentioned in the thirteenth premise—it follows necessarily, according to this opinion,[8] that the first cause of the movement of the sphere conforms to the second possibility; I mean to say that it is separate from the sphere according to what is required by the above division.[9] It accordingly has been demonstrated that it is necessary that the mover of the first sphere, if the movement of the latter is regarded as eternal and perpetual, should not at all be a body or a

[6] This appears to be the probable meaning of the phrase. However, if one keeps to the letter of the text, it would seem that that which is at rest in the circumstances under discussion is "the mover" rather than "that which may be moved." There are certain considerations that seem to favor the latter interpretation.

[7] In the singular in Arabic. In the context the Arabic word may mean the faculty of representation.

[8] Namely, the opinion that regards the movement of the sphere as eternal.

[9] The one posing four prima facie possible hypotheses regarding the nature of the mover of the sphere.

force in a body; in this way the mover of this sphere would have no movement, either according to essence or to accident, and would not be subject to division or to change, as has been mentioned in the seventh and the fifth of the premises. Now this is the deity, may His name be sublime; I am referring to the first cause moving the sphere. And it is absurd that there should be two or more of them because it is absurd that there should be multiplicity in the separate things, which are not bodies, except when one of them is a cause and the other an effect, as has been mentioned in the sixteenth premise. It has also been made clear that this first cause does not fall under time because it is impossible that there should be movement with regard to it, as has been mentioned in the fifteenth premise. Accordingly this speculation has led by means of a demonstration to the knowledge that it is impossible that the sphere should move itself in an eternal motion; that the first cause to which its being set in motion is due, is not a body or a force in a body; and that this first cause is one and unchangeable because its existence is not conjoined with time. These are the three problems with regard to which the most excellent among the philosophers gave demonstrations.

A second speculation made by them. Aristotle propounded, by way of introduction, a premise that runs as follows: Supposing that there exists a thing composed of two things and that one of these two things exists separately outside this compound thing, it follows necessarily that the other thing also must exist outside the compound thing.[10] For if the existence of these two things had required that they exist only together, as do matter and natural form, one of them would not have existed in any way without the other. Accordingly, the fact that one of them exists separately is a proof for the absence of an obligatory mutual connection. Consequently the second thing, which enters into the compound thing, must necessarily exist separately. The following example for this may be adduced: if oxymel exists and honey likewise exists by itself, it follows necessarily that vinegar must exist by itself. After having explained this premise, he says: We find that many things are composed of a mover and a moved. He means to say thereby that these things move other things, and, when moving the latter, are themselves moved by other things. This is manifest with regard to all the things that have an intermediate

---

[10] I.e., the second element entering into the makeup of the compound thing.

status as far as causing to move is concerned. Now we find that there exists a thing that is moved and does not at all cause to move; this is the last of the moved things. It follows accordingly that there must exist a mover that is not moved at all; this is the first mover.[11] And inasmuch as no motion is possible in it, it is not divisible and not a body, and it does not fall under time, as has become clear in the preceding demonstration.

A third philosophic speculation about this subject is taken over from Aristotle's argumentation, even though he sets it forth with a view to another purpose. This is how the argument is ordered. There is no doubt that there are existent things. These are the existent things that are apprehended by the senses. Now there are only three possible alternatives,[12] this being a necessary division: namely, either no existents are subject to generation and corruption, or all of them are subject to generation and corruption, or some of them are subject to generation and corruption whereas others are not. Now the first alternative is clearly absurd, for we perceive many existents that are subject to generation and corruption. The second alternative is likewise absurd, the explanation of this being as follows: if every existent falls under generation and corruption, then all the existents and every one of them have a possibility of undergoing corruption. Now it is indubitable, as you know, that what is possible with regard to a species must necessarily come about. Thus it follows necessarily that they, I mean all existents, will necessarily undergo corruption. Now if all of them have undergone corruption, it would be impossible that anything exists, for there would remain no one who would bring anything into existence. Hence it follows necessarily that there would be no existent thing at all. Now we perceive things that are existent. In fact we ourselves are existent. Hence it follows necessarily, according to this speculation that if there are, as we perceive, existents subject to generation and corruption, there must be a certain existent that is not subject to generation and corruption. Now in this existent that is not subject to generation and corruption, there is no possibility of corruption at all; rather, its existence is necessary, not possible. He also says that, with reference to this existent's being necessary of existence,

---

[11] In this passage, Maimonides appears to be referring to one of Alexander of Aphrodisias' commentaries rather than to Aristotle himself.

[12] Literally: And the matter is not free from three divisions.

there are two possibilities: this may be either in respect to its own essence or in respect to the cause of this existent. In the latter case, its existence and nonexistence are possible in respect to its own essence, but necessary in respect to its cause. Thus its cause would be necessary of existence, as has been mentioned in the nineteenth premise. Now it has been demonstrated that, of necessity, there can be no doubt that there is an existent that is necessary of existence in respect to its own essence. For without it, there would be no existent at all, neither one that is subject to generation and corruption, nor one that is not subject to them—if there is a thing that exists in this manner, as Aristotle states; I mean to say a thing that is not subject to generation and corruption because of its being an effect caused by a cause that is necessary of existence. This is a demonstration concerning which there can be no doubt, no refutation, and no dispute, except on the part of one who is ignorant of the method of demonstration. After this we shall say that it follows necessarily that the existence of everything that is necessary of existence with respect to its own essence can have no cause, as has been set forth in the twentieth premise; and that in anything that is necessary of existence there cannot be a multiplicity of notions, as has been mentioned in the twenty-first premise. Hence it follows necessarily that, as has been set forth in the twenty-second premise, it is not a body or a force in a body. It thus has been demonstrated in this speculation that there is an existent that is necessary of existence and is so necessarily with respect to its own essence, and that this existent has no cause for its existence and has no composition in itself, and for this reason is neither a body nor a force in a body. It is He who is the Deity, may His name be sublime. Similarly it can be easily demonstrated that it is impossible that necessity of existence in respect to essence should exist in two beings. For the species, necessity of existence, is a notion that would be superadded to the essence of each one of these two supposed beings. Accordingly, none of them would be necessary of existence in virtue only of itself, but it would be necessary of existence in virtue of the notion representing the species—necessity of existence—a species subsisting both in that particular being and in another one. Now it has been made clear in a number of ways that no duality at all, nor the existence of an equal or of a contrary, can be true with reference to the necessary of existence. The cause

of all this is the latter's absolute[13] simplicity and absolute[13] perfection—leaving no residue outside its essence that pertains to the
species, the necessary of existence—as well as the nonexistence in
any way of a primary or secondary cause[14] for it. Accordingly,
nothing at all can be associated with the necessary of existence.

The fourth speculation, likewise philosophic. It is well known
that we constantly see things that are in potentia and pass into
actuality. Now everything that passes from potentiality into actuality
has something outside itself that causes it to pass, as has been mentioned in the eighteenth premise. It is also clear that this something,
which in one particular case causes to pass from potentiality to
actuality, had been a cause of this passage in potentia and then only
became such a cause in actu. Now the reason for its having been in
potentia might lie either in an obstacle subsisting in its own right
or in a relation—which had been absent before—between it and
the thing it is to cause to pass from potentiality to actuality. When
this relation is realized, it actually causes the thing to pass from
potentiality to actuality. Now these two explanations necessarily
require something that causes to pass from potentiality to actuality
or a factor that puts an end to a hindrance. And the same thing
must necessarily be said of the second something that causes to pass
from potentiality to actuality or of the second factor that puts an
end to hindrance. And this series of causes or factors cannot continue to infinity. There is no doubt that, in the last resort, one must
come to something that causes the passage from potentiality to
actuality, that is perpetually existent in one and the same State, and
in which there is no potentiality at all. I mean to say that in it, in its
essence, there is nothing in potentia. For if there were possibility[15]
in its essence, the thing in question would at some time become
nonexistent, as has been mentioned in the twenty-third premise. It
is further impossible that the thing in question should be endowed
with matter; rather is it separate from matter, as has been mentioned
in the twenty-fourth premise. Now the being that is separate from
matter, in which there is no possibility whatever, but that exists in

---

[13] Literally: pure.

[14] *al-'illa wa'l-sabab.* These two terms are often synonymous, both of them
meaning "cause." Sometimes, however, each may have a distinctive shade of
meaning; in that case *sabab* tends to mean secondary cause.

[15] In the sense of potentiality.

virtue of its essence, is the deity. And it has already been made clear that He is not a body and that He is one, as has been mentioned in the sixteenth premise.

All these are demonstrative methods of proving the existence of one deity, who is neither a body nor a force in a body, while believing at the same time in the eternity of the world.

There is also a demonstrative method of refuting the belief in the corporeality of [God] and of establishing [God's] unity. For if there were two deities it would follow necessarily that they must have one separately conceivable thing in which they participate, this being the thing in virtue of which each one of them merits being called a deity. They also must necessarily have another separately conceivable thing in virtue of which their separation came about and they became two. Now in virtue of the fact that in each of them there must be a separately conceivable thing other than the one subsisting in the other deity, each one of them must be composed of two separately conceivable things. Accordingly, as has been explained in the nineteenth premise, none of them can be a first cause or necessary of existence in respect to its own essence, but each of them must have several causes. If, however, the separately conceivable thing causing the separation between them exists in only one of them, the one in which the two separately conceivable things[16] exist, is not according to his essence, existent of necessity.

Another method with regard to the belief in unity. It has already been established as true by means of a demonstration that all that exists is like one individual whose parts are bound up with each other, and that the forces of the sphere pervade this lowly matter and fashion it. At the same time it is impossible—and this has already been established as true—that one deity should be exclusively concerned with one part of what exists, and the other deity[17] with another part; for one part is bound up with the other. According to the division of possibilities, the only hypotheses that remain open are that one deity acts during a certain time and the other during another time, or that both of them always act together so that no act is perfect unless it has been carried out by both of them together. Now the supposition that one of them acts during a certain time

---

[16] Namely, necessity of existence and the separately conceivable thing causing separation between the two hypothetical deities.

[17] Assumed to exist ex hypothesi.

and the other during another time is absurd from several points of view. For if it were possible that during the time in which one of them acts the other should act also, what could be the cause necessitating that one of them acts during that time whereas the other remains inactive? If, however, it were impossible for one of them to act during the time in which the other acts, there consequently must be another cause that necessitates that at a given time it is possible for one of them to act whereas for the other it is impossible. For there is no differentiation in time as a whole; and the substratum for the action[18] is one, and its parts are bound up with one another, as we have made clear. Furthermore, according to this supposition, each one of them would fall under time inasmuch as his work would be tied up with time. Furthermore, each one of them, at the time of his action, would have to pass from potentiality to actuality, and, in consequence, each one of them would need something that would cause him to pass from potentiality to actuality. Furthermore, possibility would subsist in the essence of each of them. If, however, they were supposed always to make together everything that is in existence, so that one of them would not act without the other, that also would be absurd, as I shall set forth. For in the case of any complex composed parts, which cannot cause a certain act to become perfect except through the cooperation of each one of its parts, none of these parts is an agent in respect to its own essence or the first cause of the act; that first cause is the coming-together of the parts of the complex. Now it has been demonstrated that it is a necessary conclusion that what is necessary of existence can have no cause. Moreover the coming-together of the parts of the complex represents a certain act, which requires another agent, namely, one who causes the parts of the complex to come together. Now if the agent who causes the parts of the complex to come together—without which the act cannot become perfect—is one, he is indubitably the deity. If, however, this agent who causes the parts of this complex to come together is another complex, the same conclusions follow necessarily with regard to this second complex as with regard to the first. Thus there can be no doubt about ultimately reaching One who is the cause of the existence of this existent, which is one,[19] whatever the manner of

---

[18] To be accomplished by the two deities whose existence is supposed.
[19] I.e., the cause of the universe.

this may have been: whether through creating it in time after it had been nonexistent, or because it proceeds necessarily from this One. It has thus become clear, also according to this method, that the fact that all that exists is one, indicates to us that He who caused it to exist is one.

Another method of refuting the belief in the corporeality [of God]. As has been mentioned in the twenty-second premise, every body is a compound. Now there can be no doubt that every compound requires an agent, which is the cause of the subsistence of its form in its matter. Now it is most clear that every body is divisible and has dimensions. Accordingly, it is indubitably something to which accidents must be attached. Hence a body cannot be one, both because of its being a compound—I mean to say, because of its being two as far as statement is concerned. For every body is a certain body only because of some separately conceivable thing subsisting in it that is superadded to the fact of its being a body. In consequence, every body is necessarily provided with two separately conceivable things. Now it has been demonstrated that in the necessary of existence there is no composition in any way at all.

After having first set forth these demonstrations, I shall start to give an epitome of that method which is emphatically ours, as we have promised.

30. MAIMONIDES: The Meaning of Wisdom*

The term *wisdom* [*ḥokhmah*] is applied in Hebrew in four senses. It is applied to the apprehension of true realities, which have for their end the apprehension of Him, may He be exalted. It says: *But wisdom, where shall it be found? and so on.*[1] It says: *If thou seek her as silver, and so on.*[2] This usage is frequent. The term is applied to acquiring arts, whatever the art might be: *And every wise-hearted among you;*[3] *And all the women that were wise-hearted.*[4] It is ap-

* See Introduction to Selection 29.
[1] Job 28:12.
[2] Prov. 2:4.
[3] Exod. 35:10.
[4] Exod. 35:25.

plied to acquiring moral virtues: *And teach his elders wisdom;*[5]
Is wisdom with aged men?[6]—for the thing that is acquired through
mere old age is a disposition to achieve moral virtues. It is applied
to the aptitude for stratagems and ruses: *Come, let us deal wisely
with them.*[7] According to this meaning it says: *And fetched thence
a wise woman,*[8] meaning thereby that she had an aptitude for
stratagems and ruses. In this sense it is said: *They are wise to do
evil.*[9] It is possible that the meaning of *wisdom* in Hebrew indicates
aptitude for stratagems and the application of thought in such a way
that the stratagems and ruses may be used in achieving either rational
or moral virtues, or in achieving skill in a practical art, or in working evil and wickedness. It has accordingly become plain that the
term *wise* can be applied to one possessing the rational virtues, to
one possessing the moral virtues, to everyone skilled in a practical
art, and to one possessing ruses in working evil and wickedness.
According to this explanation, one who knows the whole of the Law
in its true reality is called *wise* in two respects: in respect of the
rational virtues comprised in the Law and in respect of the moral
virtues included in it. But since the rational matter in the Law is
received through traditions and is not demonstrated by the methods
of speculation, the knowledge of the Law came to be set up in the
books of the prophets and the sayings of the *Sages* as one separate
species and wisdom,[10] in an unrestricted sense, as another species.
It is through this wisdom, in an unrestricted sense, that the rational
matter that we receive from the Law through tradition, is demonstrated. All the texts that you find in the [scriptural] books that
extol wisdom and speak of its wonder[11] and of the rarity of those
who acquire it—*Not many are wise;*[12] *But wisdom, where shall it be
found? and so on;*[13] and many other texts of this kind—treat of

5 Ps. 105:22.
6 Job 12:12.
7 Exod. 1:10.
8 II Sam. 14:2.
9 Jer. 4:22.
10 It is not quite clear whether Maimonides uses here the Hebrew word
ḥokhmah or the Arabic word *ḥikma*, spelled in the same way. The Arabic
word also connotes "philosophy." The Hebrew word may also have this connotation, and if Maimonides used it here, he undoubtedly had this connotation
in mind.
11 Or: its strangeness.
12 Job 32:9.
13 Job 28:12.

that wisdom which teaches us to demonstrate the opinions of the
Torah. This is also frequent in the sayings of the *Sages, may their
memory be blessed;* I mean that they set up the knowledge of the
Torah as one separate species and wisdom as another species. They,
may their memory be blessed, say of *Moses our Master: He was
father in wisdom, father in the Torah, father among the prophets.*[14]
And with reference to its dictum concerning *Solomon, And he was
wiser than all men,*[15] they say: *Not [wiser] than Moses;*[16] for the
dictum, *than all men,* means: than his contemporaries. Therefore
you will find that it mentions *Heman and Khalkol and Darda, the
sons of Mahol,*[17] who were celebrated then as wise men. The *Sages,
may their memory be blessed,* mention likewise that man is required
first to obtain knowledge of the *Torah,* then to obtain wisdom, then
to know what is incumbent upon him with regard to the legal science
of the Law—I mean the drawing of inferences concerning what one
ought to do. And this should be the order observed: The opinions
in question should first be known as being received through tradition;
then they should be demonstrated; then the actions through which
one's way of life may be ennobled, should be precisely defined. This
is what they, *may their memory be blessed,* literally say regarding
man's being required to give an account with respect to these three
matters in this order. They say: *When man comes to judgment, he
is first asked: Have you fixed certain seasons for the study of the
Torah? Have you ratiocinated concerning wisdom? Have you
inferred one thing from another?*[18] It has thus become clear to you
that, according to them, the science of the *Torah* is one species and
wisdom is a different species, being the verification of the opinions
of the *Torah* through correct speculation. After we have made all
these preliminary remarks, hear what we shall say:

The ancient and the modern philosophers have made it clear that
the perfections to be found in man consist of four species. The first
and the most defective, but with a view to which the people of the
earth spend their lives,[19] is the perfection of possessions—that is,
of what belongs to the individual in the manner of money, garments,
tools, slaves, land, and other things of this kind. A man's being a

---

[14] B.T., Megillah, 13a.
[15] I Kings 5:11.
[16] B.T., Rosh Hashanah, 21b.
[17] I Kings 5:11.
[18] B.T., Shabbath, 31a.
[19] Or: mutually destroy each other.

great king also belongs to this species of perfection. Between this perfection and the individual himself there is no union whatever; there is only a certain relation, and most of the pleasure taken in the relation is purely imaginary. I refer to one's saying: This is my house; this is my slave; this money is mine; these are my soldiers. For if he considers his own individual self, he will find that all this is outside his self and that each of these possessions subsists as it is by itself. Therefore when the relation referred to has been abolished, there is no difference between an individual who has been a great king and the most contemptible of men, though nothing may have changed in any of the things that were attributed to him. The philosophers have explained that the endeavor and the efforts directed by man toward this kind of perfection are nothing but an effort with a view to something purely imaginary, to a thing that has no permanence. And even if these possessions should remain with him permanently during the whole of his life, he would by no means thereby achieve perfection in his self.

The second species has a greater connection than the first with the individual's self, being the perfection of the bodily constitution and shape—I refer to that individual's temperament being most harmonious, his limbs well proportioned and strong as they ought to be. Neither should this species of perfection be taken as an end, for it is a corporeal perfection and does not belong to man qua man, but qua animal; for man has this in common with the lowest animals. Moreover even if the strength of a human individual reached its greatest maximum,[20] it would not attain the strength of a strong mule, and still less the strength of a lion or an elephant. The end of this perfection consists, as we have mentioned, in man's transporting a heavy burden or breaking a thick bone and in other things of this kind, from which no great utility for the body may be derived. Utility for the soul is absent from this species of perfection.

The third species is a perfection that to a greater extent than the second species subsists in the individual's self. This is the perfection of the moral virtues. It consists in the individual's moral habits having attained their ultimate excellence.[21] Most of the *commandments* serve no other end than the attainment of this species of perfection. But this species of perfection is likewise a preparation for

[20] Literally: finality and end.
[21] The Arabic word *faḍīla,* translated "excellence," is the singular of the word translated in the preceding sentence as "virtues."

something else and not an end in itself. For all moral habits are concerned with what occurs between a human individual and someone else. This perfection regarding moral habits is, as it were, only the disposition to be useful to people; consequently it is an instrument for someone else. For if you suppose a human individual is alone, acting on no one, you will find that all his moral virtues are in vain and without employment and unneeded, and that they do not perfect the individual in anything; for he only needs them and they again become useful to him in regard to someone else.

The fourth species is the true human perfection; it consists in the acquisition of the rational virtues—I refer to the conception of intelligibles, which teach true opinions concerning the divine things. This is in true reality the ultimate end; this is what gives the individual true perfection, a perfection belonging to him alone; and it gives him permanent perdurance; through it man is man. If you consider each of the three perfections mentioned before, you will find that they pertain to others than you, not to you, even though, according to the generally accepted opinion, they inevitably pertain both to you and to others. This ultimate perfection, however, pertains to you alone, no one else being associated in it with you in any way: *They shall be only thine own, and so on.*[22] Therefore you ought to desire to achieve this thing, which will remain permanently with you, and not weary and trouble yourself for the sake of others, O you who neglect your own soul so that its whiteness has turned into blackness through the corporeal faculties having gained dominion over it—as is said in the beginning of the poetical parables that have been coined for these notions; it says: *My mother's sons were incensed against me; they made me keeper of the vineyards; but mine own vineyard have I not kept.*[23] It says on this very same subject: *Lest thou give thy splendor unto others, and thy years unto the cruel.*[24]

The prophets too have explained to us and interpreted to us the selfsame notions—just as the philosophers have interpreted them—clearly stating to us that neither the perfection of possession nor the perfection of health nor the perfection of moral habits is a perfection of which one should be proud or that one should desire;

[22] Prov. 5:17.
[23] Song of Songs 1:6.
[24] Prov. 5:9.

the perfection of which one should be proud and that one should desire is knowledge of Him, may He be exalted, which is the true science. *Jeremiah* says concerning these four perfections: *Thus saith the Lord: Let not the wise man glory in his wisdom, neither let the mighty man glory in his might, let not the rich man glory in his riches; but let him that glorieth glory in this, that he understandeth and knoweth Me.*[25] Consider how he mentioned them according to the order given them in the opinion of the multitude. For the greatest perfection in their opinion is that of *the rich man in his riches,* below him *the mighty man in his might,* and below him *the wise man in his wisdom.* [By the expression, "the wise man in his wisdom,"] he means him who possesses the moral virtues; for such an individual is also held in high esteem by the multitude, to whom the discourse in question is addressed. Therefore these perfections are arranged in this order. The *Sages, may their memory be blessed,* apprehended from this *verse* the very notions we have mentioned and have explicitly stated that which I have explained to you in this chapter: namely, that the term *wisdom [ḥokhmah],* used in an unrestricted sense and regarded as the end, means in every place the apprehension of Him, may He be exalted; that the possession of the treasures acquired, and competed for, by man and thought to be perfection are not a perfection; and that similarly all the actions prescribed by the Law—I refer to the various species of worship and also the moral habits that are useful to all people in their mutual dealings—that all this is not to be compared with this ultimate end and does not equal it, being but preparations made for the sake of this end. Hear verbatim a text of theirs dealing with all these notions; it is a text in *Bereshith Rabbah.* It is said there: *One scriptural dictum says: And all things desirable are not to be compared unto her.*[26] *Another scriptural dictum says: And all things thou canst desire are not to be compared unto her.*[27] *The expression, things desirable, refers to commandments and good actions; while things thou canst desire, refers to precious stone and pearls. Neither things desirable nor things thou canst desire are to be compared unto her, but let him that glorieth glory in this, that he understandeth*

25 Jer. 9:22-23.
26 Prov. 8:11.
27 Prov. 3:15.

and knoweth Me.[28] Consider how concise is this saying, how perfect is he who said it, and how he left out nothing of all that we have mentioned and that we have interpreted and led up to at length.

As we have mentioned this *verse* and the wondrous notions contained in it, and as we have mentioned the saying of the *Sages, may their memory be blessed,* about it, we will complete the exposition of what it includes. For when explaining in this *verse* the noblest ends, he does not limit them only to the apprehension of Him, may He be exalted. For if this were his purpose, he would have said: *But let him that glorieth glory in this, that he understandeth and knoweth Me,* and have stopped there; or he would have said: *that he understandeth and knoweth Me that I am One;* or he would have said: *that I have no figure,* or *that there is none like Me,* or something similar. But he says that one should glory in the apprehension of Myself and in the knowledge of My attributes, by which he means His actions, as we have made clear with reference to its dictum: *Show me now Thy ways, and so on.*[29] In this *verse*[30] he makes it clear to us that those actions that ought to be known and imitated are *loving-kindness, judgment,* and *righteousness.* He adds another corroborative notion through saying, *in the earth*[31]—this being a pivot of the Law. For matters are not as the overbold opine who think that His providence, may He be exalted, terminates at the sphere of the moon and that the earth and that which is in it are neglected: *The Lord hath forsaken the earth.*[32] Rather is it as has been made clear to us by the Master of those who know: *That the earth is the Lord's.*[33] He means to say that His providence also extends over the earth in the way that corresponds to what the latter is, just as His providence extends over the heavens[34] in the way that corresponds to what they are. This is what he says: *That I am the Lord who exercise loving-kindness, judgment, and righteousness, in the earth.*[35] Then he completes the notion by saying: *For in these things I delight, saith the Lord.*[36] He means that it is My purpose

---

[28] Genesis Rabbah, XXXV *in fine.*
[29] Exod. 33:13.
[30] Jer. 9:23 is referred to.
[31] Jer. 9:23.
[32] Ezek. 9:9.
[33] Exod. 9:29.
[34] In the singular in Arabic.
[35] Jer. 9:23.
[36] Jer. 9:23.

that there should come from you *loving-kindness, righteousness, and judgment in the earth* in the way we have explained[37] with regard to the *thirteen attributes*: namely, that the purpose should be assimilation to them and that this should be our way of life. Thus the end that he sets forth in this *verse* may be stated as follows: It is clear that the perfection of man that may truly be gloried in is the one acquired by him who has achieved, in a measure corresponding to his capacity, apprehension of Him, may He be exalted, and who knows His providence extending over His creatures as manifested in the act of bringing them into being and in their governance as it is. The way of life of such an individual, after he has achieved this apprehension, will always have in view *loving-kindness, righteousness,* and *judgment,* through assimilation to His actions, may He be exalted, just as we have explained several times in this Treatise.

This is the extent of what I thought fit that we should set down in this Treatise; it is a part of what I consider very useful to those like you. I hope for you that through sufficient reflection you will grasp all the intentions I have included therein, with the help of God, may He be exalted; and that He will grant us *and all [the people of] Israel, being fellows,* that which He has promised us: *Then the eyes of the blind shall be opened, and the ears of the deaf shall be unstopped.*[38] *The people that walked in darkness have seen a great light; they that dwelt in the land of the shadow of death, upon them hath the light shined.*[39]

AMEN

God is very near to everyone who calls,
If he calls truly and has no distractions;
He is found by every seeker who searches for Him,
If he marches toward Him and goes not astray.

THE THIRD PART

HAS BEEN COMPLETED WITH THE HELP OF GOD
AND WITH ITS COMPLETION THERE HAS BEEN COMPLETED
THE GUIDE OF THE PERPLEXED

[37] Cf. I 54.
[38] Isa. 35:5.
[39] Isa. 9:1.

VI.

*Meeting of East
and West*

THE renaissance of the twelfth century in France requires simultaneous analysis of intellectual, religious and social developments. Men's wills and emotions were in the course of new formation and their actions shaped with new motivations.

In this rebirth of learning, the thought of the whole period of twelve centuries may be brought into focus. The relatedness of earlier and later centuries, and the coming together of East and West, is evident in three areas: religious reform, educational advance, and crusade. Of particular interest are the religious reform led by Bernard of Clairvaux and the educational advances exemplified by Peter Abelard and John of Salisbury. As part of their time one must keep in mind the vast social movements which were engendered in connection with the Crusades.

The religious efforts to establish practices of simplicity and poverty, and to find a place for prophetic and mystical teaching, are common to both the early centuries in the East with the teachings of the New Testament and the example of the monks in the desert, and to the twelfth century with the teachings of Arnold of Brescia, a disciple of Abelard, and Bernard of Clairvaux, prophet of the Cistercian reform. The influence of Gregory of Nyssa on Bernard of Clairvaux is a special instance of continuity within the traditions of mysticism. The new monastic movement in the West is also a renewal of the communal developments fostered in the West by Augustine and Benedict, and inherited in part by them from Gregory's contemporary in the East, Basil the Great.

Both Peter Abelard and John of Salisbury influenced notable educational advance and contributed greatly to the tradition of grammatical and logical studies. They provided a development of the study of the liberal arts fostered in the schools of the Alexandria of Philo and Origen, and continued in the earlier centuries in the

West by Augustine and Boethius. A separate continuation within the world of Islamic and Jewish culture achieved a climax in the application of logical and linguistic studies within the theology of Maimonides. Setting out from those portions of the older heritage which were available, Abelard and John of Salisbury were to provide important stimuli to a new age of disciplined and creative work. In sustaining rigorous intellectual life, and in criticism of existing institutions, they continued within the world of the religious establishment much of what had been valued by secular and separatist movements.

In the vast social developments which were the Crusades—led from the West to recover the holy lands in the East—we may see a parallel to the earlier vast efforts of Justinian in seeking the recovery of the Roman provinces of the West from the barbarian invasions and establishments. More striking was the establishment in Asia Minor of principalities by Western crusaders in the face of the rise of Islam. In the renaissance of the twelfth century in France we are indeed close to alternative meetings of East and West.

Peter Abelard (A.D. 1079-1142), was in his time famous as a teacher of Christian theology. He is perhaps best remembered today as a champion of rational inquiry. While he is an important early figure in the scene which was to develop that most characteristic of Western institutions, the University of Paris, there is much in his manner and in the very content of his teaching to remind us of the early tradition of philosophy in the Athens of classical antiquity.

His versatility and audacity as philosopher and theologian contributed much to the intellectual renaissance of the Paris of his day. He is best known in the history of thought for his "nominalism" in the philosophical controversy over the status of universal concepts. Abelard is remembered for this as Anslem of Canterbury is remembered for the "ontological" argument. The issues addressed by both men continue explicitly in the history of thought.

The history of Abelard's life, in part recounted by himself, includes strong intellectual and religious conflict with Bernard of Clairvaux. It is too simple by far to say that Bernard and Abelard represent respectively the traditions of "mysticism" and "reason," respectively the Church and the University. The problem of Abelard's life within the religious and intellectual community calls to mind similar problems with Islam and Judaism, the response of the forces of religio-intellectual traditionalism in the face of efforts to develop, not supplant, religious teaching through different intellectual modes of communication. The problem has many analogues in our time quite apart from any specific religious context.

Bernard of Clairvaux (1091-1153) was a great Christian mystic and father of a whole school of monasticism. He was the champion who once again was to call the vast military forces of Western Europe to crusading battle in Asia Minor. What is especially interesting is the immediate contact and conflict between the thought and the persons of the two men. In the person of Bernard of Clairvaux there is much to remind us of that coming together of the life of the mind and the life of the church and the life of society at large which was sought in the sacral society of Byzantium in the person of the emperor. The presence of these various dimensions in one life is reminiscent of the greatest of the Hebrew prophets. Thus, while Abelard in a way recalls something of the spirit of ancient Athens, Bernard recalls something of the spirit of ancient Israel. The greatness of life in the twelfth century in the area we now call France, and in succeeding centuries as well, can be seen in a sense of universal mission—the gathering together into some kind of transcendent unity of the historic missions of Jerusalem and Athens and Rome.

Bernard is known as the author of a mystical theology, as the leader of the Cistercian movement of monastic and related reform, as the leading force behind the Second Crusade, as the leading figure in the world of his day. Much of his work is reminiscent of developments in earlier centuries. Nevertheless, it would be a mistake to view him simply as conservative or traditionalist. On the other hand, his sermons and letters especially testify to his power in speaking specifically to the men of his day, and his life's work was the hoped for inauguration of a new Europe.

John of Salisbury (1125-1180), confidant of Thomas à Becket, Bishop of Chartres, is, perhaps, the most attractive figure in his period. He shared in the zeal of Bernard and in the art of Abelard. He shared in high religion, high politics and high learning. He is most often remembered for his advance and defense of the study of the liberal arts. His greatest attractiveness, however, judged in view of the rich and varied history of the thought of his period, may lie in his efforts to come to terms with variety and disagreement in the circle of learned men. In his work one finds some use of historical approach, a moderate eclecticism, and a measure of skepticism. There is sympathy. Explicitly and deeply concerned with intellectual, political, and religious issues, he brings, with his zeal and art, taste and tact.

We have moved, then, in these twelve centuries from Alexandria and Cappadocia and Byzantium, to Paris and Clairvaux and Chartres. These twelve centuries, with their successive renewals of learning, provide the long formative phase of the seventeen centuries which comprise the central period of Western civilization. The thirteenth through the seventeenth centuries contain the further phases. Built upon the legacy of the ancient world this central period provided the transition to the contemporary world of the last three centuries.

The importance of France in the twelfth century should not cause us to overlook the importance of events at the other end of Europe where another meeting of East and West was at hand. In Russia, in twelfth century Novgorod, then one of the most populous cities of Europe, one could see coming into Slavic lands great numbers of colonizers or invaders from Western Europe. Novgorod in the twelfth century, with its thirty-seven monasteries, its great cathedral modeled after Santa Sophia in Constantinople, and its commanding governmental and trade position, stood as a second Byzantium, or as a third Rome.

The meeting of East and West was not to take place in Mediterranean Europe alone, not in the West alone. The development in the East was to be left in good part in the hands of Slavic peoples as the development of the West had come clearly to be in the hands of Franks, Visigoths, Lombards, and other "barbarian" peoples.

These first twelve centuries, from Philo of Alexandria to John of Salisbury, have seen a confluence of intellectual and social and religious movements which have produced ideas inevitably present in the life of man today. To man belonging to Western civilization these ideas are part of himself, and knowledge of them belongs to the beginning of his wisdom.

31. ABELARD: A Beleaguered Professor

Peter Abelard (1079-1142) was a brilliant teacher at the Cathedral School of Notre Dame, from which the University of Paris developed. The story of his tragic romance with Héloïse has been told and retold in many versions. He wrote notable treatises in logic, ethics, theology, and patristic exegesis. His pioneering work, *Sic et Non*, is a landmark of the history of theology. His work on the Trinity was condemned at the Council of Soissons in 1121. He was again condemned at the Council of Sens in 1141 where Bernard of Clairvaux was one of his accusers. Abelard died in 1142 while on his way to Rome to appeal to the Pope.

In reading Abelard's *Historia Calamitatum* (*The Story of My Misfortune*),* his account of his tribulations, it should be remembered that Abelard is pleading his own case. At times he candidly accepts his own guilt, but for the most part he cries out against what he considers the unjust treatment he has suffered. Abelard's book is, in short, a moving human document and a rather unusual autobiography.

In the second of the two chapters (Selection 32) presented here,† Abelard recounts the story of his condemnation at the Council of Soissons.

It so happened that at the outset I devoted myself to analysing the basis of our faith through illustrations based on human understanding, and I wrote for my students a certain tract on the unity and trinity of God. This I did because they were always seeking for rational and philosophical explanations, asking rather for reasons they could understand than for mere words, saying that it was futile to utter words which the intellect could not possibly follow, that nothing could be believed unless it could first be understood, and that it was absurd for any one to preach to others a thing which neither he himself nor those whom he sought to teach could comprehend. Our Lord Himself maintained this same thing when He said: "They are blind leaders of the blind" (Matthew, xv, 14).

* From *Historia Calamitatum*, chap. 9, trans. Henry Adams Bellows, 1923.
† *Ibid.*, chap. 10.

Now, a great many people saw and read this tract, and it became exceedingly popular, its clearness appealing particularly to all who sought information on this subject. And since the questions involved are generally considered the most difficult of all, their complexity is taken as the measure of the subtlety of him who succeeds in answering them. As a result, my rivals became furiously angry, and summoned a council to take action against me, the chief instigators therein being my two intriguing enemies of former days, Alberic and Lotulphe. These two, now that both William and Anslem, our erstwhile teachers, were dead, were greedy to reign in their stead, and, so to speak, to succeed them as heirs. While they were directing the school at Rheims, they managed by repeated hints to stir up their archbishop, Rodolphe, against me, for the purpose of holding a meeting, or rather an ecclesiastical council, at Soissons, provided they could secure the approval of Conon, Bishop of Praeneste, at that time papal legate in France. Their plan was to summon me to be present at this council, bringing with me the famous book I had written regarding the Trinity. In all this, indeed, they were successful, and the thing happened according to their wishes.

Before I reached Soissons, however, these two rivals of mine so foully slandered me with both the clergy and the public that on the day of my arrival the people came near to stoning me and the few students of mine who had accompanied me thither. The cause of their anger was that they had been led to believe that I had preached and written to prove the existence of three gods. No sooner had I reached the city, therefore, than I went forthwith to the legate; to him I submitted my book for examination and judgment, declaring that if I had written anything repugnant to the Catholic faith, I was quite ready to correct it or otherwise to make satisfactory amends. The legate directed me to refer my book to the archbishop and to those same two rivals of mine, to the end that my accusers might also be my judges. So in my case was fulfilled the saying: "Even our enemies are our judges" (Deut. xxxii, 31).

These three, then, took my book and pawed it over and examined it minutely, but could find nothing therein which they dared to use as the basis for a public accusation against me. Accordingly they put off the condemnation of the book until the close of the council, despite their eagerness to bring it about. For my part, every day before the council convened I publicly discussed the Catholic faith in the light of what I had written, and all who heard me were enthusiastic in their approval alike of the frankness and the logic of my words. When the public and the clergy had thus learned something of the real character of my teaching, they began to say to one another: "Behold, now he speaks openly, and no one brings any charge against him. And this council, summoned, as we have heard, chiefly to take action upon his case, is drawing toward its end. Did the judges realize that the error might be theirs rather than his?"

As a result of all this, my rivals grew more angry day by day. On one occasion Alberic, accompanied by some of his students, came to me for the purpose of intimidating me, and, after a few bland words, said that he was amazed at something he had found in my book, to the effect that, although God had begotten God, I denied that God had begotten Himself, since there was only one God. I answered unhesitatingly: "I can give you an explanation of this if you wish it." "Nay," he replied, "I care nothing for human explanation or reasoning in such matters, but only for the words of authority." "Very well," I said; "turn the pages of my book and you will find the authority likewise." The book was at hand, for he had brought it with him. I turned to the passage I had in mind, which he had either not discovered or else passed over as containing nothing injurious to me. And it was God's will that I quickly found what I sought. This was the following sentence, under the heading "Augustine, On the Trinity, Book I": "Whosoever believes that it is within the power of God to beget Himself is sorely in error; this power is not in God, neither is it in any created thing, spiritual or corporeal. For there is nothing that can give birth to itself."

When those of his followers who were present heard this, they were amazed and much embarrassed. He himself, in order to keep his countenance, said: "Certainly, I understand all that." Then I added: "What I have to say further on this subject is by no means new, but apparently it has nothing to do with the case at issue, since you have asked for the word of authority only, and not for explanations. If, however, you care to consider logical explanations, I am prepared to demonstrate that, according to Augustine's statement, you have yourself fallen into a heresy in believing that a father can possibly be his own son." When Alberic heard this he was almost beside himself with rage, and straightway resorted to threats, asserting that neither my explanations nor my citations of authority would avail me aught in this case. With this he left me.

On the last day of the council, before the session convened, the legate and the archbishop deliberated with my rivals and sundry others as to what should be done about me and my book, this being the chief reason for their having come together. And since they had discovered nothing either in my speech or in what I had hitherto written which would give them a case against me, they were all reduced to silence, or at the most to maligning me in whispers. Then Geoffroi, Bishop of Chartres, who excelled the other bishops alike in the sincerity of his religion and in the importance of his see, spoke thus:

"You know, my lords, all who are gathered here, the doctrine of this man, what it is, and his ability, which has brought him many followers in every field to which he has devoted himself. You know how greatly he has lessened the renown of other teachers, both his masters and our own, and how he has spread as it were the offshoots of his vine from sea to sea. Now, if you impose a lightly considered judgment on him, as I cannot believe you will, you well know that even if mayhap you are in the right there are many who will be angered thereby, and that he will have no lack of defenders. Remember above all that we have found nothing in this book of his that lies before us whereon any open accusation can be based. Indeed it is true, as Jerome says: 'Fortitude openly displayed always creates rivals, and the lightning strikes the highest peaks.' Have a care, then, lest by violent action you only increase his fame, and lest we do more hurt to ourselves through envy than to him through justice. A false report, as that same wise man reminds us, is easily crushed, and a man's later life gives testimony as to his earlier deeds. If, then, you are disposed to take canonical action against him, his doctrine or his writings must be brought forward as evidence, and he must have free opportunity to answer his questioners. In that case, if he is found guilty or if he confesses his error, his lips can be wholly sealed. Consider the words of the blessed Nicodemus, who, desiring to free Our Lord Himself, said: 'Doth our law judge any man before it hear him and know what he doeth?' " (John, vii, 51).

When my rivals heard this they cried out in protest, saying:

"This is wise counsel, forsooth, that we should strive against the wordiness of this man, whose arguments, or rather, sophistries, the whole world cannot resist!" And yet, methinks, it was far more difficult to strive against Christ Himself, for Whom, nevertheless, Nicodemus demanded a hearing in accordance with the dictates of the law. When the bishop could not win their assent to his proposals, he tried in another way to curb their hatred, saying that for the discussion of such an important case the few who were present were not enough, and that this matter required a more thorough examination. His further suggestion was that my abbot, who was there present, should take me back with him to our abbey, in other words to the monastery of St. Denis, and that there a large convocation of learned men should determine, on the basis of a careful investigation, what ought to be done. To this last proposal the legate consented, as did all the others.

Then the legate arose to celebrate mass before entering the council, and through the bishop sent me the permission which had been determined on, authorizing me to return to my monastery and there await such action as might be finally taken. But my rivals, perceiving that they would accomplish nothing if the trial were to be held outside of their own diocese, and in a place where they could have little influence on the verdict, and in truth having small wish that justice should be done, persuaded the archbishop that it would be a grave insult to him to transfer this case to another court, and that it would be dangerous for him if by chance I should thus be acquitted. They likewise went to the legate, and succeeded in so changing his opinion that finally they induced him to frame a new sentence, whereby he agreed to condemn my book without any further inquiry, to burn it forthwith in the sight of all, and to confine me for a year in another monastery. The argument they used was that it sufficed for the condemnation of my book that I had presumed to read it in public without the approval either of the Roman pontiff or of the Church, and that, furthermore, I had given it to many to be transcribed. Methinks it would be a notable blessing to the Christian faith if there were more who displayed a like presumption. The legate, however, being less skilled in law than he should have been, relied chiefly on the advice of the archbishop, and he, in turn, on that of my rivals. When the Bishop of Chartres got wind of this, he reported the whole conspiracy to me, and strongly urged me to endure meekly the manifest violence of their enmity. He bade me not to doubt that this violence would in the end react upon them and prove a blessing to me, and counseled me to have no fear of the confinement in a monastery, knowing that within a few days the legate himself, who was now acting under compulsion, would after his departure set me free. And thus he consoled me as best he might, mingling his tears with mine.

32.   ABELARD: The Burning of His Book*

Straightway upon my summons I went to the council, and there, without further examination or debate, did they compel me with my own hand to cast that memorable book of mine into the flames. Although my enemies appeared to have nothing to say while the book was burning, one of them muttered something about having seen it written therein that God the Father was alone omnipotent. This reached the ears of the legate, who replied in astonishment that he could not believe that even a child would make so absurd a blunder. "Our common faith," he said, "holds and sets forth that the Three are alike omnipotent." A certain Tirric, a schoolmaster, hearing this, sarcastically added the Athanasian phrase, "And yet there are not three omnipotent Persons, but only One."

This man's bishop forthwith began to censure him, bidding him desist from such treasonable talk, but he boldly stood his ground, and said, as if quoting the words of Daniel: " 'Are ye such fools, ye sons of Israel, that without examination or knowledge of the truth ye have condemned a daughter of Israel? Return again to the place of judgment,' (Daniel, xiii, 48—The History of Susanna) and there give judgment on the judge himself. You have set up this judge, forsooth, for the instruction of faith and the correction of error, and yet, when he ought to give judgment, he condemns himself out of his own mouth. Set free today, with the help of God's mercy, one who is manifestly innocent, even as Susanna was freed of old from her false accusers."

Thereupon the archbishop arose and confirmed the legate's state-

* See Introduction to Selection 31.

ment, but changed the wording thereof, as indeed was most fitting. "It is God's truth," he said, "that the Father is omnipotent, the Son is omnipotent, the Holy Spirit is omnipotent. And whosoever dissents from this is openly in error, and must not be listened to. Nevertheless, if it be your pleasure, it would be well that this our brother should publicly state before us all the faith that is in him, to the end that, according to its deserts, it may either be approved or else condemned and corrected."

When, however, I fain would have arisen to profess and set forth my faith, in order that I might express in my own words that which was in my heart, my enemies declared that it was not needful for me to do more than recite the Athanasian Symbol, a thing which any boy might do as well as I. And lest I should allege ignorance, pretending that I did not know the words by heart, they had a copy of it set before me to read. And read it I did as best I could for my groans and sighs and tears. Thereupon, as if I had been a convicted criminal, I was handed over to the Abbot of St. Médard, who was there present, and led to his monastery as to a prison. And with this the council was immediately dissolved.

The abbot and the monks of the aforesaid monastery, thinking that I would remain long with them, received me with great exultation, and diligently sought to console me, but all in vain. O God, who dost judge justice itself, in what venom of the spirit, in what bitterness of mind, did I blame even Thee for my shame, accusing Thee in my madness! Full often did I repeat the lament of St. Anthony: "Kindly Jesus, where wert Thou?" The sorrow that tortured me, the shame that overwhelmed me, the desperation that wracked my mind, all these I could then feel, but even now I can find no words to express them. Comparing these new sufferings of my soul with those I had formerly endured in my body, it seemed that I was in very truth the most miserable among men. Indeed that earlier betrayal had become a little thing in comparison with this later evil, and I lamented the hurt to my fair name far more than the one to my body. The latter, indeed, I had brought upon myself through my own wrongdoing, but this other violence had come upon me solely by reason of the honesty of my purpose and my love of our faith, which had compelled me to write that which I believed.

The very cruelty and heartlessness of my punishment, however, made every one who heard the story vehement in censuring it, so that those who had a hand therein were soon eager to disclaim all responsibility, shouldering the blame on others. Nay, matters came to such a pass that even my rivals denied that they had had anything to do with the matter, and as for the legate, he publicly denounced the malice with which the French had acted. Swayed by repentance for his injustice, and feeling that he had yielded enough to satisfy their rancour, he shortly freed me from the monastery whither I had been taken, and sent me back to my own. Here, however, I found almost as many enemies as I had in the former days of which I have already spoken, for the vileness and shamelessness of their way of living made them realize that they would again have to endure my censure.

After a few months had passed, chance gave them an opportunity by which they sought to destroy me. It happened that one day, in the course of my reading, I came upon a certain passage of Bede, in his commentary on the Acts of the Apostles, wherein he asserts that Dionysius the Areopagite was the bishop, not of Athens, but of Corinth. Now, this was directly counter to the belief of the monks, who were wont to boast that their Dionysius, or Denis, was not only the Areopagite but was likewise proved by his acts to have been the Bishop of Athens. Having thus found this testimony of Bede's in contradiction of our own tradition, I showed it somewhat jestingly to sundry of the monks who chanced to be near. Wrathfully they declared that Bede was no better than a liar, and that they had a far more trustworthy authority in the person of Hilduin, a former abbot of theirs, who had travelled for a long time throughout Greece for the purpose of investigating this very question. He, they insisted, had by his writings removed all possible doubt on the subject, and had securely established the truth of the traditional belief.

One of the monks went so far as to ask me brazenly which of the two, Bede or Hilduin, I considered the better authority on this point. I replied that the authority of Bede, whose writings are held in high esteem by the whole Latin Church, appeared to me the better. Thereupon in a great rage they began to cry out that at last I had openly proved the hatred I had always felt for our monastery, and that I was seeking to disgrace it in the eyes of the whole kingdom, robbing it of the honour in which it had particularly gloried, by thus denying that the Areopagite was their patron saint. To this I answered that I had never denied the fact, and that I did not much care whether their patron was the Areopagite or some one else, provided only he had received his crown from God. Thereupon they ran to the abbot and told him of the misdemeanour with which they charged me.

The abbot listened to their story with delight, rejoicing at having found a chance to crush me, for the greater vileness of his life made him fear me more even than the rest did. Accordingly he summoned his council, and when the brethren had assembled he violently threatened me, declaring that he would straightway send me to the king, by him to be punished for having thus sullied his crown and the glory of his royalty. And until he should hand me over to the king, he ordered that I should be closely guarded. In vain did I offer to submit to the customary discipline if I had in any way been guilty. Then, horrified at their wickedness, which seemed to crown the ill fortune I had so long endured, and in utter despair at the apparent conspiracy of the whole world against me, I fled secretly from the monastery by night, helped thereto by some of the monks who took pity on me, and likewise aided by some of my scholars.

I made my way to a region where I had formerly dwelt, hard by the lands of Count Theobald (of Champagne). He himself had some slight acquaintance with me, and had compassion on me by reason of my persecutions, of which the story had reached him. I found a home there within the walls of Provins, in a priory of the monks of Troyes, the prior of which had in former days known me well and shown me much love. In his joy at my coming he cared for me with all diligence. It chanced, however, that one day my abbot came to Provins to see the count on certain matters of business. As soon as I had learned of this, I went to the count, the prior accompanying me, and besought him to intercede in my behalf with the abbot. I asked no more than that the abbot should absolve me of the charge against me, and give me permission to live the monastic life wheresoever I could find a suitable place. The abbot, however, and those who were with him took the matter under advisement, saying that they would give the count an answer the day before they departed. It appeared from their words that they thought I wished to go to some other abbey, a thing which they regarded as an immense disgrace to their own. They had, indeed, taken particular pride in the fact that, upon my conversion, I had come to them, as if scorning all other abbeys, and accordingly they considered that it would bring great shame upon them if I should now desert their abbey and seek another. For this reason they refused to listen either to my own plea or to that of the count. Furthermore, they threatened me with excommunication unless I should instantly return; likewise they forbade the prior with whom I had taken refuge to keep me longer, under pain of sharing my excommunication. When we heard this both the prior and I were stricken with fear. The abbot went away still obdurate, but a few days thereafter he died.

As soon as his successor had been named, I went to him, accompanied by the Bishop of Meaux, to try if I might win from him the permission I had vainly sought of his predecessor. At first he would not give his assent, but finally, through the intervention of certain friends of mine, I secured the right to appeal to the king and his council, and in this way I at last obtained what I sought. The royal seneschal, Stephen, having summoned the abbot and his subordinates that they might state their case, asked them why they wanted to keep me against my will. He pointed out that this might easily bring them into evil repute, and certainly could do them no good, seeing that their way of living was utterly incompatible with mine. I knew it to be the opinion of the royal council that the irregularities in the conduct of this abbey would tend to bring it more and more under the control of the king, making it increasingly useful and likewise profitable to him, and for this reason I had good hope of easily winning the support of the king and those about him.

Thus, indeed, did it come to pass. But in order that the monastery might not be shorn of any of the glory which it had enjoyed by reason of my sojourn there, they granted me permission to betake myself to any solitary place I might choose, provided only I did not put myself under the rule of any other abbey. This was agreed upon and confirmed on both sides in the presence of the king and his councillors. Forthwith I sought out a lonely spot known to me of old in the region of Troyes, and there, on a bit of land which had been given to me, and with the approval of the bishop of the district, I built with reeds and stalks my first oratory in the name of the Holy Trinity. And there concealed, with but one comrade, a certain cleric, I was able to sing over and over again to the Lord: "Lo, then would I wander far off, and remain in the wilderness." (Ps. IV, 7).

33. BERNARD OF CLAIRVAUX:
Reform and Crusade

Bernard of Clairvaux (1091-1153), preacher of the Second Crusade (1147), and implacable enemy of what he considered the dangerous rationalism of Abelard, joined the strict Cistercian Order at the age of twenty-one. Within three years he was abbot of Clairvaux, from which office he was able to influence popes and kings. A man of great literary ability, Bernard, like Jerome and others of similar talent combined with a severe affective religious attitude, consciously avoided the stylistic graces of classical Latin. Perhaps because of this, Bernard's letters and sermons often manifest the perfect vital blend of religious fervor and literary beauty.

The four letters* presented here manifest some of these qualities of warmth, religious affectivity, together with the stern attitude of the religious reformer who is sometimes moved to the anger of righteousness.

TO THE UNIVERSAL DOCTOR, GILBERT, BISHOP OF LONDON†

The fame of your life has spread far and wide, and it has been as a most sweet odour for all unto whom it has come. Your avarice has been stifled: who would not delight in this? Charity rules in its stead: who does not relish this? All men know you to be wise because you have crushed the chief enemy of wisdom. This is something worthy of your priesthood and your great name. The witness of your life well becomes your philosophy; it is a fitting crown of your studies. Yours has been the true wisdom which scorns filthy lucre and refuses to consort with the service of idols. For you it was no great thing to be a bishop, but to be a bishop of London and yet to live as a poor man, this is something clearly magnificent.

---

* From *St. Bernard of Clairvaux*, ed. Bruno Scott James (Chicago: Henry Regnery Company, 1953). Used by permission.

† Gilbert was Bishop of London from 1128 to 1135. It is therefore probable that this letter was written about the year 1130. He was called the "Universal Doctor" because he excelled in all branches of learning. St. Bernard congratulates him in his letter for overcoming avarice by living as a poor man while Bishop of London. Henry of Huntingdon, however, attributes the spartan life of the bishop to miserliness.

The dignity of high office could have added little to the lustre of your fame, but the humility of your poverty has added much. To bear poverty with resignation argues great patience; to seek it of one's own free will is the highest wisdom. The Scriptures acclaim and praise the man who does not set his heart on riches, but you have deserved even higher praise by scorning them. Unless cold reason can see nothing wonderful in a wise man acting wisely. And without any doubt you are a wise man, taking your pleasure in all the books and studies of the wise men of the world, and studying all the divine Scriptures so as to give life to their meaning and apply it to the present day. For have you not "dispersed and given to the poor"? But it is money you have given. And what is money in comparison with the justice for which you have exchanged it? "His justice remaineth for ever and ever." Can the same be said of money? It is certainly a desirable and worthy sort of commerce to exchange what passes for what lasts for ever. O admirable and praiseworthy Master, may you always be able to do business in this way! It only remains for you to finish the good work you have begun, so that the tail of the victim may be joined to the head. I gladly accept your blessing, especially as it comes recommended by the joy I take in your high perfection. Although the bearer of this letter is a most worthy person in himself, yet I wish him to be acceptable to you for my sake as well, because he is very dear to me by reason of his integrity and piety.

TO DAVID, KING OF SCOTLAND*

To the Lord David, the most excellent King of Scotland, worthy of all love in Christ, greetings and eternal life, from Bernard, styled Abbot of Clairvaux.

I have long since learned to love you, most illustrious king, your fair renown has for long stirred in me the desire to meet you in person. This is my desire and relying on the words, "The Lord has heard the desire of the poor", I am confident in the Lord that one day I shall see you in the body whom even now I delight to gaze upon in spirit and imagination, and whom I constantly think of with such pleasure and joy. Our brothers at Rievaulx were the first

* This letter was written about 1134 in favour of the new foundation at Fountains.

to experience the effects of your mercy. You opened to them the treasury of your good will and anointed them with the oil of your compassion and kindness, so that the house of the King of heaven was filled with the odour of your ointments. I am not ungrateful for this, I am as grateful as if you had shown your favours to me personally. And now there are other brothers in the same neighbourhood who have lately joined us. I do not think that your Highness can be ignorant of how these brothers, inspired from on high, came forth into a desert place from the Church of the blessed Mary at York where the observance was perfunctory. They have had to endure many persecutions and injuries inflicted on them sometimes with force and sometimes with guile. They were rich and they abounded in the goods of this world, but they have chosen to become poor for the love of Christ, true followers of the apostolic life and sanctity. If they had been of the world, the world would have loved them, according to the words of the Lord. But now that they are not of the world, the world persecutes them. With the help of God they bear patiently whatever the world does to them but we, who fear God, should help his servants in their troubles. To you therefore, most merciful king, I commend these aforesaid servants of Christ that you may comfort them in their poverty, looking to Christ, the King of Kings, for the meed which he will distribute to the just in his eternal kingdom.

TO THE BRETHREN IN IRELAND, ON THE PASSING OF BLESSED MALACHY*

To his brother religious in Ireland, and especially to those houses founded by Bishop Malachy of blessed memory, the consolation of the Holy Spirit, from Brother Bernard, styled Abbot of Clairvaux.

1. If we had here an abiding city we might rightly shed many tears at the loss of such a fellow citizen as Malachy; and if we look, as we should, for the one that is to come, the loss of such a valuable leader will still be an occasion for sorrow, yet nevertheless in this case knowledge should moderate our feelings and sure hope set a limit to our grief. It ought to be no matter for wonder if our affection

* St. Malachy died on November 2nd, 1148. He had been an intimate friend of St. Bernard since first meeting him when he stopped at Clairvaux on his way to Rome in the year 1139.

wrings a groan from our hearts, if our sense of bereavement expresses itself in tears, yet there should be measure in our grief, we should, in fact, find some consolation for it in the contemplation, not of what we can see, but of what we cannot see, for we see only what passes, what endures we cannot see. We must be glad for the sake of this holy soul, otherwise he would accuse us in the words of our Lord to the Apostles: "If you really loved me you would be glad to hear that I am on my way to my Father". The spirit of our father has gone ahead of us to the "Father of a world of spirits". We would prove ourselves not only wanting in charity but also ungrateful for all that we have received through him, were we not glad for his sake that he has passed from his many labours to everlasting repose, from the dangers of the world to the safety of heaven, from the world to the Father. It is an act of filial piety to grieve for the death of Malachy, but it were an act of even greater filial piety to rejoice with him in the life that he has found. Has he not found life? Surely he has, and a blessed life: "In the eyes of fools he seemed to die, but all is well with him".

2. Even considerations of our own advantage suggest that we should rejoice and be glad that we have such a powerful patron in the court of heaven, a faithful advocate whose deep love will not permit him to forget us, and whose well tried holiness will obtain for him the favour of God. Who would dare to believe that the holy Malachy loves his sons less now or is less able to help them than he was? There is no doubt that since God loved him before he died he now enjoys a deeper and more sure experience of God's love; and that since he loved his own, he loved them to the end. May it be far from us, O holy soul, to consider your prayers less helpful to us now that you are offering them to the Divine Majesty with even greater eagerness, now that you are no longer living by faith but reigning by vision! Far may it be from us to believe that your charity is in any way less active that it was, now that you sit at the very fount of charity and are able to draw deep draughts of it instead of the drops for which you used to thirst. Charity is strong and cannot yield to death, it is even stronger than death. When he lay dying he remembered you and lovingly commended you to God, and he begged even me, a person of no consequence, always to remember you. For this reason I thought it well to write and tell you that I am ready with all my heart to give you such help as I can both in

spiritual matters, if my incompetence in such things can achieve anything through the prayers of our blessed father, and in material matters if any opportunity should arise.

3. And also, dear sons, I feel the deepest compassion for the Irish Church in her great bereavement, and my sympathy for you is all the greater for my realization of the debt I owe you. The Lord has highly honoured us by favouring our place with the blessed death of Malachy and enriching it with the treasure of his precious body. Do not take it ill that he should have his tomb with us, since God out of his abundant mercy has so ordained it that you should have him while he lived and we when he was dead. For both you and us he was a common father, and still is, for this was the wish he expressed to us on his death-bed. Wherefore we embrace you all with deep affection as our true brothers for the sake of this great father of ours, just as we are inspired to regard you as such by the very spirtual relationship by which we are united.

4. I exhort you, my brethren, to follow carefully in the footsteps of our father, and all the more zealously for knowing from daily experience his holy way of life. You will prove yourselves his true sons by manfully keeping his teaching; and as you saw in him and received from him a pattern of how you ought to live, live by that pattern, and make more of it than ever: "Wise sons are the pride of their father". Even I have been stirred from my sloth and imbued with reverence by the pattern of perfection he set before me. May he so draw me after him that I may run willingly and eagerly in the fragrance of his virtues, while the memory of them is still fresh. May Christ have you all in his safe keeping praying as you are for us! . . .

TO THE ENGLISH PEOPLE

[1.] I address myself to you, the people of England, in the cause of Christ, in whom lies your salvation. I say this so that the warrant of the Lord and my zeal in his interests may excuse my hardihood in addressing you. I am a person of small account, but my desire for you in Christ is not small. This is my reason and motive for writing, this is why I make bold to address you all by letter. 1 would have preferred to do so by word of mouth had I but the strength to come to you as I desire.

2. Now is the acceptable time, now is the day of abundant salvation. The earth is shaken because the Lord of heaven is losing his land, the land in which he appeared to men, in which he lived amongst men for more than thirty years; the land made glorious by his miracles, holy by his blood; the land in which the flowers of his resurrection first blossomed. And now, for our sins, the enemy of the Cross has begun to lift his sacrilegious head there, and to devastate with the sword that blessed land, that land of promise. Alas, if there should be none to withstand him, he will soon invade the very city of the living God, overturn the arsenal of our redemption, and defile the holy places which have been adorned by the blood of the immaculate lamb. They have cast their greedy eyes especially on the holy sanctuaries of our Christian Religion, and they long particularly to violate that couch on which, for our sakes, the Lord of our life fell asleep in death.

3. What are you doing, you mighty men of valour? What are you doing, you servants of the Cross? Will you thus cast holy things to dogs, pearls before swine? How great a number of sinners have here confessed with tears and obtained pardon for their sins since the time when these holy precincts were cleansed of pagan filth by the swords of our fathers! The evil one sees this and is enraged, he gnashes his teeth and withers away in fury. He stirs up his vessels of wrath so that if they do but once lay hands upon these holy places there shall be no sign or trace of piety left. Such a catastrophe would be a source of appalling grief for all time, but it would also be a source of confusion and endless shame for our generation. What think you, my brethren? Is the hand of the Lord shortened and is he now powerless to work salvation, so that he must call upon us, petty worms of the earth, to save and restore to him his heritage? Could he not send more than twelve legions of angels, or even just say the word and save his land? Most certainly he has the power to do this whenever he wishes, but I tell you that God is trying you. "He looks down from heaven at the race of men, to find one soul that reflects, and makes God its aim," one soul that sorrows for him. For God has pity on his people and on those who have grievously fallen away and has prepared for them a means of salvation. Consider with what care he plans our salvation, and be amazed. Look, sinners, at the depths of his pity, and take courage. He does not want your death but rather that you should turn to him and live.

So he seeks not to overthrow you but to help you. When Almighty God so treats murderers, thieves, adulterers, perjurers, and such like, as persons able to find righteousness in his service, what is it but an act of exquisite courtesy all God's own? Do not hesitate. God is good, and were he intent on your punishment he would not have asked of you this present service or indeed have accepted it even had you offered it. Again I say consider the Almighty's goodness and pay heed to his plans of mercy. He puts himself under obligation to you, or rather feigns to do so, so that he can help you to satisfy your obligations towards himself. He puts himself in your debt so that, in return for your taking up arms in his cause, he can reward you with pardon for your sins and everlasting glory. I call blessed the generation that can seize an opportunity of such rich indulgence as this, blessed to be alive in this year of jubilee, this year of God's choice. The blessing is spread throughout the whole world, and all the world is flocking to receive this badge of immortality. . . .

34. JOHN OF SALISBURY: The Difference Between a Prince and a Tyrant

John of Salisbury (1115-1180) was educated in France under some of the most brilliant men of the time. He was later to serve as secretary to the famous Archbishop of Canterbury, Thomas à Becket. In 1176 John of Salisbury was made Bishop of Chartres. Having studied at the school of Chartres many years before, he was thoroughly conversant with the masterpieces of classical Latin literature. Virgil, Cicero, Seneca, Ovid, Horace, Juvenal, and Terence not only perfected his literary style, but also influenced him as philosophers and moralists whose work he thought should be taken seriously in Christian thinking; he especially admired Cicero.

John of Salisbury's most important works are the *Stateman's Book* (*Polycraticus*) and the *Metalogicon*. The *Statesman's Book** is a treatise

* The selection entitled "The Difference between a Prince and a Tyrant" is from the first chapter of *The Statesman's Yearbook of John of Salisbury* (*Polycraticus*), trans. John Dickinson (New York: Appleton-Century-Crofts, 1927). Used by permission.

on political theory, one of the first in Christian Europe. One of the notable theses in this work is John of Salisbury's insistence that the ruler, or prince, is not above the law. The ruler is not only subject to law—his legislating is to be regarded as subject to a higher law, i.e., the natural law of right reason. Salisbury brings the stoic notion of natural law together with particular themes derived from Cicero, and from Augustine's *City of God*, into the new synthesis represented by his outlook on the nature of the state.

John of Salisbury's noted *Metalogicon* is a treatise on education. It shows him to be an urbane, cultured, and informed commentator on the educational situation of his day. In the sections from this work presented below,* he defends the importance of the classical authors, i.e., secular studies, to Christian education.

CHAPTER I

OF THE DIFFERENCE BETWEEN A PRINCE AND A TYRANT AND OF WHAT IS MEANT BY A PRINCE

Between a tyrant and a prince there is this single or chief difference, that the latter obeys the law and rules the people by its dictates, accounting himself as but their servant. It is by virtue of the law that he makes good his claim to the foremost and chief place in the management of the affairs of the commonwealth and in the bearing of its burdens; and his elevation over others consists in this, that whereas private men are held responsible only for their private affairs, on the prince fall the burdens of the whole community. Wherefore deservedly there is conferred on him, and gathered together in his hands, the power of all his subjects, to the end that he may be sufficient unto himself in seeking and bringing about the advantage of each individually, and of all; and to the end that the state of the human commonwealth may be ordered in the best possible manner, seeing that each and all are members one of another. Wherein we indeed but follow nature, the best guide of life; for nature has gathered together all the senses of her microcosm or little world, which is man, into the head, and has subjected all the members in obedience to it in such wise that they will all function properly so long as they follow the guidance of the head, and the

---

* Selection 35 is from *The Metalogicon,* trans. Daniel B. McGarry (Berkeley: The University of California Press, 1955). Used by permission.

head remains sane. Therefore the prince stands on a pinnacle which is exalted and made splendid with all the great and high privileges which he deems necessary for himself. And rightly so, because nothing is more advantageous to the people than that the needs of the prince should be fully satisfied; since it is impossible that his will should be found opposed to justice. Therefore, according to the usual definition, the prince is the public power, and a kind of likeness on earth of the divine majesty. Beyond doubt a large share of the divine power is shown to be in princes by the fact that at their nod men bow their necks and for the most part offer up their heads to the axe to be struck off, and, as by a divine impulse, the prince is feared by each of those over whom he is set as an object of fear. And this I do not think could be, except as a result of the will of God. For all power is from the Lord God, and has been with Him always, and is from everlasting. The power which the prince has is therefore from God, for the power of God is never lost, nor severed from Him, but He merely exercises it through a subordinate hand, making all things teach His mercy or justice. "Who, therefore, resists the ruling power, resists the ordinance of God,"[1] in whose hand is the authority of conferring that power, and when He so desires, of withdrawing it again, or diminishing it. For it is not the ruler's own act when his will is turned to cruelty against his subjects, but it is rather the dispensation of God for His good pleasure to punish or chasten them. Thus during the Hunnish persecution, Attila, on being asked by the reverend bishop of a certain city who he was, replied, "I am Attila, the scourge of God." Whereupon it is written that the bishop adored him as representing the divine majesty. "Welcome," he said, "is the minister of God," and "Blessed is he that cometh in the name of the Lord," and with sighs and groans he unfastened the barred doors of the church, and admitted the persecutor through whom he attained straightway to the palm of martyrdom. For he dared not shut out the scourge of God, knowing that His beloved Son was scourged, and that the power of this scourge which had come upon himself was as nought except it came from God. If good men thus regard power as worthy of veneration even when it comes as a plague upon the elect, who should not venerate that power which is instituted by God for the punishment of evil-doers and for the reward of good men, and which is promptest in devotion and

[1] Rom., xiii., 2.

obedience to the laws? To quote the words of the Emperor, "it is indeed a saying worthy of the majesty of royalty that the prince acknowledges himself bound by the Laws."[2] For the authority of the prince depends upon the authority of justice and law; and truly it is a greater thing than imperial power for the prince to place his government under the laws, so as to deem himself entitled to do nought which is at variance with the equity of justice. . . .

Although all defer to the supreme pontificate as the very apex of things, still in my own opinion, I think that so far as is consistent with the safety of religion a wise man ought to shun it rather than take it upon him. For, to speak the truth from my own knowledge, it seems to me the most laborious and wretched post, so far as pertains to the condition of the present age. For if he pursues his own avarice, it is death to him; but if not, he will not escape the hands and tongues of the Romans. For unless he has that wherewith he may stop up their mouths and restrain their hands, he must harden his eyes, his ears, his heart to endure their revilings, their outrages and their sacrileges. Now there are three things which beyond others pervert utterly the judgment even of wise men, namely love of gifts, respect of persons, and credulity. For no one can at the same time be influenced by these things and administer justice. Therefore it is needful that the Roman pontiff should be immune from these things, since it is his duty to curb the excesses of all. But if he hates gifts, who will force presents upon him against his will? And how then, if he does not receive, will he be able to bestow? And how, if he does not bestow, will he be able to please the Romans? If he does not show personal favoritism to those who are prominent among them, how will he be able to hold his ground in the face of them? For he will scarcely be able to judge of a sacerdotal cause in conclave without being compelled to admit them into all his councils. And what of the fact that he must condemn simony, the taking of gifts, and the receipt of compensation? If he follows these practices, must he not condemn himself with his own voice? If in supreme power there is the least freedom from restraint, verily he who is over the laws is subjected to no law, but is all the more strictly obliged not to commit unlawful acts. And for this reason the Roman pontiff has the least lawful liberty by virtue of the very fact that he has the most. And what is a heavier burden than the care of all the churches?

[2] Justin., Cod., I., 14, § 4.

The privilege of the apostle descends to his successors, and clearly a part of the privilege is that whereof the apostle speaks to the Corinthians: "Who is weak," he says, "and I am not weak? Who is caused to stumble, and I burn not?"[3] If you do not wish to go through all aspects of the matter, let him who contends for the primacy once prove his right to such a post, and I think he will speedily surrender the place. Besides, he who is pontiff of Rome must of necessity, because of the condition the Church is now in, be the "servant of servants"; and not merely nominally and for the sake of glory, as some think, but actually and in substance, as one who must serve the servants of God, even though unwillingly. For each of the three persons of the Godhead is a servant and a dispenser of His mercy or justice. The angel is a servant, the human being is a servant, good men are servants, bad men are servants, and the devil himself, the prince of the world, is a servant. Therefore even the Romans are servants of God, although they are tyrants whose servant the Roman pontiff must necessarily be, to the point that unless he is their servant he must of necessity cease to be either pontiff or Roman. Who then doubts that he is the servant of servants? I call upon Lord Adrian, whose times may God render fortunate, to bear witness to this fact, namely that no one is more wretched than the Roman pontiff, that the plight of no man is more miserable than his. And though there were no other cause of harm, he must necessarily sink down speedily under the burden of labor alone. For he confesses that he has found so many miseries upon that throne that on making a comparison of the present with the past, all the bitterness of his preceding life seems as joy and the greatest felicity. He says that the throne of the Roman pontiff is a prickly seat, his mantle sewed together everywhere with the sharpest thorns, and of such great weight that it weighs down, exhausts and crushes the strongest shoulders; and that the crown and mitre rightly seem bright only because they are of fire. And he says that he wishes that he might never have left his native soil of England, and had remained forever unknown in the cloisters of blessed Rufus, rather than to have exposed himself to such great anguish, were it not that he dare not resist the dispensation of God. While he is still alive, make inquiry of him directly and believe one who speaks from experience. And the wisest thing of all that he said to me was when

[3] II Cor. xi. 20.

he added that as he ascended step by step from a simple clerk of the cloister through all the offices up to the supreme pontiff, he never found that anything worth while was added to his previous happiness and tranquil peace by his ascent. And, to use his own words (for when I am with him, his graciousness never wishes that anything shall be hid from my eyes), he says, "God has ever enlarged me upon the anvil and with the hammer; but now may He support with His right hand, if He pleases, the weight which He has laid on my weakness, for of myself I cannot support it."

Is not the man most deserving of misery who fights to attain such misery? Let the richest of men be chosen, on the following day he will be poor and burdened by obligations to almost countless creditors. What then will happen to him who is called by no election, but against the will of Christ as expressed in His members forcibly intrudes with blind and bloody ambition, and not without the shedding of fraternal blood? This is verily to succeed Romulus among parricides, not Peter in the care and management of the fold entrusted to him.

35. JOHN OF SALISBURY: The Defense of Secular Learning*

PROLOGUE

I believe that there is hardly anything human, which is so free from defect as to be completely immune from detraction. For what is bad is deservedly denounced; while what is good is maliciously slandered. Reconciled to this, I have steeled myself to bear with patience the darts of detractors. Which resignation is especially necessary, since, in accordance with the divine plan, mother nature has brought us forth in our present day, and in this region of the world, while fate has assigned us the lot of being associated with those who would rather criticize the works of others than look after, order, and reform their own lives. [To the latter applies the saying:]

> Not a one attempts to examine his own conscience,
> Rather, each stares at the bag on the back of the fellow in front.

* See Introduction to Selection 34.

While it is true that, by keeping silent, I might have avoided being criticized by scholars and those who make a profession of philosophy, I was utterly at a loss to evade the snapping teeth of my fellow members of the court. Being respectful to all and injuring no one used, of yore, to assure one of popularity. Such was the formula given by the comic poet, whereby "One can gain praise unmixed with envy, and win for himself friends." In our day, however, the aforesaid policy rarely even suffices to repress the envy of one's comrades. The habit of obedience is branded as a stigma of servility, and the absence of guilt is deemed an admission of impotence. A person who is quiet is accused of ignorance, one who is fluent is classed with the garrulous. A man whose manner is serious is suspected of dark designs, one of less gravity is charged with levity and incompetence. Anyone who makes an effort to be modest in word and action is adjudged to be a sycophant, who is courting popularity. Even where actual bickering is absent, ill feeling is hardly ever at rest. Had I wasted my every moment in the company of my fellow members of the court, frittering away all my time in gambling, hunting, and like frivolous pastimes, they could not now be slandering my writings, just as I cannot find any of theirs to challenge. However, I am little concerned if what I write is criticized by persons who magnify the judgment of comedians and actors, and quake as groveling slaves for fear Thais or Thraso, Callirrhoe, or Bathyllus may say or think something deprecatory about them. On the other hand, if professors of philosophy persecute an admirer of those who philosophize, clearly they are doing me an injustice and are poorly repaying my devotion. Even though I cannot be one of them, I am certainly endeavoring to love, honor, and respect them. The support of scholars is due me, inasmuch as I am defending, to the full extent of my capabilities, what they are or what they have been. If I have succeeded, thanks and a reward are due me for the happy event; whereas even if I have failed, I still deserve the same for my good intentions, in accordance with the quotation:

> You declare that I have accomplished naught, and have lost the case;
> But so much the more are you indebted to me, O Sextus, because I
> have been put to shame.

I do not exclude abler men from pleading the cause of scholarship, when I attest my own devotion. Let the more distinguished authoritatively lend their mighty hand to silence all opposition, and to incline the scales in favor of the logicians. Since, however, the labors of the latter [logicians] were being lampooned as a waste of time, and my opponent was goading me on by his almost daily controversies, finally, indignant and objecting, I took up his challenge and determined to strike down his calumnies even as they issued from his mouth. Hence, I have planned my work to answer his objections. I have thus often omitted more important points in order to refute his arguments. It was he, indeed, who determined the course of our discussion. My friends pressed me to compose this work, even if I had practically to throw the words together. For I had neither the leisure nor energy to enter into a subtle analysis of opinions, much less to polish my style. My regular duties have consumed all my time, save that required for eating and sleeping. By the commission of my lord, whom I cannot disappoint, the responsibility for the whole of Britain, as far as ecclesiastical matters are concerned, is on my shoulders. Administrative concerns and the [time-consuming] trifles of court life have precluded study, and the interruptions of friends have used up practically all the time I had left. Consequently, I do not think I should be too harshly judged if any of my statements seem insufficiently considered. On the other hand, the credit for anything that I may say which seems more apt is to be referred to Him without Whom human weakness is powerless. I am by nature too dull to comprehend the subtleties of the ancients; I cannot rely on my memory to retain for long what I have learned; and my style betrays its own lack of polish. This treatise, which I have taken care to divide into four books for the reader's refreshment, is entitled THE METALOGICON. For, in it, I undertake to defend logic. According to the wont of writers, I have included various points, which each reader is at liberty to accept or reject as he sees fit:

> Some things you will read herein are excellent, some mediocre, and
> several defective;
> But this is inevitable—as otherwise, dear Avitus, there would be no
> book.

So says Martial, and I echo him. I prefer thus to speak in lighter vein, rather than to "start hares" with Ganymede, or to "Reek of strong wine both night and day." I have not been ashamed to cite moderns, whose opinions in many instances, I unhesitatingly prefer over those of the ancients. I trust that posterity will honor our contemporaries, for I have profound admiration for the extraordinary talents, diligent studies, marvelous memories, fertile minds, remarkable eloquence, and linguistic proficiency of many of those of our own day. I have purposely incorporated into this treatise some observations concerning morals, since I am convinced that all things read or written are useless except so far as they have a good influence on one's manner of life. Any pretext of philosophy that does not bear fruit in the cultivation of virtue and the guidance of one's conduct is futile and false. Being an Academician in matters that are doubtful to a wise man, I cannot swear to the truth of what I say. Whether such propositions may be true or false, I am satisfied with probable certitude. It is hoped that, at your convenience, you will examine all the points that I have made in detail, since, to rest assured that my labor and expenses will not be unavailing, I have constituted you the judge of my little works. But should (as heaven forbid) my Alexis prefer any stageplayer, no matter whom, to a would-be philosopher, then, "If this Alexis spurns me, I will find another." There are (more fully to explain my purpose) three things that cause me to fear, and that constitute for many writers a danger to their salvation or a loss of merit. These (three) are: ignorance of the truth, misled or wanton statement of falsehood, and the haughty assertion of fact. I concur with the author of the saying that "It is safer to hear the truth than to state it ourselves, for humility is guarded when we listen," while pride often insinuates itself when we speak. I confess that I am at fault in all three respects. Not only am I handicapped by ignorance, but also frequently—indeed, too frequently—I make false statements, or maintain the truth with arrogance and pride, until reproved and corrected by God. Hence it is that I earnestly beseech my reader and listener to remember me in his prayers to the Most High, and to petition God to grant me pardon for my past offenses, security against future falls, knowledge of the truth, love of what is good, and devotion to Himself, as well as that we may accomplish, in thought, word, and action, what is pleasing to His divine will.

END OF PROLOGUE

BOOK ONE

CHAPTER 3

When, how, and by whom Cornificius was educated

I am not at all surprised that Cornificius, although he has been hired at a high price, and has been thrashing the air for a long time, has taught his credulous listeners to know nothing. For this was the way in which he himself was "untaught" by his own masters. Verbose, rather than eloquent, he is continually tossing to the winds verbal leaves that lack the fruit of meaning. On the one hand, he assails with bitter sarcasm the statements of everyone else, without any concern as to who they may be, in the effort to establish his own views and overthrow the opinions of others. On the other hand, he carefully shuns engaging in hand-to-hand combat, and avoids basing his arguments on reason or consenting to walk together in the field of the scriptures. Really, I cannot imagine what extraordinary thing, hidden from all the wise, Cornificius has conceived in the swollen bellows of his windy lungs, wherefore he disdains to answer or to listen with patience to anyone else. No matter what proposition is advanced, he rejects it as false, or laughs it to scorn. If you expect him to prove his propositions, he puts you off, and when the day has ended, you find you have been defrauded of what you were awaiting. For he does not want to cast his pearls, so he says, before strange swine. Meanwhile he pastures his [sheepish] listeners on fictions and foibles. He boasts that he has a shortcut whereby he will make his disciples eloquent without the benefit of any art, and philosophers without the need of any work. He himself learned from his own teachers what he is today passing on to his pupils. He is ladling out the very same kind of instruction that he himself received. He will make his disciples his equals in philosophy. What more [could they wish]? Will they not thus, in accordance with the saying, be perfect? Do we not read in the Gospel: "Every disciple who becomes like his master is perfect?" What he now teaches, Cornificius learned at a time when there was no "letter" in liberal studies, and everyone sought "the spirit," which, so they tell us, lies hidden in the letter. He has carefully preserved this, to be heard only by the fortunate and by "the ears of Jove" (as the saying goes). When Cornificius went to school, it was a dominant principle that "Hercules begets

Hyllus": namely, that the strength and vigor of the disputant add up to a valid argument, and that sovereignty resides in the five vowel sounds. At that time this was considered the proper way to teach everything. The philosophers of that day argued interminably over such questions as whether a pig being taken to market is held by the man or by the rope; and whether one who buys a whole cape also simultaneously purchases the hood. Speech in which the words "consistent" and "inconsistent," "argument" and "reason" did not resound, with negative particles multiplied and transposed through assertions of existence and non-existence, was entirely unacceptable. So true was this that one had to bring along a counter whenever he went to a disputation, if he was to keep apprized of the force of affirmation or negation. For generally a double negative is equivalent to affirmation, whereas the force of a negation is increased if it is repeated an uneven number of times. At the same time, a negation repeated over and over usually loses its effect, and becomes equivalent to contradiction, as we find stated in the rules. In order, therefore, to discriminate between instances of even and uneven numbers, it was then the custom of those who had prudent foresight to bring a bag of beans and peas to disputations as a reasonable expedient. Even though one might try to get to the root of a question, noisy verbosity would suffice to win the victory, regardless of the kind of arguments advanced. Poets who related history were considered reprobate, and if anyone applied himself to studying the ancients, he became a marked man and the laughingstock of all. For he was deemed both slower than a young Arcadian ass, and duller than lead or stone. Everyone enshrined his own and his master's inventions. Yet even this situation could not abide. Students were soon swept along in the current, and like their fellows in error, came to spurn what they had learned from their teachers, and to form and found new sects of their own. Of a sudden, they blossomed forth as great philosophers. Those newly arrived in school, unable to read or write, hardly stayed there any longer than it takes a baby bird to sprout its feathers. Then the news masters, fresh from the schools, and fledglings, just leaving their nests, flew off together, after having stayed about the same length of time in school and nest. These "fresh-baked" doctors had spent more hours sleeping than awake in their study of philosophy, and had been educated with less expenditure of effort than those who, according to mythology, after sleeping on [Mount]

Parnassus, immediately became prophets. They had been trained more rapidly than those who, after imbibing from the Castalian Fountain of the Muses, directly obtained the gift of poetry, or those who, after setting eyes on Apollo, merited not only to be classed as musicians, but even to be accepted into the company of the Muses. What, now did they teach? How could they allow anything to remain crude and unpolished, old and obsolete? Behold, all things were "renovated." Grammar was [completely] made over; logic was remodeled; rhetoric was despised. Discarding the rules of their predecessors, they brought forth new methods for the whole Quadrivium from the innermost sanctuaries of philosophy. They spoke only of "consistence" or "reason," and the word "argument" was on the lips of all. To mention "an ass," "a man," or any of the works of nature was considered a crime, or improper, crude, and alien to a philosopher. It was deemed impossible to say or do anything "consistently" and "rationally," without expressly mentioning "consistence" and "reason." Not even an argument was admitted unless it was prefaced by its name. To act with reference to an art and according to the art were (for them) the same. They would probably teach that a poet cannot write poetry unless he at the same time names the verse he is using; and that the carpenter cannot make a bench unless he is simultaneously forming on his lips the word "bench" or "wooden seat." The result is this hodgepodge of verbiage, reveled in by a foolish old man, who rails at those who respect the founders of the arts, since he himself could see nothing useful in these arts when he was pretending to study them.

BOOK TWO

[PROLOGUE]

It has been sufficiently proved in the preceding book, I believe, that grammar is not useless. I feel that we have adequately demonstrated that, in the absence of grammar, not only is perfect eloquence precluded, but also the gateway to other philosophical pursuits is blocked to those who would engage in them. Attention has also been called to the fact that grammar is to be judged leniently, since it is subject both to nature and to the will of man. In like manner, civil laws frequently derive their force from human constitution while what is deemed expedient for the common welfare is considered equivalent to natural justice. But they [the Cornificians] are still not silenced, and refuse to acquit logic. Though maimed, and destined to be yet further mutilated, Cornificius, beating against a solid wall like a blind man, rashly brings to trial, and still more brazenly accuses logic. One who [really] loves the truth hates wrangling, whereas one who is charitable instinctively and spontaneously withdraws from contention. I will pass over the question whether grammar is a part of logic, although logic certainly treats and serves words, despite the fact that it does not, of course, discuss them from every angle. I will leave it to you, who are informed on this matter, to judge the extension of the term [logic], and to decide whether logic includes all speech, or is limited to the critical evaluation of reasoning. I have no misgivings as to your decision. For I have confidence in both the equity of my cause, and the capability and fairness of my judge. Let us pass over the question whether what relates to reasoning is useful, and let us consider the power of logic, notwithstanding the unwillingness of our opponent. My task here will be lightened, since my reader is favorably disposed and does not need persuasion. For all take pride in being logicians: not only those who have become engaged to the science with a few sweet pleasantries, but even those who have not yet made her acquaintance. . . .

CHAPTER 6

That all seek after logic, yet not all are successful in their quest

From what has been said, it can be seen that logic gives great promise. For it provides a mastery of invention and judgment, as well as supplies ability to divide, define, and prove with conviction. It is such an important part of philosophy that it serves the other parts in much the same way as the soul does the body. On the other hand, all philosophy that lacks the vital organizing principle of logic is lifeless and helpless. It is no more than just that this art should, as it does, attract such tremendous crowds from every quarter that more men are occupied in the study of logic alone than in all the other branches of that science which regulates human acts, words, and even thoughts, if they are to be as they should be. I refer to philosophy, without which everything is bereft of sense and savour, as well as false and immoral. All are shouting to one another: "Let him who is last catch the itch"; and let him who does not come to logic, be plagued by continuous, everlasting filth. Therefore: "I hate to be left behind,"—a plight that is also embarrassing and dangerous. I crave to behold the light, revealed only to these public criers of logic. I approach, and with humble supplication, beseech them to teach me, and if [at all] possible, to make me like themselves. They promise great things, but meanwhile they command me to observe a Pythagorean silence, for they are disclosing the secrets of Minerva, of which according to their boasts, they are custodians. However, they permit and even require that I converse with them in childish prattle, which for their kind is to dispute. When, after long association, I come to know them better, so that they will finally deign to heed me, I ask more firmly, knock more insistently, and implore more ardently that the door of the art be opened to me. At long last [they comply, and] we begin with definition. They tell me to define in a few words whatever I have in mind. First I must give the genus of the subject, and then add the latter's substantial differences until I have enough of these to be able to convert the proposition. Highest and lowest concepts cannot be defined: the former because they are without genus, the latter because they lack differences. Such are, nonetheless, described by their properties, the same aggregate of which is not found elsewhere. There cannot be, however, any definition of a substance, unless we state its genus and enumerate some substantial differences. Behold, I have so been taught the art of defining; and I am directed to go ahead and adequately define, or at least describe, whatever is proposed. We move on to treat the science of division. I am [similarly] admonished to apportion a genus adequately into its species by means of differences, or by affirmation and negation. The whole should be entirely resolved into its parts, the universal into its subjects, the virtual into its powers. When we want to divide a word, we should enumerate either its meaning or its forms. I am instructed to divide an accident according to its subjects, and to show what subjects can possess this accident. Conversely, I am directed to divide a subject according to its accidents, as it is pertinent to point out the various accidents that a subject is capable of possessing. I am even told to divide according to the coaccidents of accidents, since for a variety of subjects these are shown to be numerous or even excessive. I have thus been rapidly conducted through two-thirds of the course. There still remains the final third, whose mastery is even more essential for the aspirant [to logic], and which it takes longer to explain. This [last] is the art of drawing inferences, useful for defeating an opponent in argument, or for demonstrating philosophical truth without regard to what one's listeners may think. A few precepts for this are presented, and these I still further synopsize for brevity's sake. We are to take careful note that, if we wish to win assent to a given proposition, we must first posit something from which it may be inferred as probable or necessary. Thus we may posit a genus in order to establish its species; or eliminate one of two contraries in order to posit the other. I proceed accordingly, for I have a rather dull mind, and am one for whom "belief comes through hearing," and who [alas] all too often fails to comprehend what I hear or read. Since therefore the rules are being brought out into the light, I beseech my very learned teachers, who will never admit ignorance of anything, to take sample passages found in books, and demonstrate the application of the rules. For it is no great matter for one who has mastered this art to review the findings of others in definitions composed at an earlier date. If logic is definitive because it possesses a certain number of definitions, other disciplines are still more so, since they have a still greater number of them. These unadulterated philosophers, who despise everything save logic, and are ignorant of grammar, physics, and ethics alike, grow furious. They accuse me of being a reprobate, a dullard, a blockhead, a stone. What they have told me [they insist] should adequately take care of the three functions of the art. They demand that I [now] pay them their stipulated fee. If I take exception, and object, quoting the moralist: "What is this talk about payment? What have I learned?" Immediately they rejoin, in the words of the same moralist:

> The teacher is blamed, forsooth,
> For the lack of wit
> In the boorish youth.

"That's just it," they taunt: "Everyone desires knowledge, but no one is willing to pay the price." Since I blush at the thought of being branded an ingrate, I decide to repay them [in full measure]: doctrine for doctrine, the essential for the essential. I present them [in return] with a compendium of rules, instructing them how to apply the latter. Since they have taught me three useful arts, I will also teach them three other arts, still more useful. One should know the arts of military science, medicine, and law, both civil and canon. Thus one will become a master of moral philosophy. [I therefore proceed:] Whenever you have to fight an enemy, your primary precaution should be not to let him wound you in any way. At the very outset, while you are as yet uninjured, charge in upon him, and wound him, until either your vanquished opponent himself acknowledges defeat, or onlookers acclaim you as the victor over your breathless adversary. In medicine, first ascertain the cause of the sickness, then cure and eliminate it. Subsequently, restore and build up the health of your patient by remedial and preventive medicine until he has fully recuperated. In cases involving civil law, always make justice your object, and be affable with everyone. Then, as the comic poet says: "Praise free of envy will be yours, and many will be your friends." What further? In all things "be clothed with charity." Note that I have ready the keys to these latter arts, in the same way that they had the rules for the aforesaid ones. Alas, they are the more to be pitied in that they are blind to their own want. They deceive themselves, with the consequence that, in their very quest of the truth, they come to know nothing. The only sure road to truth is humility. Pilate, for example, on hearing the word "truth," asked: "What is truth?" But his incredulity prompted the proud man to turn away from the master before he could be enlightened by the revelation of the sacred reply.

BOOK THREE

[PROLOGUE]

Almost twenty years have elapsed since I was forced to forsake the workshop and gymnasium [or school] of the logicians because of straitened circumstances, and the advice of friends whom I could not disregard. Since then, to confess the truth as I myself know it, not once have I consulted the writings of the dialecticians. Not even in passing have I glanced at their treatises on the arts, or commentaries, or glossaries, wherein this science [of logic] is begotten, preserved, and revised. Meanwhile, I have been preoccupied with other concerns, which have been, not merely diverse from, but even well nigh diametrically opposed to dialectic. I have hardly been able to find time to philosophize even an hour, and then only by dint of snatching [occasional] moments like a thief. Leaving England, I have crossed the Alps [no less than] ten times, journeyed to Apulia twice, and repeatedly handled negotiations with the Roman Church for my superiors and friends. I have, also, on numerous occasions, traveled about Gaul as well as England, in connection with various cases which have arisen. A host of business concerns, numerous responsibilities, and the pressure of work that had to be done have consumed all my attention, and have left me no time for learning. Hence I hope that my reader will see fit to pardon me for parts of this work that may seem somewhat dull or crude. The dryness of my tongue and the slowness of my wits are due partly to the facts I have mentioned above, partly to my responsibilities in the court, partly to the deceit and effrontery of my adversary, who has goaded and provoked me, unarmed and reluctant though I am, to make some sort of rebuttal. The saying of the moral poet has been fulfilled in me:

> Age makes off with everything, even one's mind:
> I remember how, as a boy, I used to sing the whole day through;
> But today I can no longer recall the many songs I once knew,
> And even his voice itself now fails Moeris.

Would it not, therefore, be unjust to expect of me the mental spryness of youth, the quick comprehension of glowing natural talent, and an exact memory, always sure of itself? Immersed in a busy turmoil of affairs, I have reached an age at which one is occupied only with more serious things, except so far as this seriousness may be diminished or extinguished by the infirmity of the flesh or the negligence of the spirit, or the malice which has flamed up from these as a result of the smoldering fire of sin. Just as that virtue which is out of proportion to tender youth is acknowledged, so that virtue which does not desert those who are becoming feeble with age is also acceptable. Ascanius won renown because, while yet a mere boy, he overcame Numanus. On the other hand, the veteran Entellus, as an old man, increased his repute by vanquishing Dares, who was famous for many victories. It is a wonderful thing to see virtue victorious over nature. But although I am already a deserving veteran, who should rightfully be exempt from attack, because of both my age and my state of life, I am in a way dragged into the arena, and forced to engage again in combats, which I had [long ago] set aside, and to which I am no longer used. I find myself confronted with the dire and harsh alternative of either fighting, inexpedient as this may be, or surrendering, and, by so doing, acquiescing to foul falsehood. The second possibility is utterly abhorrent. I have refused to become an accomplice in evil, to which alone, or above all else, philosophizing is opposed. Because I lack sufficient weapons of my own, I make use of those of all my friends without distinction. I am not, as [some of] our contemporaries, contemptuous of the means that are here and now at hand. Rather I employ the latter with greater confidence, so far as I am more certain that they are the gifts of faithful friends. The truth of things endures, impervious to corruption. Something that is true in itself does not melt into thin air, simply because it is stated by a new author. Who, indeed, except someone who is foolish or perverse, would consider an opinion authoritative, merely because it was stated by Coriscus, Bryso, or Melissus? All of the latter are alike obscure, except so far as Aristotle has used their names in his examples. And who, except the same sort of person, will reject a proposition simply because it has been advanced by Gilbert, Abelard, or our own Adam? I do not agree with those who spurn the good things of their own day, and begrudge recommending their contemporaries to posterity. None of the latter [none of our contemporaries] has, so far as I know, held that there is no such thing as a contradiction. None of them has denied the existence of movement and asserted that the stadium is not traversed. None of them has maintained that the earth moves because all things are in motion, as did Heraclitus, who, as Martianus puns, is red hot, because he is all afire, since he maintains that everything was originally composed of fire. But these opinions of the ancients are admitted, simply because of their antiquity, while the far more probable and correct opinions of our contemporaries are, on the other hand, rejected merely because they have been proposed by men of our own time. Everyone can say what he thinks: I believe that such procedure frequently springs from envy. Each jealously imagines that his own opinion is belittled to the degree in which the slightest praise is conceded to that of anyone else. For my part, I seek not my own glory, but only that of Him from Whom proceeds everything that is good, whether it be in myself or in others. And I also desire that credit be given those to whom I owe what little I know or think. For I am an Academician, and am not ashamed to acknowledge the authors of my own progress. As Pliny says: "It is the laudable sign of good character to admit the author of one's progress." Even those who at present criticize my viewpoint on this, will one day, God being the source, be praised for their worthwhile contributions. While the envy of their contemporaries will melt away with the passage of time, the glory of their virtues will endure untarnished. Let us now proceed with our discussion. I will briefly summarize what I can recall at an advanced age concerning what I studied in my youth. Happy days are brought back to mind, as I reminisce with pleasure as to what books should be read in preference to others, and how they should be studied. If I overlook anything, or make any mistakes in what I say, this should be attributed to the limitations of my memory, the lapse of time, and my [many] occupations.

BOOK IV

CHAPTER 31

The nature of original reason, and some observations
concerning philosophical sects

Reason in creatures is a spiritual force that examines the natures of things and acquires a knowledge, not only of material entities, but also of concepts perceptible by the intellect alone. In addition to reason in creatures, there is also that original reason which efficaciously comprehends all things, whether they be material or perceptible only by the intellect. Fully and accurately, that is without any error whatsoever [this] original reason determines the exact nature and precise power of everything. If I describe [this] original reason as the divine wisdom or power, and the firm foundation of all things, I am undoubtedly correct. This original reason embraces the nature, development, and ultimate end of all things. It is the sphere, which Martianus, speaking under a veil of poetical fiction, describes as comprised of all the elements, and lacking nothing of which any nature may be conceived to consist. It includes all heaven and air, the seas, the various parts of the earth, the infernal regions, and towns as well as crossroads, with their [manifold] activities and fortunes, as well as every sort of thing, particular or general, that may be mentioned. This sphere is evidently an image, as well as an idea of the world. Plato raises the question whether there is but one idea or [there are] several ideas. If, on the one hand, we consider the substance of scientific knowledge or reason, there is only one idea. But if, on the other hand, we consider the numerous diverse things that reason contemplates in its council chamber, ideas are countless. In view of the aforesaid [unity of scientific knowledge or reason] the Stoic reveres *Pronoen,* which we may translate as "Providence," and maintains that all things are bound by its necessary laws. Epicurus, on the other hand, impressed by the mutability of [the numerous] things [reason considers], does away with Providence, and relieves everything from subjection to necessary laws. The Peripatetic, for his part, shuns the precipice of error on either side. He will fully accept neither the "paradoxical teachings" of the Stoic, nor the "authentic dogmas" of Epicurus. While he admits the Providence of the Stoics, he explains it in such a way that he does not bind things by necessity. And while, with Epicurus, he frees things from the shackles of necessity, he does so without denying the reality of Providence. The Peripatetic thus maintains that, although things are, on the one hand, partly necessary, they are also, on the other hand, partly subject to natural changes and to free will. The Academician, however, wavers. He will not presume to state definitely what is true in each and every case. His sect [of the Academicians] is divided into three camps. By excessive caution, the right to be called philosophers has been forfeited [by some]. A [second] group admit only knowledge of things that are necessary and self-evident, namely, things that one cannot fail to know. A third type [of Academicians] consists in those of us who do not [venture to] precipitate an opinion concerning questions that are doubtful to a wise man.

CHAPTER 41

[The limitations of reason and the function of faith.]

Many things exceed our comprehension: some because of their august dignity, some because of their great number or vast extent, some because of their mutability and instability. Accordingly, Ecclesiasticus instructs us as what should be our principal concern, and what is to our greatest advantage. "Seek not," he says, "things that are beyond your reach, and do not fret over questions that exceed your comprehension." Note how he restrains the rashness of those who, with irreverent garrulity, discuss the secrets of the Divine Trinity and mysteries whose vision is reserved for eternal life. While the impression may be created that knowledge is increased by such a procedure, devotion is certainly diminished. "Refrain," Ecclesiasticus warns us, "from being inquisitive about numerous unnecessary things, and do not be curious about too many of the divine works. . . . For consideration of such things has caused the fall of many, and has enslaved their minds to vanity." The holy writer represses the audacity of those who stick their nose into everything, and want to account for all things. We know, on the authority of Solomon in Ecclesiastes, that man cannot fully explain the least object on earth, much less give a complete account of heavenly and supracelestial things. The son of Sirac makes clear to what the philosopher should direct his mental abilities: "Ever bear in mind God's commandments, and you will not be curious about too many of his works." We know that our knowledge flows ultimately from our senses, which are frequently misled, and that faltering human infirmity is at a loss to know what is expedient. Accordingly, God, in His mercy, has given us a law, to make evident what is useful, to disclose how much we may know about Him, and to indicate how far we may go in our inquiries concerning Him. This law displays the divine power in the creation, the divine wisdom in the orderly plan, and the divine goodness in the conservation of the world. The latter [attributes of God] are especially evident in the redemption of man. This law further clearly discloses God's will, so that everyone may be certain about what he should do. Since not only man's senses, but even his reason frequently err, the law of God has made faith the primary and fundamental prerequisite for understanding of the truth. Which is appropriately epitomized by Philo in the Book of Wisdom: "Those who trust in the Lord shall understand the truth, and those who persevere faithfully in love shall rest tranquil in Him, For God's elect shall enjoy grace and peace."

SUGGESTIONS FOR FURTHER READING

C. J. Barry, *Readings in Church History,* vol. I. The editor provides a collection of key readings which are particularly helpful with respect to the Tradition of the East.

Émile Brehier, *The Middle Ages and the Renaissance.* One volume of a widely read, standard French history of philosophy. The bibliographies are extensive.

Frederick Copleston, *A History of Philosophy,* Vol. II. A widely read, standard account of medieval philosophy.

Christopher Dawson, *Religion and the Rise of Western Culture.* This work argues the role of religion in determining intellectual and social and cultural life in the middle ages.

Denis de Rougemont, *Love in the Western World.* The author provides a detailed argument relating the courtly love of the troubadours to the teachings of the Albigensians.

Étienne Gilson, *History of Christian Philosophy in the Middle Ages.* The extraordinary notes make this a book for scholars, though the text itself provides a readable account of the author's thesis with respect to the unity of medieval thought.

Charles Homer Haskins, *The Renaissance of the Twelfth Century.* This classic, first printed in 1927, provides a helpfully varied account of twelfth century culture.

Friedrich Heer, *The Medieval World, Europe* 1100-1350. Although covering much general material, the author opens up many relatively untouched areas in medieval social life.

J. Husik, *A History of Medieval Jewish Philosophy.* First published in 1916, this has been a standard work.

David Knowles, *The Evolution of Medieval Thought.* The book is an especially well written summary.

Armand Maurer, *Medieval Philosophy.* The work was written with college students in mind, yet it makes clear the resources of scholarship.

Richard McKeon, *Selections from Medieval Philosophers.* 2 volumes. This work has been most widely read and has the standing of a classic.

Herman Shapiro, *Medieval Philosophy.* This book of selections provides an admirable complement to McKeon's selections listed above.

H. O. Taylor, *The Medieval Mind,* 2 volumes. This has been a standard work in the English-speaking world.